D1431761

Luminos is the Open Access monograph publishing program
from UC Press. Luminos provides a framework for preserving
and reinvigorating monograph publishing for the future and
increases the reach and visibility of important scholarly work. Titles
published in the UC Press Luminos model are published with the
same high standards for selection, peer review, production, and
marketing as those in our traditional program. www.luminosoa.org

This research was made possible by an ESRC studentship
PTA-031–2006–00143 and by a British Academy Postdoctoral
Fellowship.

The Stranger at the Feast

THE ANTHROPOLOGY OF CHRISTIANITY

Edited by Joel Robbins

1. *Christian Moderns: Freedom and Fetish in the Mission Encounter*, by Webb Keane

2. *A Problem of Presence: Beyond Scripture in an African Church*, by Matthew Engelke

3. *Reason to Believe: Cultural Agency in Latin American Evangelicalism*, by David Smilde

4. *Chanting Down the New Jerusalem: Calypso, Christianity, and Capitalism in the Caribbean*, by Francio Guadeloupe

5. *In God's Image: The Metaculture of Fijian Christianity*, by Matt Tomlinson

6. *Converting Words: Maya in the Age of the Cross*, by William F. Hanks

7. *City of God: Christian Citizenship in Postwar Guatemala*, by Kevin O'Neill

8. *Death in a Church of Life: Moral Passion during Botswana's Time of AIDS*, by Frederick Klaits

9. *Eastern Christians in Anthropological Perspective*, edited by Chris Hann and Hermann Goltz

10. *Studying Global Pentecostalism: Theories and Methods*, by Allan Anderson, Michael Bergunder, Andre Droogers, and Cornelis van der Laan

11. *Holy Hustlers, Schism, and Prophecy: Apostolic Reformation in Botswana*, by Richard Werbner

12. *Moral Ambition: Mobilization and Social Outreach in Evangelical Megachurches*, by Omri Elisha

13. *Spirits of Protestantism: Medicine, Healing, and Liberal Christianity*, by Pamela E. Klassen

14. *The Saint in the Banyan Tree: Christianity and Caste Society in India*, by David Mosse

15. *God's Agents: Biblical Publicity in Contemporary England*, by Matthew Engelke

16. *Critical Christianity: Translation and Denominational Conflict in Papua New Guinea*, by Courtney Handman

17. *Sensational Movies: Video, Vision, and Christianity in Ghana*, by Birgit Meyer

18. *Christianity, Islam, and Orisa Religion: Three Traditions in Comparison and Interaction*, by J. D. Y. Peel

19. *Praying and Preying: Christianity in Indigenous Amazonia*, by Aparecida Vilaça

20. *To Be Cared For: The Power of Conversion and Foreignness of Belonging in an Indian Slum*, by Nathaniel Roberts

21. *A Diagram for Fire: Miracles and Variation in an American Charismatic Movement*, by Jon Bialecki

22. *Moving by the Spirit: Pentecostal Social Life on the Zambian Copperbelt*, by Naomi Haynes

23. *The Stranger at the Feast: Prohibition and Mediation in an Ethiopian Orthodox Christian Community*, by Tom Boylston

The Stranger at the Feast

*Prohibition and Mediation in an Ethiopian
Orthodox Christian Community*

———

Tom Boylston

UNIVERSITY OF CALIFORNIA PRESS

University of California Press, one of the most distinguished university presses in the United States, enriches lives around the world by advancing scholarship in the humanities, social sciences, and natural sciences. Its activities are supported by the UC Press Foundation and by philanthropic contributions from individuals and institutions. For more information, visit www.ucpress.edu.

University of California Press
Oakland, California

Suggested citation: Boylston, T. *The Stranger at the Feast: Prohibition and Mediation in an Ethiopian Orthodox Christian Community*. Oakland: University of California Press, 2018. doi: https://doi.org/10.1525/luminos.44

Chapter 5 was first published in different form in *Africa* Vol. 87, No. 2, 11.04.2017, p. 387–406, under the title "From sickness to history : Evil spirits, memory, and responsibility in an Ethiopian market village." (2017)

Material from Chapter 6 was first published in *Material Religion* 11(3): 281–302, under the title: "'And Unto Dust Thou Shalt Return': Death and the Semiotics of Remembrance in an Ethiopian Orthodox Christian Village." (2015).

Chapter 8 was first published under the title: "Sharing Space: On the Publicity of Prayer, between an Ethiopian Village and the Rest of the World" in *Praying with the Senses*: Contemporary Orthodox Christian Spirituality in Practice. Ed. Sonja Luehrmann. Bloomington: Indiana University Press (2018).

Library of Congress Cataloging-in-Publication Data

Names: Boylston, Tom, 1980- author.
Title: The stranger at the feast : prohibition and mediation in an Ethiopian Orthodox Christian community / Tom Boylston.
Description: Oakland, California : University of California Press, [2018] | Includes bibliographical references and index. |
Identifiers: LCCN 2017038245 (print) | LCCN 2017041872 (ebook) | ISBN 9780520968974 (ebook) | ISBN 9780520296497 (pbk. : alk. paper)
Subjects: LCSH: Christianity—Ethiopia—Case studies. | Taboo—Ethiopia—Case studies. | Mediation—Religious aspects—Christianity—Case studies. | Ethiopia—Church history.
Classification: LCC BR1370 (ebook) | LCC BR1370 .B69 2018 (print) DDC 281/.75—dc23
LC record available at https://lccn.loc.gov/2017038245

CONTENTS

Map   vi
Note on Amharic Pronunciation and Transliteration   vii
Acknowledgments   viii

  Introduction   1

1. A History of Mediation   22

2. Fasting, Bodies, and the Calendar   37

3. Proliferations of Mediators   56

4. Blood, Silver, and Coffee: The Material Histories of
   Sanctity and Slavery   72

5. The *Buda* Crisis   86

6. Concrete, Bones, and Feasts   103

7. Echoes of the Host   119

8. The Media Landscape   131

9. The Knowledge of the World   144

  Conclusion   156

Reference List   159
Index   173

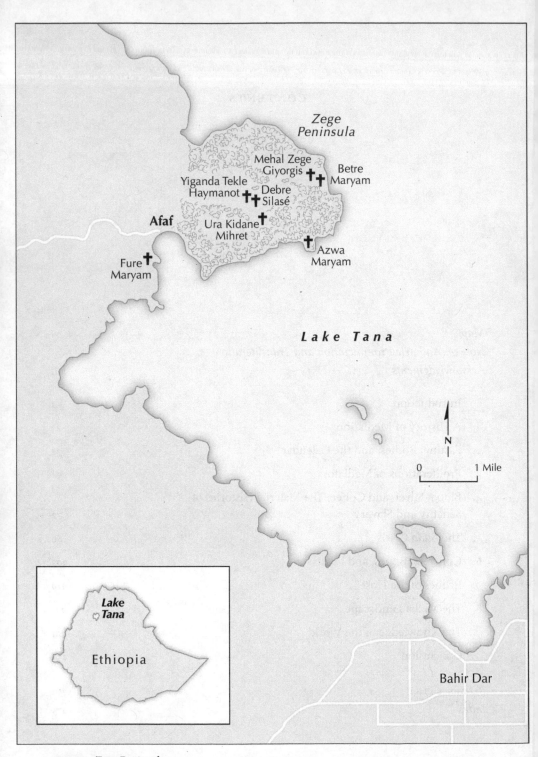

MAP 1. Zege Peninsula.

NOTE ON AMHARIC PRONUNCIATION AND TRANSLITERATION

Amharic transliteration is based on the system used by A. Pankhurst (1992). This system minimizes diacritics and is more approachable to nonspecialists than those used for technical linguistic work.

The vowels are represented as follows:

1st order: e (pronounced as in democracy)

2nd order: u (as in lunar

3rd order: í (as in Fiji)

4th order: a (as in father)

5th order: é (as in fiancé)

6th order: i (as in medicine)

7th order: o (as in vote)

Explosive consonants are represented by q, t', s', ch', and p'. Gemination is indicated by doubling of the consonant where appropriate.

ACKNOWLEDGMENTS

I have run up far too many intellectual debts to count since this research began. First of all I am grateful to everyone in Zege who has looked after me and put up with my questions: to Thomas and Haregwa, Abebe and Zebirhan, Abbo, Antihun and Askay, Eyayehu and Yekaba, Kassahun and Wibayé, to Menilek, Babbi, and Masti, to Aderaw and Getaneh, to Temesgen, Tillik Sew, Selam, Beza, Endalew, Yitayal, Mulet, Abderajah, to Taddesse and to *gashé* Tesfaye. I am grateful to Yilekal for his help in starting this work, and to Amare for introducing me. I thank everybody in the Ethiopian Orthodox Church who has assisted me with such patience: *Abba* S'om and *Abba* Melake Gennet; *Abba* Haylemaryam, *Mergéta* Worqé, *Mislené* Fantahun, *Memhir* Abbi, and in Addis Ababa to *Memhir* Daniel, who was always willing to explain things. Tefera Ewnetu has shared his expertise and time with unmatched generosity. *Igzíabhér yist'illiñ lehullachihu.* I owe special debts to the works of Tihut Yirgu Asfaw, Binayew Tamrat, and Abdussamad Ahmad, who have set the standard for studying Zege.

In Bahir Dar I am also tremendously grateful for the friendship of Anna, Kyle, Saul and Juliet, John Dulin, Anita, Caitlin, Stef, and all the Peace Corps folks. In Addis Ababa Makeda Ketcham, Yodit Hermann-Mesfin, Stéphane Ancel, Alula Pankhurst, and many others have provided generous guidance, and Brook Beyene introduced me to Amharic language and literature with flair and wit. Izabela Orlowska was a gracious host and an academic inspiration. Ralph Lee has shared freely his immense knowledge of the Ethiopian Orthodox Tewahido Church. Sara Marzagora has been an inspirational scholar.

At the LSE, Matthew Engelke and Michael Lambek offered assured guidance and intellectual inspiration. Fenella Cannell was a wonderful mentor, as were

Maurice Bloch and Adam Kuper. It was my privilege to share my work with Alanna, Agnes, Miranda, Alex, Gustavo, Dave, and many others. Special thanks to the Funktionalists, Deborah, Max, George, Jonah, and Hans, for bringing the fun, and to Insa, Tom G, Charlotte, Nico, and Andrew. And to Stephan Feuchtwang, a model of intellectual generosity and kindness.

Steven Kaplan showed exceptional generosity in reading an earlier draft of this manuscript, and Wendy James and Charles Stewart have been insightful commentators on earlier parts of the work.

I am grateful to Joel Robbins for his support for this project, and to Naomi, Jon, Andreas, James B, and the other friends who have made the anthropology of Christianity such a vibrant field to be a part of.

Jordan Haug, Koreen Reece, Lucy Lowe, Casey High, Beckie Marsland, Magnus Course, Maya Mayblin, Alex Nading, and many others have read parts of this manuscript and helped the work become what it is today. Jonathan Spencer and Janet Carsten have provided welcome and guidance, and everyone at Edinburgh has contributed to a wonderful intellectual environment. Diego Maria Malara has been the best reader and interlocutor I could have hoped for over the decade that I have worked on this project.

I am grateful to Nick, Rachel, Steve, Anne, Charlotte, Geoff, Maggie, Amanda, Justin, and to Dave W and Ben, there is nothing I can say that will do justice except thank you for being there.

To my parents for their endless support and to Nick and Latifeh and Cuz Jim and Lucy and Mainie, Bridge and Jim, Celia and Tim, Boz and Ella and Jess and Melissa.

And for Emily, Cassie, and Sam. Of course.

Introduction

A RITUAL REGIME I: PROHIBITION AND THE
CONNECTION OF THINGS

On the Zege peninsula it is forbidden to plough the land or to keep cattle or horses. The prohibition dates from a covenant *(kídan)* made between God and a wandering monk named *Abune* Betre Maryam sometime in the fourteenth century.[1] The covenant states that so long as nobody cuts trees, ploughs the land, or keeps large animals, God will provide the people of Zege with a living and protect them from natural disasters and wild animal attacks. As a result, Zege is covered by a dense coffee forest, in marked contrast to the arable and ploughlands that dominate most of northern Ethiopia. Nine church-monasteries maintain the prohibition on ploughing to this day, and residents of Zege (known as *Zegeña*) state clearly that the forest is tangible evidence of their continued observance of the covenant.[2]

The prohibition makes Zege ecologically unique as well as sacred. Forests have a long association with churches in Ethiopia (Tsehai 2008). They connote the Garden of Eden, and the fact that they are unploughed marks them apart from the curse of Adam, to eat bread "by the sweat of your brow" (Genesis 3:19). Forests also provide shade and shelter for the church, lending seclusion and modesty in the same way that clothes shelter the naked human body (Orlowska 2015). Images of shelter and seclusion predominate. And yet this same forest has made Zege an important node in long-distance trade routes and, for a significant period, an importer of slaves (Abdussamad 1997, Tihut 2009).

The prohibition of ploughing and the existence of the coffee forest, therefore, do not isolate Zege from the surrounding farmlands. Quite the opposite, they create interdependence, where inhabitants of the peninsula need a market to sell their coffee and fruit and obtain food staples. Moreover, as the church-monasteries have gained fame as sites of blessing, they have attracted pilgrims, kings, and lately foreign tourists to visit in search of blessing, political legitimacy, and historical experience. What initially appears as an isolating move, the prohibition of ploughing and the growth of the forest, turns out to create a dense web of spiritual and earthly connections. This close, seemingly paradoxical relationship between prohibition and interconnection lies at the heart of this book and, I argue, of contemporary socioreligious practice in Zege.

This book takes prohibition as a starting point for understanding the religious life of Orthodox Christians in Zege. I want to highlight how prohibitions create lasting, material states of affairs (such as the existence of the forest in Zege), but also how they build meaningful distinctions into the fabric of social life: here, between the forest, where ploughing is prohibited, and the surrounding farmlands, where it is not. The prohibition of ploughing is only one example of a religious regime in which eating, work, and sexuality are continuously subject to various fasts, avoidance rules, and periodic proscriptions. And yet prohibition is always accompanied by mediation: if refusing to plough creates a distinction between forestland and farmland, it also enables a relationship with God, via the intervention of the saint who made the original divine compact.

This is a place that has seen massive political upheaval since 1974: the fall of the emperor and rise of the socialist Derg; the land reforms that stripped the church of most of its holdings and deeply impacted local class relations; and the rise in 1991 of the secular-federal Ethiopian People's Revolutionary Democratic Front (EPRDF) government, which has rendered the Orthodox Church constitutionally equal to Islam and Protestantism, while reimagining Ethiopia along ethnic lines under the aegis of the developmental state (Clapham 2017, Donham 2002). And yet these developments have not seen a breakdown of the prohibitions and practices that organized religious-economic life in Zege. Rather, such practices have been reorganized and in some cases reemphasized in line with constantly developing local understandings of the proper arrangement of power and blessing. This proper arrangement revolves around the observance of prohibitions and the importance of mediators.

Alongside the emphasis placed on the religious protection of the forest, Orthodox Christians in Zege highlight the importance of fasting, of priestly and saintly intermediaries between humans and God, and of the protection and seclusion of ritual objects and spaces, in what amounts to a general theory of mediation. This theory explicitly opposes secular, modern, Protestant practices of leveling and breaking down distinctions with the properly Orthodox regulation and mediation of boundaries, whether these be the boundaries between humans and God, the distinction between the Orthodox community and other peoples, or the interface between a human body and the world.

This boundary work, based on prohibitions and their mediation, produces something approaching a total framework for social life: what I term a *ritual regime*. We have already seen how the prohibition of ploughing ties work, labor, and the environment to the work of the church-monasteries. In this and the following chapters it will become clear that the Orthodox calendar and its timetable of fasting and feasting incorporate human bodies into a structured religious life-world at a very basic experiential level, so that the daily life of the body and its rhythms becomes hard to separate from the calendrical rhythm of Orthodox ritual.

At times it appears that Orthodox life in Zege is totally bound up in this regime, and almost entirely defined by the remarkable continuity of practice engendered by the fasts and other forms of prohibition. But we will also see that this encompassing ritual regime is never total, and that it coexists with unorthodox practices and ideas of impressive diversity. To pick one example, it is common knowledge in Zege that poor and landless men often cut down trees to sell as firewood, violating the church's edict of protection and threatening the health of the forest as a whole (Tihut 2009: 63). They do so out of a sheer and immediate need that is impossible to square with the dominant narrative of the sacred forest, and the depth of such contradictions will become clear in chapters 4 and 5. We will also see that the structure of political authority in Zege has undergone significant transformation in recent decades, but that core principles of prohibition and mediation remain intact or even enhanced.

ANTHROPOLOGY AND ORTHODOXY

To speak of a kind of religious system built from pervasive, structured practices of prohibition and mediation puts this ethnography on quite a different footing from existing work in the anthropology of Christianity. Much of that work has taken as its theme the search for directness and immediacy in the religious practices of global Protestant and Pentecostal churches, while making efforts to trace the development of distinctly Protestant-modern ideologies of interiority and sincerity (e.g., Engelke 2007, Keane 2007, Bielo 2011). Even works that focus on mediation and the use of media show how intermediaries between humans and God become effaced in the search for direct, nonmediated, instant communication (Mazzarella 2004, Meyer 2011, Eisenlohr 2012). From such a perspective, intermediaries such as saints and priests may appear as obstructions to clear and sincere religious communication, while the observance of fasts and prohibitions looks like unthinking (and therefore insincere) deference to tradition.

Indeed, this is a criticism I have heard Protestants in Ethiopia make of Orthodox Christians: that Orthodox Christians do not read the Bible for themselves, but only follow rules and priests. My Orthodox friends in Zege respond that Protestants show arrogance in denying the need for intercession, and say that not follow-ing the fasts is tantamount to having no religion at all. Orthodox Christians in Ethiopia do not efface the medium, but valorize and sanctify it.

It has often been noted that the anthropology of Christianity has been weighted heavily toward the study of Protestantism and Pentecostalism, due in part to the pre-dominance of these churches in the places that anthropologists traditionally study (Hann 2007, Hann & Goltz 2010). Orthodox churches have seemed to lack that global scope, and it has not been obvious how to locate them within conversations about the anthropology of Christianity. The Orthodox affirmation of mediation is to some extent articulated as a response to Protestantism. But I want to avoid the assumption that Protestantism represents a modernizing, globalizing, rationalizing force, while Orthodoxy is simply reactionary, taking refuge in tradition, ritual, and institutional authority. It seems more useful to ask what are the starting premises from which Orthodox Christians in Zege approach the contemporary world.

One way to begin is to consider some of the distinctive ways that Orthodox Christians understand materiality and the relationship between God and the tan-gible world. Anthropologists of Christianity have tended to define Christianity's driving problem, following Hegel, as the difficulty of making the divine present in a fallen world, or of accessing that which is present but intangible (Cannell 2006: 14–15). What Engelke (2007) calls the "problem of presence" is taken to begin from absence: we cannot see or feel God, so we must somehow make him present.

I would suggest that Ethiopian Orthodox Christianity begins from the opposite problem: the boundary between God and humans is insufficiently stable (as are the boundaries of human bodies in general). There is a prevailing sense that divin-ity unbound is a profound physical danger to humans—those who enter the sanc-tum of a church while in an impure state are likely to be struck down or become sick; a thief who attempts to steal a sacred object may become frozen to the spot.

A large number of Orthodox practices in Zege concern themselves either with the boundaries of the holy, as in the seclusion of ritual objects, or with the bound-aries of bodies, as with restrictions around menstruation and bleeding. Prohibitive practices also mark out certain times as inappropriate for particular activities such as eating meat or working the fields. The boundary between God and humans, in all their physicality, is never totally closed, but is subject to careful and ongoing management.

God can seem less like an absence than an overwhelming presence. This goes along with a distinctive theory of materiality and mediation common to many Orthodox churches: the potential sanctity of all matter, including flesh (Hanganu 2010). Painted icons can be true points of contact with saints, and holy water, imbued with divine power, is a regular part of daily practice. As Engelhardt (forthcoming) puts it, "The mediatic nature of Orthodox Christianity is sensible everywhere—in the materials and prototypes of icons; the sacred language, script, and chant notation of service books; the intercessory power of saints; the bodies and voices of clergy; the architectural acoustics of churches; the Eucharist; and, ultimately, in Christ as the hypostatic union of God and humanity." Things, substances, and sensations can be not just ethically charged, in Keane's (2014) terms, but divinely charged.

But the potential sanctity of matter is subject to close regulation, and is understood to be granted from the top down. This is especially the case in Ethiopian Orthodoxy. Emanations of divine power on earth are due solely to God's grace (s'ega). The principal and perhaps only way for humans to access grace is through the seven sacraments (mistírat, "mysteries" or "secrets"): baptism, confirmation, matrimony, communion, unction of the sick, confession, and holy orders. Only clergy, empowered by the sacrament of holy orders, may perform these, and only bishops may ordain priests (Boylston 2017).

The use of holy water is not included among the sacraments, but in practice water is almost always made holy through the prayers of the clergy—that is, it is enabled by holy orders. In those cases where divine power irrupts in the world without the intervention of the clergy, it is usually through angelic action, as in Zege when the whole of Lake Tana becomes holy on the annual day of the Archangel Raphael. God's power, therefore, can be anywhere, but by the same token is subject to hierarchical mediation. Prohibition, mediation, and hierarchy, then, indicate a practical theory of matter, spirit, and authority. Mediation between humans and God is not simply an act of reaching out, but has a regulatory and restrictive function, which is most clearly evident in the practice of the Eucharist.

A RITUAL REGIME II: PURITY AND TIME

According to Orthodox doctrine, the Eucharist is fully transubstantial: through the performance of the liturgy and by divine grace, bread and wine become the actual body and blood of God. This is the one point in Orthodox life when Christians and God come into direct contact. It may come as a surprise, then, to learn that most Orthodox Christians do not take the Eucharist throughout most of their adult lives. This is because of concerns about purity, and especially the assumption that sexually mature adults are generally not in a fit state for communion.[3] The actual transformation of the Eucharist demands stringent regulations to preserve the purity of the host: communicants must fast completely for eighteen hours beforehand and abstain from sexual activity; they must have no open wounds or flowing mucus; menstruating and postpartum women may not enter the church building at all; and, I have been told, you must not take Communion if a fly has entered your mouth by accident. After taking Communion, you must not speak or spit or work or wash or blow on a fire or otherwise open the border between your body and the world.

These prohibitions have spatial correlates: Orthodox churches are divided into three concentric areas separated by walls: the inner holy of holies (meqdes or qiddiste qiddusan), accessible only to priests and deacons and home to the tabot, on which the Eucharist is consecrated; around this the qiddist, in which the liturgy is performed and communion is given; and outside of this, the qiné mahlét, where votive hymns are sung. Men and women must enter by separate doors and remain in separate areas at all times while within the church. Outside of this is the churchyard, an open space surrounded by a wall of its own.

The practical result is that, during any liturgical service, people will arrange themselves in a concentric pattern according to the degree of prohibitions they are in accord with: celebrants in the middle; then those in a state to take communion; then, outside the walls, large numbers of people attending the liturgy and performing prostrations but not actually entering the church building. Outside the churchyard wall, passers-by may stop to kiss the church gate and cross themselves. As was the case with the Zege forest, the existence of a prohibition creates a specific geographical arrangement among people and the environment. Note, however, one distinction whose importance will become clear: while the prohibition of ploughing is permanent, the Eucharistic prohibitions are temporary and rhythmical—fasting and purity are required at certain times and places and for certain actions, but are understood to be part of wider social and biological temporalities. If there is a time and place for abstinence, there are other times and places for feasting and the reproduction of life.

Eucharistic restrictions coexist with a raft of prohibitions derived from Leviticus, which have tremendous importance across Orthodox Ethiopia. Orthodox Christians may not eat pork or shellfish; men must be circumcised; boys must be baptized after forty days and girls after eighty, and until that time the mother may not enter church space because, as was repeatedly explained to me, of her bleeding.[4] The strong gendering of these prohibitions is evident; female reproductive bodies emerge as a special concern in a manner not unusual among patriarchal societies (Hannig 2014). Nonetheless and as we will see, this should not lead us to assume that women are entirely excluded from discourses and practices of holiness.

An important point about prohibitions is that you do not need to know the reasoning behind them in order to maintain them. In a casual situation I asked a group of friends, including some sons of priests, why boys were baptized after forty days and girls after eighty. A lively debate ensued: one man said that Jesus had been baptized after forty days; another said that girls gestate for five days longer than boys, though he could not say how this had become a forty-day differential; another suggested that girls were baptized after eighty because Mary had spent eighty days in exile in Egypt. I then asked a woman, who told me that her son and daughter had spent the same amount of time in the womb, and so she was unconvinced by those arguments. She was also unimpressed by the idea that women bleed longer after giving birth to girls. Finally, we all went to ask *Abba* S'om,[5] the local expert in exegesis, who explained that Jesus had been baptized at thirty years old, because Adam was thirty years old when he came to the world. The split between forty and eighty days for baptism was because Adam entered the Garden of Eden forty days after his creation, and Eve after eighty.[6]

All of my interlocutors agreed that the forty-eighty rule was important, though most were open about the fact that they were unsure exactly why it existed. But there is something to be learned from the form of their guesses: each assumed that there must be some parallel or archetype in the biblical story, and that the baptism rule would be explained by virtue of its formal resemblance to that archetype—rather than using a causal deduction. This is an example of what Mary Douglas (1999: 27) in her work on Leviticus calls "the analogical mode of reasoning," in which "what is true is so by virtue of its compliance with a microcosm of the world and of society; to be convincing, what is true must chime with justice; it looks to match microcosm with macrocosm in ever-expanding series."[7]

The prominence of analogical reasoning in esoteric traditions within Ethiopian Orthodoxy has been remarked on by both Young (1977) and Mercier (1997). The latter points to the numerological and symbolic work of authors of magico-religious scrolls as evidence of a "Hellenistic" theory of associations in which formal patterns are understood to reflect the nature of authority in the universe (cf. Lloyd 1996). I would suggest that logical systems based on analogy stretch much wider and deeper into Ethiopian Orthodox practical culture than either author has suggested, and that analogy is the mechanism by which everyday practice comes to be associated with the authority of church tradition. Here my approach is informed by Descola (2013), who proposes that "analogism" is the organizing ontological schema for a large portion of the world's societies. The implications of Descola's argument are too broad for this book to pursue in full, but I have drawn freely on his ideas, especially concerning the ways in which analogistic thought tends to produce totalizing models of the social cosmos.

Formal resemblances, rules based on analogy, and prohibitions share this quality: they can be understood by their logic of dividing and organizing the world, and can be maintained, without further exegetical investigation.[8] This is not to say that Ethiopian Orthodox Christians do not reflect on their practices, or that they do not care about the intention behind religious action. They certainly do. But prohibitions and analogical rules can continue to do their work without such examination (see Fortes 1966: 11, Bloch 2005).

In addition to the prohibitions derived from Leviticus, and perhaps most importantly, Orthodox Christians follow a calendar of fasts. Officially, there are seven major fasts (Fritsch 2001); minimally, you must avoid meat, animal products, and sexual activity on Wednesdays and Fridays, and throughout Lent. Most people avoid any food or water for a certain period of time on fasting days (usually until the liturgy has finished), and those who attend church must abstain from food and water completely. But there are in total more than 250 fasting days in the year, and it is expected that clergy will keep to these, while for lay Christians observance of the noncompulsory fasts will be largely a matter of "conscience and reputation" (Ephraim 2013: 81). The fasts are the core of Ethiopian Orthodox practice, and regarded by most Christians in Zege as the main point of distinction between Orthodox Christians and others.

The fasts are extensive and regular enough that prohibitions become a part of the everyday experience of having a body: even nonfasting days become meaningful by opposition to fasting days. In this way temporary, rhythmic prohibitions become a way of maintaining and managing one's bodily state of being. But prohibitions also come to define boundaries of the collective.

The clearest example is the prohibition on Christians eating Muslim meat and vice versa (Ficquet 2006). I learned this after attending a wedding in the local Muslim community, which is based in Afaf town and the area to the south around Fure Maryam church (see map). Many Christians attended and were fed vegetarian dishes. I temporarily forgot that I had, through my practices and associations, marked myself as a Christian, and had some of the main meat dish. A friend of mine approached me that evening and told me that I had done a bad thing and people were talking: the meat had been blessed in the name of Allah, and now if I were to enter church I would certainly become extremely unwell. In the general mood of conviviality I had let my guard down. Later when asking Muslim friends what they would do in Christian festivals, they said that they would always visit people and eat nonmeat food and drink nonalcoholic drink, and that Christians would always be sure to have these on hand. The importance of neighborly hospitality, however, coexisted with an equally important prohibition. The rules, then, may draw a sharp distinction between collectives at one level (that of meat, because meat must be divinely blessed when it is prepared), while allowing relations at another level (that of visiting and hospitality) (see Dulin 2016).

The Amharic term for *prohibition* or *taboo, newir,* has a range of important applications not obviously associated with Orthodox doctrine. Incest is *newir,* traditionally tracing relations back seven generations (Hoben 1973), although three generations are often considered sufficient. Also prohibited according to *Abba Siom* is marriage between God-kin, who are "just like blood relations."[9] But equally *newir* is marriage between a "clean" (*nes'uh*) or "proper"(*chewa*) person and a descendant of potters, weavers, Muslims, slaves, or Weyto (a marginalized ethnic group associated with hunting and canoe-making). Slave descent, in particular, is a point of deep division, as will become clear in the following chapters. Often respondents have described marriage prohibitions in terms of food prohibitions: weavers were thought to have been Muslims and so to follow the wrong fasts and eat the wrong meat; Weyto are widely denigrated as pagan eaters of hippopotamus flesh. As one friend told me, many *chewa* people would also refuse to share a table with descendants of slaves, even though these divisions are not usually publicly acknowledged; this could make seating at weddings a tricky procedure, though he stated that this was more true of his father's generation, and that he felt his own peers were more relaxed. This was a young man who had several close friends rumored to be of slave descent, but who nonetheless described the idea of marrying a slave as deeply *newir*. As is often the case with Muslim neighbors, friendship and cooperation are one thing; eating together and marriage quite another. But prohibitions or stigmas around sharing substance vary in their severity: while Christians may share vegetables but not meat with Muslims, they are supposed to throw away any cup or plate that has been used by a Weyto.[10]

Finally, cannibalism is profoundly *newir*, but turns out also to relate to marriage prohibitions. The idiom of the cannibal in Zege is the *buda*, an evil spirit that inhabits certain people and magically feeds on the flesh of others. As we will see in great detail, the idiom of *buda* is in fact closely associated with those marginal groups with whom marriage is also *newir*.

It would be possible to write a whole book dissecting the logic principles by which marriage and food prohibitions relate to classes of people, things, and spirits. But it is important to recognize that prohibitions do not just map out, describe, and impose order on socioreligious classifications: they also enforce and bring them into being as ongoing states of affairs. Marriage prohibitions, for example, create two de facto and unequal endogamous classes in Zege; to be *chewa* is to define the terms of prohibition. While this is rarely acknowledged, it has an extremely durable effect on social relations. These marriage prohibitions coexist, in an incommensurable way, with fasting and dietary prohibitions, which include all Orthodox Christians (including all slave descendants) within the same code of practice. It is one thing to deduce the logics behind prohibitions (whether they relate to blood or to ideas of proximity and distance, for example) and quite another to understand how prohibitions create durable relations of inclusion and exclusion within a society.

Prohibitions can organize relations between human groups, between the genders, between humans and God, and between bodies and the environment. They can become operative at certain times and in certain places and situations, and they lend a certain sense that life itself has a structure, and has certain kinds of difference imbued into it. These differences always possess a moral quality: to threaten them becomes an act of pollution. For Orthodox Christians in Zege, prohibitions are explicitly mechanisms by which humans demonstrate control over desire and pride. At the same time they draw distinctions between "proper," "clean," *chewa* people who refuse improper desires and connections and other people who do not. And yet, as the example of interreligious hospitality shows, the distinctions that prohibitions create are always capable of being mediated. Indeed, that mediation may be part of the process of prohibition itself.

The anthropological tradition offers a wealth of resources for thinking about prohibition; ambivalence around sex, death, and eating animals seems to be a human universal. Anthropologists have tended to focus on the symbolic and logi cal orders that underlie prohibition, in a manner that is, explicitly or implicitly, structuralist: treating prohibitions as basically synchronic and concerned with symbolic order and classification. Even Valeri (2000), who is critical of "intellec-tualist" approaches, still devotes most of his wide-ranging analysis to the logical patterns that underlie taboo practices.

This tradition, most famously represented by Lévi-Strauss (e.g., 1964, 1966) and Douglas (1966), considers prohibition at its heart as part of the human quest to classify and order the world and to render anomalies and contradictions manage-able. This work is foundational: there is no doubt that prohibitions produce clear binary distinctions (fasting/nonfasting, sacred/profane, Christian/non-Christian, human/animal, or human/God) from which logical orders can be built. But there is cause for dissatisfaction with models that would interpret prohibition in purely structural-conceptual terms. As Lambek (1992), Gell (1996), Valeri (2000: 95), Descola (2013), and others have pointed out, matters of identity and difference are not just taxonomic exercises; they are produced in everyday acts of practical and ethical identification and distinction.[11]

We have seen that prohibitions on ploughing actively shape the living environ-ment in Zege, as well as set the temporal and spatial conditions in which labor and consumption may take place. Prohibitions create ways of being in time and ways of being with others: they make ongoing states as well as conceptual oppositions. This state-maintaining capacity is largely a result of the negative nature of prohi-bitions. Not doing something (eating meat, ploughing the land) is not so much a clearly definable action as an open-ended state of being. Abstaining from some-thing has a different temporal quality than doing something: there are an infinite number of things I am not doing right now (household chores, reading fiction, retraining as a chemical engineer), but my not doing them only becomes salient when I *might* do them, or I want to do them, or other people around me are doing them.[12] In Ethiopia, it may not be clear whether I am fasting or simply between meals, until we sit down to eat together.[13]

Michael Lambek (1992: 246) discusses this definition-by-negation with regard to Malagasy taboo: "Self-identity or self knowledge is predicated not on substance, but on that which the other is not." Lambek (1992: 253–55) goes on to show how this not doing becomes an embodied status, a "continuously vibrant" moral condition. He draws on Fortes's (1966: 16) account of taboos as a kind of living rule set, where "eating lends itself uniquely to the imposition of rules." Because food is a regular, intimate, and recurring need, food prohibitions must be continuously reaffirmed through practice.

The idea of taboo as making states of being is perhaps most pronounced in Gell (1996: 137): "Taboos on eating, on killing, on sexual intercourse, on looking at, touching, etc., together circumscribe a 'hole' in the texture of shareable intersubjective reality which, privileged with respect to a specific individual, constitutes his soul or ego or personality. Taboo does more than express the self: it constitutes the self" (cited in Valeri 2000: 98). Likewise in Zege, to keep the fasts is to be an Orthodox Christian; to refuse marriage to slaves is to be *chewa*. But in the case of marriage, a profound asymmetry is present: only the "proper" get to constitute themselves in this way, as observers of prohibition. The definition of social reality itself is deeply one-sided.

This presents significant ethnographic problems. I have worked over a number of years to try to elicit accounts from slave descendants and other marginal figures of how life works in Zege, and these are presented in this book. But they are extremely partial, not just because it is difficult to interview marginal people in the presence of others who define the terms of the encounter, but because the isolating dimensions of stigma impede the formulation of any kind of stable counterdiscourse. At the same time, Orthodox Christianity and Islam do offer potent ways for marginal people to claim to belong, and to mark themselves as correct followers of prohibitions in their own right. It is a point enshrined in the Fetha Negest, the Law of Kings, that a Christian's slaves must be baptized, suggesting that the rejection of identity with slaves has never been total (Pankhurst 2011).

The embodied nature of prohibitions around eating, reproduction, and sexuality, furthermore, lends them a profound and important affective dimension (Valeri 2000: 48, 101). This is true in two respects: First, as with my consumption of Muslim meat, the violation of prohibitions around the body tends to produce reactions of disgust or fear. Second, through acts of abstention, we work on and shape our own feelings of hunger or sexual desire. As Valeri has it, "what are the relations between object and subject that taboo regulates? Principally eating, touching, and penetrating. . . . All these involve the body as desiring, that is, feeding on its objects, consuming them" (2000: 101). (To these Valeri might have added being eaten, being touched, being penetrated, and the like.) This aspect is particularly important for Ethiopian Orthodox understandings of fasting as an act that, in weakening the flesh, suppresses sinful desires and pridefulness and encourages more spiritual yearnings (Malara 2017, Ephraim 2013, Levine 1965).

Fortes likewise notes that avoidance frequently appears as evidence of self-possession, and a degree of control over the appetites that distinguishes humans from beasts. From this perspective, to abstain from killing, or from eating certain foods, or from certain sexual acts is to demonstrate that you can be moral at all. To abstain is to enact a distinction between beings capable of regulating desire and those that are not. I believe that this is a premise of Ethiopian Orthodox prohibitions, and that we can thus add something to Lambek's account of how taboo enacts and marks the self by negating the other. Following a prohibition does not just mark me as different than the other who does not; it marks me *as a negator*—as one who is in general capable of abstinence and avoidance, as opposed to those who, not observing such limits, are beholden to their appetites. But as we have seen, and as Lambek and Fortes indicate, this is not just about producing conceptual oppositions, but about living ways of being and indeed whole geographies of prohibition.

A RITUAL REGIME III: MEDIATION AND HIERARCHY

Since 1991 various forms of Protestantism have rapidly gained ground at the expense of Orthodoxy in traditionally Orthodox areas (Haustein 2011), compelling Orthodox Christians to formulate active responses and to articulate their own position. Zege remains almost entirely Orthodox, but there is nonetheless a strong sense of Protestantism as an existential threat. I asked *Abba*[14] S'om to explain the major differences between Orthodoxy and Protestantism, and received a reply: "*Maryam attamalednim yilallu*" (They say Mary does not mediate/intercede) whereas in fact "*Tamallednallech; kefit'rat belay, kefet'arí betacch*" (She mediates/ intercedes for us, above creation, below the creator). He went on to discuss how Protestants deny transubstantiation, thus denying both the role of priests and the rules of Eucharistic purity, and how Protestant ritual was therefore "worldly" *(alemawí)*. The role of specialist, ordained priests is understood here as a function of prohibition rules: the sacrament of holy orders, bestowed from on high by God's grace, is necessary for the performance of the liturgy and the handling of the Eucharist. Prohibitions are accompanied by a pervasive religious division of labor. Where there are rules and acts of avoidance, we see not just mediators, but proliferations of mediators: Mary, saints, priests, monks, and various other expert actors are required to manage the boundaries (Kaplan 1984).

Asking lay people about Protestants, I received similar responses, but with an even stronger focus on Mary. One friend, Temesgen, used the same phrase for the Protestant idea that Mary does not intercede *(attamaledim)* and also pointed out that, because they drank milk on Fridays, they were *koshasha (dirty)*, while wrinkling his nose and rubbing his shoulders in disgust. Violating fasting days and prohibitions and the denial of Mary's intercession go together, I suggest, because it is assumed that there is no need for mediators when you do not respect boundaries.[15]

Relationships between lay people and Mary take a number of practical forms in Zege. Thirty-three major annual feasts of Mary are included in the calendar, while the churches of Fure Maryam and Azwa Maryam, being consecrated in her name each observe a major festival on one of these days.

Some people have *zikir* pacts with her in which a request for assistance (for example, with fertility) is made and, if granted, the petitioner will hold a feast for her neighbors on one of Mary's annual days. On the celebration of Mary's birthday, *Ginbot Lideta,* family and neighbors gather together to eat in Mary's name and to promise to meet again one year in the future (see chapter 7). That so many of these commemorations involve eating and feasting is a defining feature of Ethiopian Orthodox relations with saints: we related to them by eating or fasting together in their names. There are also fasts specifically for Mary, most notably those commemorating *Qwisqwam*, the exile in Egypt, and *Filseta*, the Assumption. During the fast of *Filseta* there are certain hymns that women in Zege sing during the night, sometimes removing their clothes and wrapping themselves in sharp leaves to mark her suffering. An example, related to me by Tefera:

> Out of all, out of all (the grains), teff is the smallest,
> (Yet) she rises, wearing a shield
> Our mother Mary, what happened to her?
> Bowing her head, she cries
> Even if she cries, even if she lets her tears flow
> While her son hangs on the cross,
> "Hang me, let them beat me."[16]

Key themes here are the empathy of Mary with the suffering of mothers, and the protection that God offers to the meek, through her intercession (Marcus 2001). In Ethiopian Mariology Mary is fully human but possesses certain special characteristics: she was mortal but her body was not subject to putrescence. In the words of the former patriarch (Paulos 1988: 205): "Her death confirms that she is not a heavenly being but truly our human sister." However, her body did not decompose but was taken intact into heaven, as commemorated by the feast of *Filseta*, the Assumption: "the Lord did not permit the body in which He Himself had dwelt to fall prey to corruption and dissolution: though Mary as a human being underwent death, she was taken up into heaven" (Paulos 1988: 206). All humans will be returned to their bodies on judgment day, but until then "in her perfect state she intercedes for humanity until the final judgement" (Paulos 1988: 205).[17] Mary's physical incorruption contrasts with the leaky and endlessly mutable bodies of regular people, but as a human herself she can still speak to us, grieve with us, and feel pity for us (Bynum 1995: 113).

As Ethiopian Orthodox Christians make abundantly clear, Mary is due veneration not in isolation but because of her relationship to God. This brings out a rather important point: part of God's becoming human (although still divine) through the Incarnation was to gain kin, because having kin is part of the human condition. To engage with God through Christ is thus to engage with a wider web of relations that make such communion possible. A key part of such relations is the *kidan,* or covenant (Antohin 2014, Girma 2012). This is a pact made between God and a saint on behalf of humans—a mediated agreement with lasting effects.

A paradigm of the covenant is the Kidane Mihret, the Covenant of Mercy, which is also the name by which the monastery of Ura in Zege is consecrated. This refers to Mary pleading with Christ on behalf of all humanity. According to Paulos

(1988: 73),[18] Mary appeals to him, "by my womb which bore Thee nine months and five days, . . . by my breasts which gave Thee suck, and by my mouth which kissed Thee, and by my feet which walked about with Thee." On hearing this, Christ compares his mother's sufferings and grief with his own, and agrees that all who seek intercession in her name will be saved. Mary's suffering and grief as a mother make possible a connection between God and the rest of humanity.

Similar patterns of covenant and salvation are widespread. In Zege's own foundation story, *Abune* Betre Maryam does not just gain salvation in return for his devotion; he is promised that all who pray in his name will be saved, as well as receive earthly protection. The saint as mediator becomes a patron for those who follow, and one whose holy work is explicitly understood to be done on others' behalf.

Thus far this introduction has sought to lay out the foundational logics and practices of prohibition and mediation. Some important principles follow from these. First, the existence of prohibitions and purity rules means that specialists are usually required to mediate between humans and God, and so a religious division of labor is operative. Second, since it is possible to obey or enforce a prohibition without exactly knowing why, many forms of religious knowledge can be deferred upward (Bloch 2005, Bandak & Boylston 2014).

This does not mean that the clergy conspires to keep the population in ignorance; strong traditions of textual commentary exist instructing specialists how to communicate religious knowledge to lay folk (*andimta;* Cowley 1989) and today a widespread Sunday school movement exists for the religious education of the laity. Rather, it is the job of religious specialists to do certain kinds of work (performing the liturgy, keeping the calendar, passing on the textual tradition, monastic prayer for the souls of the community) for everyone else, because this work is not compatible with the mundane work of growing coffee or raising children. That incompatibility, the same logic by which adults tend not to take the Eucharist, is a basic practical tenet of Orthodox religious life in Zege. Like any boundary, it requires a huge amount of effort to maintain; and the more people work to maintain it, the more they produce intermediary figures who stand between worldly and spiritual life.

The Amharic verb *mamalled* is sometimes translated as "mediation" and is glossed by Kane as "to intercede, intervene" or "to conciliate." It may also be read as "to plead on behalf of"; grammatically it suggests doing something for someone else. This is the word used by my respondents to describe what Mary does for us. It implies that Mary's pleas on our behalf are much more likely to be heard than any effort we make on our own, because of Mary's special relationship with God.

In recent work on religion, "mediation" has come to be used in a wider sense, to denote the material underpinnings of any communicative action, but especially communication between humans and God. Here "material mediation" refers to practices of making "transcendent" or "invisible" things present to the senses through material communications (e.g., Meyer 2014, Vries 2001). Here media are understood "in the broad sense of transmitters across gaps and limits" (Meyer 2014: 24), and the problem of religious communication is understood as a material one: the "transcendent" must be made accessible to the senses.

For my friends and informants in Zege, "mediation" *(mamalled)* addresses a slightly different problem, which is that of authority. God is omnipresent but, notwithstanding Christ's sacrifice, humanity remains in a state too sinful and impure to relate to God directly. To do so would be to commit the sin of arrogance *(t'igab;* Levine 1965, Messay 1999). In the words of Roger Cowley (1972: 246): "The work of intercession belongs to created beings. The creator is prayed to, and does not himself pray to another."

For this reason we have saints, the Virgin Mary, the holy sacraments, and the hierarchy of the Orthodox Church: as people in Zege put it, to carry our prayers to God on our behalf. These intermediaries enable human-divine communication, but in going between they also keep things in their place. Saints can mediate for us because they have the quality of being listened to by others *(tesamínnet);* they represent us as diplomats, not just as messengers.

It is not always obvious whether the separation between humans and God is a metaphysical one premised on his physical difference from us, or a hierarchical one based on his exalted rank. In using the English term *mediation,* rather than the narrower "intercession," I hope to maintain the tension between these two possibilities: mediation as the material actualization of a relationship, and mediation as the maintenance of hierarchical distance. What makes mediation a particularly compelling question for religious studies is that in practice these questions of managing material difference (between flesh and spirit, for example) and status difference (between servant and master) often emerge together.

THE FIELDWORK AND THE RELIGIOUS DIVISION
OF KNOWLEDGE

The research for this book took place between February 2008 and June 2009, with return visits of up to a month every year until 2014. I arrived in Ethiopia at the beginning of 2008, looking for a place to study the relationship between Orthodox Christianity and local practices of magic and spirit possession. As my research developed and I realized the importance of daily practices such as fasting, my focus shifted toward the pervasive embeddedness of Orthodoxy: in the local material environment, in the economy, and in the complex memory work around the forest and the churches. I was interested in Zege as an important historical center of Orthodox Christianity, but one that because of its environment seemed slightly out of step with the rest of the highlands. In February 2008 I chartered a tourist boat and asked the captain, Amare, if there was somewhere I might try to live in Zege, where his father was a priest, and if he could introduce me to people.

Amare took me to Afaf (pop. c. 3000), the market town at the edge of the forest, where the Zege peninsula meets the mainland. He introduced me to Thomas and Haregwa, the owners of a local bar with a room to rent where I would stay for the next several months before moving to quieter accommodation in a compound where some schoolteachers and other incomers rented rooms.

On finding out that I was there to study Orthodoxy, most people I spoke to were encouraging; they were proud of their religious traditions, and felt they ought to be more widely known. In the afternoons I sometimes chewed *kh'at* with whoever was around, and I read Leslau's *Introductory Grammar of Amharic* cover to cover, before moving on to an Amharic translation of *Harry Potter and the Philosopher's Stone*. In the evenings, if there were no customers in the bar, I would watch Jean-Claude Van Damme movies with Thomas on the bar's TV and try to translate the events for him. Since those movies are not heavily dependent on dialogue, this was a suitable beginner's task.

The biggest methodological challenge I faced was how to negotiate the local knowledge economy: the range of different kinds of experts on religious and esoteric matters—what Harald Aspen (2001: 17) calls the "knowledge buffet"—and the range of opinions and attitudes that other people might have toward those experts. On top of this, there were differences between the market town, where I lived, and the inner peninsula. Afaf town still counts as part of Zege, but it is also the interface between Zege and the lands beyond, and is considered much less "traditional" *(bahilawi)* than the forest itself.

Over time I developed a set of routes that I would walk every few days, or whenever I felt at a loss for what to do. One would take me to Afaf's local church of Fure Maryam—off the tourist track—to speak with *Abba* S'om, a priest and expert in scripture and exegesis, to whom most people in the area deferred on questions of doctrine and of *why* certain practices were performed. *Abba* S'om was not from Zege, having arrived from near Lalibela some time ago, and had ambitions to move on in the church. He supported himself by working as a tailor on market days, and when last we spoke in 2014 he had reenrolled in secondary school, in his mid-thirties, in the hope of meeting the requirements for further theological training. He is extremely well read and always showed tremendous generosity and patience in explaining Orthodox doctrine to me while we drank coffee in his little hut outside of town. He also took responsibility for preaching at festivals and teaching Sunday school to the people of Afaf.

We would usually be joined by *Abba* Melake Gennet, an elderly priest and *mergéta*.[19] He was a specialist in *Aqwaqwam,* the votive dance and chants that accompany church services, and provided teaching to the young deacons and church students who lived in tiny, threadbare huts around the church. Many had come far from home, at ages as young as seven, to begin their church training, but when I arrived *Abba* Melake Gennet told me that student numbers were dwindling as more young people sought modern education instead. As we will see in chapter 8, recent events have reversed this trend somewhat. These students were still at the stage of learning the rote learning, going sound by sound through the Psalms in classical Ge'ez, not yet fully able to discern their meaning. I tried to interview deacons and church students where possible, but their work is famously tiring and they tended to extreme shyness and deference, so I often decided to let them be. Many adult clergy, on the other hand, were happy to reminisce about their apprenticeship.

My second route would take me into the Zege forest to the port of Ura, and then perhaps on to Mehal Zege at the tip of the peninsula. This is the main path that connects the forest to Afaf, and especially on market days (Tuesday, Thursday, and Saturday) one tends to meet a lot of people en route to and from town. Mehal Zege had the oldest two monasteries on the peninsula (Betre Maryam and Giyorgis), but Ura was closer and had the important monasteries of Ura Kidane Mihret and Azwa Maryam. I would interview monks and church-monastery assistants whenever I could, and am particularly grateful to *Abba* Haylemaryam, a senior monk at Azwa Maryam, who would frequently sit with me for long periods and explain what was going on. In these early months the then-abbot of Mehal Zege Giyorgis, one *Abba* Agumas, made sure to visit me to make sure I knew the official history of the monasteries.

In Ura I would also get to know a number of men who worked as tour guides and their families. The tour guides were knowledgeable, were used to explaining their history to outsiders, and were without exception extremely welcoming and helpful with my work. I owe a particular debt to Menilek and "Babbi" Alemu and all the members of their family, who took me in, fed me generously, and treated me always with warmth and friendship. When not actively interviewing, it was my pleasure to sit with them and others by the shores of Lake Tana, to speculate about questions that had come out of my research, to talk about life in Europe, and most importantly to argue about whether Man United or Arsenal would win the Premiership.

Many of the tour guides were also the children of church officials, and it was through them that I slowly began to learn of the class of people—the *mislené* and *liqered*, the *yewist' gebez* and the *yewicch' gebez*—not fully of the church or fully separate from it, who had been so important in the political life of Zege before the Derg. My efforts to reconstruct this system—and to explore the consequences for the local religious political economy—can be found in chapter 1.

My third route would take me by a different path up the hill into central Zege and the monastery of Yiganda Tekle Haymanot. In this area lived Beza, the traditional doctor to whom most people deferred on matters of general health and medicine, and especially on the treatment of *buda* spirit attacks (see chapter 5). On each of my walks I would try to conduct a semiformal interview, and then perhaps visit somebody in their home for food. In this way I tried to build an understanding of Zege that went beyond my placement in Afaf town. The main path through the Zege forest splits off into innumerable smaller paths that seem haphazard but effectively divide different landholdings. Residents of the forest themselves sometimes comment on the complexity of the paths, and sometimes get lost in unfamiliar areas. I would always go accompanied to interviews—so as not to get lost, but also because nobody would let me walk alone: they would consider it gross negligence to do so, because I am a guest, and because being alone one tends to depression, loneliness, or boredom *(dibirt),* which is a terrible state in which to leave another person. I also found it helpful to have people who were familiar with my project and interview style to come along and help explain me to people, to clarify my Amharic questions, and to discuss people's responses. As it turned out, I almost never conducted an interview without such accompaniment. Two young men, Abebe and Zebirhan, took the most interest in my work and ended up becoming de facto research assistants and accompanying me on a large number of interview trips. Their help made much of this research possible.

In my downtime in Afaf I would visit people's homes or sit somewhere public in one of the town's three main food and drink establishments, and either join in discussions or ask people questions that had arisen from my interviews. I also made efforts to visit different kinds of specialists: magicians and medicine purveyors, former church students, and, with less success, spirit mediums.

The natural tendency was for younger men with some school education to show more interest in talking to me, especially since I could talk competently about football. I did my best to reach out to other kinds of people, visiting older people in their homes and soliciting women's opinions as well as men's. This usually meant public places where there were other men present, and as such it is often hard to know what women really think about certain issues. But I was able to talk to older women when they hosted me, to my host Haregwa and her relatives, and to women who shared my compound in later months. I do my best to represent their perspectives in the pages that follow, though I must admit to limitations on this front, and I have been fortunate to be able to draw on work by Tihut Yirgu Asfaw (2009) and Rahel Mesfin (1999, 2002) in this area.

At the end of my initial long stint of research, in 2009, there were certain things I was not completely satisfied with. One was my understanding of the church-political organization of the peninsula; another was the history of slavery in the area and the continuing presence of slave descendants. This was the subject of many uncomfortable jokes but was difficult to discuss openly. Because of this, I made multiple return visits, attempting as best as I could to fill in some of the gaps. In this I received remarkable assistance from Tefera Ewnetu, a student and tour guide from Ura with a deep interest in local history. Tefera read my entire PhD thesis after I made it available online, and we discussed at length those things he disagreed with or thought I ought to have included. Following on from this, we conducted several interviews together across the peninsula, especially with church scholars and senior figures in Zege society. This follow-up work has vastly increased my understanding of Zege life, and I am indebted to Tefera for his help.

OUTLINE OF BOOK

The progression of this book reflects a tension between structure and history, and my attempts to represent both the powerful regulatory forces that make up the ritual regime of Zege and the deep historical transformations that have nonetheless taken place. The first three chapters are concerned with the political and especially religious organization of everyday life in Zege. Chapter 1 attempts a reconstruction of the social history of Zege, especially the complex and unique relationship between monastic and political power in the area. Chapter 2 describes the Orthodox calendar, perhaps the most significant mechanism of the religious regulation of life in Zege. The focus here is on how, through fasting and feasting, the daily experience of having a body unfolds in a framework and a material environment that are always already coordinated along religious lines. At the same time, we see how dissidence and nonconformism frequently get expressed through apparently trivial violations of the calendar. Chapter 3 considers the religious division of labor and the work of priests and other specialists. It shows how church work frequently becomes connected with more shadowy traditions, and lays out the theory of knowledge as the sole property of God that underlies the system.

Having outlined Zege's structures of authority and their transformation, I then proceed in chapters 4 and 5 to unravel the problematic parallel histories that people in Zege are well aware of: histories of slavery, exclusion, and sorcery fears. I explore how the church forest has been simultaneously the site of histories of sanctity and slavery, and how these histories have produced rifts that are still deeply felt. Chapter 5 discusses an outbreak of *buda* spirits and shows how this experience of crisis is tied to extensive histories of labor relations and notions of moral exchange. Throughout these chapters we will see the narrative of the decline of hospitality that has become a key trope by which recent social change has been understood.

Chapters 6 and 7 take us deeper into the religious-material interface in Zege, especially the transformation of hierarchical feeding practices. Chapter 6 continues the discussion of the decline of hospitality by examining changes in the use of concrete graves and the devaluing of funeral feasting. Chapter 7 compares hosting, hospitality, and eating together in the name of saints with Eucharistic practice, and argues that small-scale "echoes" of the Eucharist are foundational to relations between saints and community.

The final two chapters consider Zege's outward-looking relationship to the wider world. Chapter 8 discusses media, church building, and interreligious relations, as national and international interreligious politics has become far more tangible in the local environment of Zege. Chapter 9 investigates how church knowledge, modern education, and the know-how required for young men to find opportunity in the world fit together. The chapter shows how young men with church backgrounds are also frequently those who gain access to modern education and to the social opportunities that foreigners sometimes provide. Monastic traditions of knowledge itself as an ascetic practice have not necessarily kept people from secular, modern forms of knowledge; instead the two traditions are constantly drawn back into dialogue.

NOTES

1. *Abune,* "Our Father," is an honorific term for bishops and sometimes other holy men.

2. I refer to church-monasteries for simplicity. Every monastery *(gedam)* contains a church *(bête kristiyan)* and locals sometimes use the terms interchangeably. All churches in Zege were entirely monastic until roughly three generations ago, when a request was made for priests to serve in Ura and Yiganda. This may have been due to concerns about monks starting families.

3. As many priests in Addis Ababa have explained to me, the official church position is that any Christian may take Communion provided they have first given confession and observed the other purity restrictions. Nonetheless, the reticence of nonelderly adults to take communion is widespread.

4. The derivation of these rules is clearly not Leviticus alone, as the rules concerning baptism suggest. Many are codified in the Fetha Negest, the Law of Kings, which was codified around 1240 and translated into Ge'ez in the fifteenth century, where it became a key legal text for the Ethiopian monarchy (Pankhurst 2011). The influence of Leviticus in, for example, the forty-day and eighty-day rule and the repurification of the mother is clear (see Ullendorff 1968).

5. *Abba,* "Father," is a general term of address for priests and monks. The priest's name is actually *Abba* T'iw Melesan, but he is universally and affectionately known as *Abba* S'om, "Father Fasting." He is also a *Memhir,* "teacher."

6. Versions of this account appear in the Book of Jubilees as well as various versions of the Life of Adam and Eve (Stone 2013: 36).

7. Douglas's (1999: 18) extended explanation of the analogical mode of Leviticus helps to understand my friends' thinking about prohibition: "Leviticus' literary style is correlative, it works through analogies. Instead of explaining why an instruction has been given, or even what it means, it adds another similar instruction, and another and another, thus producing its highly schematized effect. The series of analogies locate a particular instance in a context. They expand the meaning. . . . They serve in place of causal explanations. If one asks, Why this rule? the answer is that it conforms to that other rule. If, Why both those rules? The answer is to a larger category of rules in which they are embedded as subsets or from some of which they are distinguished as exceptions. Many law books proceed in this concentric, hierarchical way. In Leviticus the patterning of oppositions and inclusions is generally all the explaining that we are going to get. Instead of argument there is analogy." This passage encapsulates the logic of the ritual regime I am describing.

8. Further discussion can be found in Lloyd (1996, 2011) and Descola (2013), who explore how the analogical mode of thought based on micro and macro resemblances and repetitions becomes, under certain conditions, the dominant logic of a broad but not exhaustive range of societies, including

premodern China and India, ancient Greece, much of Africa, and the indigenous societies of the Andes. Descola describes how sacrifice is a key practice of such "analogistic" societies (and only these societies) because of the concern they evince with global connection and disconnection. In this context, the focus on sacrifice in Christian society in Zege, along with the astonishingly, redundantly dense web of analogic symbolism surrounding Orthodox ritual and bodily practice, suggests that a sustained consideration of analogism is appropriate here. This informs my thought throughout this book, but to give a list of those practices that support a reading of Orthodox society as a whole would take a large amount of space and detract from my attempts to show not only how ritual life in Zege is logically ordered, but how many practices break from or run against this semitotalizing system of order that I term the *ritual regime*.

9. When they are born, children are assigned a Godparent of the same gender; marriage prohibitions extend to the close kin of the Godparent.

10. The prohibition of relations with Weyto does not extend to economic relations. Traditionally Weyto have made papyrus *tankwa* canoes for all residents of the area (Gamst 1979). For an account of similar economic relations and marital dietary prohibitons between Christians and Beta Israel, see Salamon (1999).

11. In fairness to Lévi-Strauss, his structuralism was never simply about drawing distinctions and making concepts. As Lambek (1992) points out, his entire theory of society as exchange is premised on the basis of the prohibition of incest, which compels men to seek wives beyond their immediate kin (rather as the prohibition on ploughing in Zege compels coffee farmers to trade with outsiders for their food). In Lévi-Strauss's theory of sacrifice, too, the aim of all the conceptual world is to build contiguity between humans and God—to make a relationship possible, before severing it through the act of death and so compelling divinity to make some kind of return (Lévi-Strauss 1966: 228).

12. Valeri (2000: 408), in contrast, argues that nonaction is actually more clearly marked than action.

13. Not all activity related to fasting is negation or nonaction: admonishing others to keep the fast, for example, is a positive form of action, as is refusing the offer of prohibited food. The point is that a state of fasting is maintained between such moments of affirmation, and that the temporal qualities of prohibitions similarly extend beyond the actions that affirm them.

14. *Abba,* "Father," term of address for priests and monks.

15. Most of my data concerning Protestantism concern Orthodox Christians' impressions and imaginings of what Protestants do, and may or may not reflect actual ideas and practice.

16. Translation by Mellatra Tamrat, who glosses the *teff* (local staple grain) metaphor as follows: "even the smallest rise, shielded by the protection of God." Original Amharic as transcribed by Tefera:

Kchulu kchulu teff tensaleeh
Geleba lebsa tenesalech,
Emye mariam men hunanalech
Angetan defeat teleksalech
Betalekse betaneba
Lja besekel singelata,
Enian Sekelugn yegerfugn.

17. Mary's special physical status was apparent during her life; she is said to have never menstruated and to have lived on mana; according to the Anaphora of St. Mary: O virgin, thou didst not eat earthly bread but heavenly bread prepared in the heaven of heavens" (Paulos 1988: 201).

18. Here Paulos draws from Arras (1974: 73–74).

19. The title of *mergéta* denotes religious knowledge, for which one does not necessarily have to be ordained; the next step, upon passing examinations in Gondar, is to become a *memhir,* "teacher."

1

A History of Mediation

Zege's monasteries have historically been notable for their high degree of autonomy from the state, and for their extensive administrative powers, serving as "the basis of administration, taxation, and court arbitration" (Binayew 2014: xi). This did not necessarily mean that the monasteries were simply felt to be extensions of the state. Several local scholars have described to me how the monasteries have acted to shelter the populace from state extraction. In one example, I was told how the Emperor Menilek had fallen sick and had relieved the peninsula of all taxation in order to gain the blessing of the monasteries. Bosc-Tiessé (2008), too, shows how adept monasteries were in holding state officials at bay through a careful mix of flattery and moral admonition. Nonetheless, their degree of authority and control over resources made the monastic associations *(mahber)* an important center of political power in their own right.

The political power of monasteries, as of the Orthodox Church as a whole, has greatly diminished since the fall of Emperor Haile Selassie in 1974, under both the military-socialist Derg regime and the current secular federalist government. Careful analysis shows that in fact the encroachment of secular bureaucratic institutions into domains of church authority has been going on for at least a century (Clapham 1969, Binayew 2014). Orthodox Christians in Zege generally present the decline of monastic authority in nostalgic terms, suggesting that recent history is marked by a generalized weakening of hospitality norms and religious ethics, and that the monasteries remain the only legitimate moral authority on the peninsula.

It is not so simple, however, to identify who has historically represented monastic authority in Zege. Alongside clerical authorities—the monks, deacons, and sometimes priests—there exists a class of high-status landholders (*balabbat,* "patriarch," literally "one who has a father") who, while not part of the clergy, have maintained close associations with the church-monasteries and have historically wielded significant political and jural power in Zege. There were also key political figures who combined church and lay authority, chiefly the *mislené*[1] and the *líqered*,[2] both of which titles still exist in Zege today, albeit with reduced scope. Both *mislené* and *líqered* have existed in two forms, one representing the church and one the society (*yager*, "of the land"), which further complicates efforts to untangle the precise relationships involved. But it is clear that *líqered*, for example, historically controlled much of the production of coffee from church lands (Binayew 2014), and therefore wielded significant political and economic power.

This chapter aims to develop an outline of historic trajectories of monastic and political power in Zege—or at least, to show how these are remembered today. In so doing I hope to give the reader a sense of how Zege fits within the broader scope of the history of Ethiopian Orthodox Christianity and the Ethiopian state, and of why fasting and prohibition have become such points of emphasis. I argue that many in Zege, especially older Orthodox Christians, remember recent history in terms of a decline of hospitality and feasting practices, especially funerary feasting. These practices were associated with landholding classes closely related to (but not identical with) the monastic authorities. I will suggest that Orthodox religious practice in Zege is not itself in decline, but has been reimagined to focus on practices such as fasting. Compared with those of the imperial era, these practices point less toward marking class relations within Orthodox society, and more to defining Orthodox Christians vis-à-vis the state and other religions (especially Islam and Protestantism). But they retain the key principles of prohibition and mediation that underpin socioreligious logic.

ZEGE WITHIN ETHIOPIAN ORTHODOX HISTORY

Some local church literature places the foundation of Zege's first monastery by *Abune* Betre Maryam around 1270 AD. Other historical sources, however, suggest that Betre Maryam lived during the reign of Emperor Amde Sion (1314–44; Cerulli 1946, Derat 2003: 507). This places the foundation of Zege's monastic community in a period marked by the consolidation of the Solomonic monarchy, whose legitimacy was tied closely to the church and the claim to descend from King Solomon. This was also a period of monastic revival and the rapid southward expansion of Orthodox-Imperial territory across Lake Tana and far beyond (Taddesse 1972b, Ephraim 2013). The monasteries of Lake Tana have since come to be considered as one of the heartlands of Orthodox territory.

The early history of Christianity in Ethiopia has been told many times, but some key points are worth mentioning here. Christianity appears to have spread in top down fashion, beginning with the conversion of King Ezana of Axum in the late 300s. This came in the context of centuries-old, bidirectional relationships between the kingdoms of the northeastern Horn of Africa and the Mediterranean, the Levant, and the Arabian Gulf (Finneran 2007). The Ethiopic script dates also from the third and fourth centuries and is associated with Ge'ez, a language extinct in the vernacular but very much alive as the language of Orthodox liturgy.

The Ethiopic script and the Orthodox Church have become closely associated with the Amharic- and Tigrayan-speaking societies that have dominated the northern highlands of Ethiopia. These societies, distinguished by Orthodox Christian dominance, plough agriculture, and a military-feudal class system, are sometimes referred to as "Abyssinian" to distinguish them from the other peoples who make up the contemporary Ethiopian nation-state. This designation, however, can obscure the diversity and historical mixture of northern Ethiopia. The area around Zege, for example, while almost entirely Amharic-speaking, has been home to speakers of Agew and to important non-Christian groups including Weyto and Beta Israel. Significant influence, and significant slave-descended populations, from Benishangul-Gumuz to the west are also evident (Taddesse 1972b, 1994, James 1986).

The Ethiopian Orthodox Tewahido Church itself is usually classified with the "Oriental Orthodox" churches of Armenia, Syria, and Egypt. These churches split from the mainstream at the Council of Chalcedon in 451, over a Christological dispute. The question was whether Christ was of two natures (phusis), divine and human, or one nature, divine and human combined (Binns 2002). The oriental churches dissented from the official two-natures declaration, and so came to be known as the "monophysites." This term is now considered derogatory, and has been replaced by "miaphysite," which means the same thing but without the insulting connotations (Fisseha 2002). Even still, there are many who question whether the Ethiopian Orthodox Church is miaphysite at all, arguing that Ethiopia was not directly represented at Chalcedon, and that the problem is one of translation (Ayala 1981, Ephraim 2013). The Ethiopian church holds that "there were, to be sure, two natures before the Incarnation, but only one after the union: the humanity being absorbed in the divinity" (Ephraim 2013: 49). The word Tewahido, "unified," in the church's name expresses this singularity.

The Tewahido concept has not gone unchallenged. Unionists were in the seventeenth century pitted against the school of Unctionists (qibat) who maintained that Christ's humanity and divinity were initially separated and only joined through the unction of the Holy Spirit (Getatchew 1990, Marcus 1994: 43–44). This school, although ultimately defeated, was influential in the Gojjam region, and there were Unctionists in Zege within living memory.[3] As explained to me by Tefera, their position was thought unacceptable because it held that Jesus did not, in his essence, share his mother's blood or flesh, meaning that Unctionism downplayed the importance of Mary—a transgression of great contemporary significance, given the rise of Protestantism in contemporary Ethiopia.

The 1200s and 1300s saw the consolidation of the Solomonic ideology that would continue to underpin imperial political philosophy until 1974. The key text was the Kibre Negest, Glory of Kings, compiled from various sources around this time (Levine 1974: 93, Orlowska 2006: 39). It describes the journey of the Queen of Sheba to visit King Solomon, how she learns religious law from him, and how he tricks her into sleeping with him. The king promises he will not take her by force if she does not take anything in his house by force, and then tricks her into taking water after feeding her a spicy meal. They sleep together, but that night Solomon has a dream in which he sees a brilliant heavenly sun withdraw from Israel and move to shine over Ethiopia (Budge 2000: 31).

The queen returns to Ethiopia and bears a son, who will become Emperor Menilek I. Menilek returns to Israel to learn the laws from his father, and on the way home he takes the Ark of the Covenant (Tabote S'ion), with God's permission via the Angel of the Lord, for "had it not been that God willed it Zion could not have been taken away forthwith" (Budge 2000: 61). The Ark, which according to Ethiopian tradition resides in Axum to this day, becomes the symbol of the transmission of divine sovereignty from Israel to Ethiopia, and subsequent monarchs will trace their legacy through descent from Solomon and through holy anointment.

The Ark remains a key symbol for Ethiopian Orthodoxy today. Each church contains at least one consecrated replica of the Ark of the Covenant, known as a *tabot*, which is understood to be the dwelling place of divinity and is the only object on which the Eucharist can be prepared. The *tabot*, usually made of wood and consecrated by a bishop, is a replica of the Ark of the Covenant and tablets of Moses, and is kept away from public view at all times (Hammerschmidt 1965, Pankhurst 1987, Getatchew 1988).

The *tabot* is, in a very real sense, what makes a church a church, and is crucial to the religious geography of Zege. It is brought out, under a shroud, to bless the waters on Epiphany (T'imqet) and local saints' days, and is guarded with intense care. It offers a kind of objectified evidence of the presence of divine grace on earth, and is absolutely integral to Orthodox practice and thinking about the matter-spirit relationship.

The *tabot* is also central to a classical scholarly question about the prevalence of Jewish-Hebraic influence in Ethiopian Orthodoxy (Rodinson 1964, Ullendorff 1969, Ephraim 2013, Afework 2014). The Kibre Negest draws an explicit connection between Ethiopian Christianity and Solomonic authority. Ephraim (2013: 26) describes the concentric tripartite structure of Ethiopian churches as an echo of the tabernacle of Solomon; the continued importance of dietary proscriptions is another compelling example, along with long-standing debates about the Ethiopian Sabbath (Getatchew 1988).[4]

It is important to recognize that the church itself is not a totally monolithic entity. Ethiopian Orthodox history is marked by factional and doctrinal debates and conflicts, and the relationship between monastics and the patriarchate has often been characterized by tension. The former patriarch *Abune* Paulos (1988: 38) describes Ethiopian monastic history as "a series of movements towards and away from the state and the church."[5]

A few other key points in Ethiopian history are relevant to understanding Zege today. One is the Christianizing agenda of Emperor Zara Yaqob (r. 1434–68), whose vigorous promotion of the cult of Mary and the feasts and fasts of the Orthodox calendar did much to shape everyday religious practice and turn Ethiopian Orthodoxy into a form of popular moral governance (Kaplan 2014). Another is the centralization of the church and state under the Neo-Solomonids from the 1850s onward, starting with Emperor Tewodros II (r. 1855–68) (Crummey 1988, Orlowska 2006). Orthodox Christians in Zege regard Tewodros as a modernizer who also placed the Orthodox Church at the center of Ethiopian nationhood. Even his suicide after the Napier invasion of 1868 is seen as an act of heroic defiance. Tewodros has come to encapsulate imperial nostalgia (Marcus 2002) and the half-remembered dream of an Orthodox nation that stood proudly alongside others without aping the secular West. It is not for nothing, as friends proudly told me, that Tewodros was voted Ethiopian of the millennium. His combination of a centralizing, modernizing agenda and an overtly Orthodox Christian state project stands in tacit contrast to the contemporary state based upon constitutional religious equality, state secularism, and ethnic federalism.

"A COIN HAS TWO SIDES": ZEGE AND THE MONASTERIES

My efforts to reconstruct Zege's institutional history have relied on interviews with local church scholars and dignitaries, conducted with the help of Tefera Ewnetu. The resulting picture is necessarily partial and sometimes difficult to triangulate, but it nonetheless gives a strong impression of how public memory about the past operates in Zege, and how narratives of religious transformation emerge. I have been fortunate to be able to draw on the works of Binayew Tamrat (2014), Tihut Yirgu Asfaw (2009), Rahel Mesfin (2002, 1999), and Abdussamad Ahmad (1997), on whom I rely in particular for my understanding of land politics over time. I gratefully acknowledge my debt to these scholars and to Tefera, whose own knowledge has been indispensable to this study.

We have seen that Zegeña trace the history of the forest to the founding of the monasteries in the 1300s. Early hagiographies refer to the "fruit" of the forest; it seems coffee is only introduced much later, in perhaps the early 1800s (Cerulli 1946; Pankhurst 1968: 202; Merid 1988). Between the foundation of the monasteries and the mid-1800s, the Zege forest became a significant economic entity, based around the long-distance coffee trade. A key event appears to have occurred between 1680 and 1700, when a number of Amhara settlers arrived from somewhere to the north and received land rights from the monasteries (Binayew 2014: 8). According to *Mergéta* Worqé Dibebu, a seventy-two-year-old priest, church painter, and scholar resident in Mehal Zege, it was the arrivals of the late 1600s who became the *mentarí*, or forest clearers. Sixteen settled in Mehal Zege and sixteen in Ura (the two parishes of the peninsula). These were the *aqní abbatocch*, "original fathers," whose descendants are known as *balabbatocch* (sing. *balabbat*), "those with fathers," and would, according to one key respondent, later claim the status of the true Zegeña "of the bone" *(be at'int)*. Subsequent to these arrivals, two more groups would be recognized: the purchasers, and the former sharecroppers who had gained inheritance rights. If you could show descent from one of these groups, you could claim *rist* land.[6]

On one side were the *balabbatocch*, then. Alongside these was the *mahber*, which generally means "association" but here refers to the associated clergy. Alongside the land whose *rist* rights were held by the *balabbatocch*, *mahber* land was available to members of the clergy (Binayew 2014: 22). This included, according to *Mislené* Fantahun Tsegaye, land for *yesét mahber*, the "women's association": the nuns who resided in and around the peninsula. *Mergéta* Worqé also described the phenomenon of *dinkwan merét*, "tent land": this was for hosting visiting dignitaries, but was slowly taken over by local *balabbatocch*.

Finally, we come to the *mislené* and *líqered*, who worked with and represented the monasteries.[7] These figures are the key to understanding the relationship between church and secular power. I once asked Aderaw, secretary of the local tour guides' cooperative and a descendant of church dignitaries himself, to explain *mislené* and *líqered*. I told him I was confused because there seemed to be multiple roles, and I wanted to know how to distinguish church power from *yager* power, power of the land. He replied, "*And santimm hulett ges'ita alle*" (A coin has two sides). Those who held power in the land were not separable from the monasteries, but were part of the same institutional setup, encapsulated in the *mefraq*, the church dining room in which monastic and community leaders would sit in strict hierarchical order around the *memhir*, the abbot of the monastery. The importance of the dining hall as the space in which hierarchy was legitimized should not be underestimated. Throughout this book we will see how eating and feeding in religious contexts have been the core practices by which social status was made and displayed.

There are two types of *líqered: yager* (of the land) and *yemahber* (of the church association). The *yager líqered* was elected from among the laity, held a high seat in the dining hall, and would organize taxation of the market, especially the coffee trade. Importantly, in Zege, this taxation was primarily due to the church rather than the crown, and so the *yager líqered* served under the abbot of the monastery, and had to wear the white headcloth symbolic of priesthood. This position was closely related to the *chiqa shum*, the tax collector, and neither role is filled nowadays. The *yemahber líqered*, by contrast, still exists, though with limited jural roles. This figure was selected by the clergy and seems to have controlled the coffee output from church lands (Binayew 2014). His key role was to organize the feeding and burial of the monks, becoming something of a benefactor and political patron. The *mislené*, finally, had to have a solid church education and sat at the right hand of the abbot. There are still *mislené* in Zege, with important roles as scholars and mediators of disputes.

The *mislené* and *líqered* both played key roles in the judgment of disputes, for which they received a fee. They served important roles as moral leaders, and were expected to be *chʼewa*, "proper." As we will see, this term has come to be associated with a more essentialized idea of noble descent by blood, as well as a certain kind of moral quality: the terms *chʼewa* and *mislené* sometimes denote the opposite of slaves. They remain influential figures today, but in the past they had significant economic and political power, whose moral justification was understood in terms of either their religious learning or their material and financial service to the church.

Binayew Tamrat (2014: 14) offers a useful summary of the system as a whole: under the authority of the *memhir*, "supreme administrator over his parish and the people residing within its territory," were two chains of authority, one more secular than the other. On the church side was the *qése gebbez*, the priest who guarded the *tabot* and (according to my interviews) kept the keys for the holy of holies. Below him were the other priests and deacons including *yewicchʼ gebez*, or "keeper of the outside," who provided wheat and wine for communion and wood for charcoal for the church. Below these was the *deway*, "bellringer," a church servant with some administrative responsibilities. In the other chain of authority, still below the *memhir* and above the laity, were the *mislené* and *líqered*, and below them the *chʼiqa shum*, the tax collector.

According to *Mergéta* Worqé, landlords *(balabbatocch)* began to appropriate positions in the church administration quite soon after their arrival. During the reign of Eyasu I (r. 1682–1706), the emperor made a visit to the peninsula, and was greeted not only by monks, but also by local *balabbatocch*, who bound their heads in white like priests. The emperor blessed the peninsula, saying *mehalwan gennet darwan isat* (her border is like fire, her middle like heaven). At this point the local dignitaries who had worn priestly headgear were given official leadership over the parishes. As Binayew (2014: 8) puts it, "In return for their loyalty or spiritual support to his administration, Emperor Iyasu I . . . endowed the chief church officials of Zägé power for administration, tribute collection and court arbitration." My understanding of this story is that it captures a sense of the ambiguity of the parachurch authorities who would become so important in the political-religious life of Zege.

This ambiguity remains in contemporary discourse about these figures. Most knowledgeable people—tour guides and local scholars—emphasize the respect that was due to men of all these positions, how they had the quality of *tesamínet,* being listened to, and *masmammat,* being able to bring others to agreement. They had to be servants of the church, and, as Tefera told me, no *líqered* would ever use the church's coffee for personal enrichment—they had too much respect for the church, and would only use the proceeds for church upkeep, gifts, and supplies.

The same people tell me how control of land was concentrated in these men's hands. But at least one respondent told me that someone who did not wield power in the proper fashion would not be a *balabbat* but an autocrat. He gave the example of one well-known and controversial local dignitary who had made large donations to churches but had also used his power to unfairly amass large amounts of wealth. This man was rich but supposedly lacked the religious knowledge and behavior befitting a proper dignitary. Instead, he used his wealth to abuse people and lord it over them. As the story has it, after the Derg confiscated his lands, he defiantly named his son Minattan, meaning "What have we lost?" (Implication: nothing, because our wealth was in cash and assets that the government did not have access to.)

From the 1880s a clearer history of the forest as an economic entity emerges. The long-range coffee trade became increasingly lucrative, due to increased British and Italian demand across trade routes in northeast Africa and the growth of Addis Ababa as a trade hub (Fernyhough 2010). Until the 1930s the slave trade expanded greatly, especially under the local kings Tekle Haymanot and Ras Hailu of Gojjam (roughly 1870–1930; Fernyhough 2010, Triulzi 1981). Agew and Muslim traders would bring slaves from Benishangul and Gumuz to the west, and they would be sold by Muslim traders in private houses in Afaf town (Abdussamad 1997). Orthodox Christians were forbidden by the Fetha Negest, the Law of Kings, from selling slaves but not from owning them (so long as they were baptized), and large numbers of slaves ended up working on church land (Pankhurst 2011). Abdussamad (1997) reports that a large number of priests were slave owners. This is quite plausible, but given what we have seen of Zege's lay-clerical power structure, it seems likely that the *líqered* were the dominant figures in the trade. Certainly, according to my interviews, it was often the *líqered* who were the largest landholders at this time.

Binayew Tamrat's (2014) history gives a vivid sense that the twentieth century was experienced in Zege as a series of secular bureaucratic encroachments on the domain of the church, long before the Derg government stripped the church of its landholdings in the mid-1970s. The Gojjamé king Ras Hailu, in particular, is remembered for exploiting the national interregnum from 1911 by appropriating large tracts of coffee land in Zege for himself (Binayew 2014: 17). After this point, the church in Zege would also become subject to land taxation in a way that it had not before, and the *chiqa shum,* the monasteries' tax collector, would report instead to the state (Binayew 2014: 46). Binayew also reports how the introduction of government schools was resisted in Zege from the 1940s until the 1960s, and how the introduction of government courts in 1947 would undermine the authority of the church and parachurch dignitaries and also deprive them of their mediators' fees.

The short Italian occupation is still well remembered in Zege. While there was certainly local resistance (Binayew 2014: 30), the story I have most often heard is that the peninsula as a whole submitted because the Italians had threatened to burn down the monasteries, as they had done in other areas. Protecting the monasteries came before anything else. There are also significant material remnants of the occupation—visiting the newly built church of Raphael, near Yiganda, Thomas, Abebe, and I were shown ruins of the walls of the Italian camp that had stood there, built, as we were told, with stones taken from the local churches.

THE DERG AND AFTER

The most abrupt change in the fortunes of the church, here as in the rest of Ethiopia, came with the socialist-military Derg government's overthrow of Emperor Haile Selassie in 1974, and their ensuing land reforms under the slogan of *merét larashu* (Land to the Tiller!; Haustein 2009). Almost all land under church control was redistributed among local families (Rahel 2002); *Mergéta* Worqé tells me that in previous generations it had been common practice for the wealthy to bequeath land to the local church. In Zege, in any case, peasants' associations were formed and land was redistributed from the church and major landlords to individual families, including many former slaves, sharecroppers, and dispossessed women. According to my friend and research assistant, Tefera, women who worked for the landlords had been "like slaves" and had to labor day and night. As he told me, beneficiaries of the reforms would sing the following lines:

> *Derg alem, Derg alem*
> *Ante techeggerk,*
> *Iññass inji ayyenalle*

> Derg world, Derg world;
> You (landowner) were troubled
> But we got to see (the world, i.e., we benefited)

Today there are, however, landless people in Zege: some who were born after the land reforms of 1975 and were unable to inherit; some who were not in Zege during the reforms; and some, especially children of woman-headed households, who were subsequently dispossessed (Tihut 2009, Rahel 2002). Subsequent attempts were made by the EPRDF government to address these issues with further redistribution, but these had little success. In general, it seems that while early land reforms in the mid-1970s brought significant benefit to the landless in Zege, accusations of corruption, preferential treatment, and sexual exploitation by association members would become widespread within a few years (Tihut 2009: 88).

The situation now is that the land in Zege is broken up into small segments of roughly 0.75 hectares, run by individual households (Rahel 2002: 139). The local government bureau (qebellé) parcels out land roughly according to family size. Tihut Yirgu Asfaw (2009) presents detailed evidence of how women-headed households, in particular, have struggled with land disputes at the hands of their neighbors. Of her sample of households, 44 percent were woman-headed, a result of high levels of male labor out-migration as coffee outputs have declined somewhat (Tihut 2009: 95). Sharecropping and work-for-inheritance arrangements have become common between women landholders and landless men; marriage arrangements based on the understanding that husbands will work the land and gain inheritance rights are also reported (Tihut 2009: 103). Each of these arrangements, however, can leave women householders vulnerable to exploitation and dispossession (Tihut 2009: 106).

In general, there appears to have been a significant liberalization of gender relations in recent decades in Zege. Tefera, who is in his mid-thirties, told me that he remembered a time in his childhood when boys and girls were forbidden to walk the paths of Zege together; today young men and women associate together quite openly, and we both wondered whether the existence of a school in Afaf town had had some effect on this. Tefera also mentioned that practices such as "forced marriage," where potential brides were kidnapped and then an arrangement was negotiated through the shimgelna (panel of elders), had completely disappeared. The more acceptable traditional practice of sending three shimaglé (elders) to negotiate betrothals has also largely disappeared in favor of informal negotiation and choice marriage. There remains a role for the elders, however, in negotiating the terms of marriage and mediating marital disputes, according to Mislené Fantahun Tsegaye of Ura.

Most of my information of how shimgelna used to work comes from Mislené Fantahun, an octogenarian church singer and respected shimaglé. His account gives a particularly clear view of the changing relationship between religious knowledge and interpersonal mediation. As he explains it, the shimgelna would usually mediate in land and family disputes, as well as marriage negotiations—he told us that there were rarely violent crimes in Zege because of the monastery and the power of the sacred tabots. In each case three men would be selected by the local mahber association (in Zege, implying a lay-clerical voluntary association with responsibility for managing the churches) or by the parties: one monk, one older lay *mahber* member, and one younger man whose role was to learn and provide an alternative perspective.

The *agubí* (marriage-making) *shimaglé* would negotiate wedding gifts from each family (which were supposed to be equal, and made in land and money rather than cattle because of Zege's ban on large livestock). The *agabí shimaglé* who had negotiated a betrothal would later be called on, if still alive, to negotiate in the case of marital troubles, and to try to reconcile them, but if necessary, to agree to a separation. In land disputes between villages, each side might appoint its own *shimaglé* to negotiate, or outsiders might be selected. A *shimaglé* would be selected on the basis of a calm and reflective personality, wisdom, and preferably a high degree of religious education. All of these would contribute to his *tesamínnet*, his quality of being listened to by others and therefore being able to bring about agreement (*masmammat*, "to cause to hear one another").

Today there are still *shimaglé* but their influence and authority are greatly reduced. As *Mislené* Fantahun told me, all land disputes now had to go to government court *(fird bét)*. There is a local social court system known as *mahberawí shengo*, in which *shimaglé* adjudicate, but this is set up by the government and largely restricted to family disputes. It also involves a great deal of paperwork that did not exist before, and the potential of sanctions for *shimaglé* who fail to bring about resolution. Even in marital disputes, separation cannot be agreed to without reference to the government court.

The *shimgelna* was a key interface between the people and the ritual institutions of the church. One of their jobs was to arrange the *sir'ate teklil*, the ceremony of the crown by which virgin couples are married with Holy Communion. This ceremony allows no divorce (though separations could be negotiated in practice); but the *mislené* explained to me that these days young people were choosing their own ceremonies, and that therefore there were far fewer Communion marriages than in the past (implying both that fewer people were marrying as virgins and that more divorces were taking place).

There are signs today that Communion marriages may be on the rise again; young Orthodox Christians are certainly engaging widely and enthusiastically with the church through fasting and public displays of faith. What has greatly lessened, with great consequences for social life in Zege, is the degree to which associations of religiously educated older men act as mediators between families and the church. This role involved both bringing people together (negotiating disputes) and keeping them apart (by acting as go-betweens so that men and women did not make their own arrangements). As we will see throughout the book, the simultaneous connection and separation are characteristic of mediation in general.

While chewing *khat* and talking to a friend in his forties (who, as a *khat*-chewer, was automatically far less reputable than the men we have been discussing), I asked what he thought was most different from his childhood. Apart from the conservatism relating to boys and girls, he lamented that the coming of the police to Afaf (a few resident officers as of the past decade) meant that people no longer resolved their own fights. In the old days, he said, if you got drunk and fought someone, you would say, "I'm sorry, I was drunk," and if necessary you would have the *shimaglé*. Now, the police simply lock you up for a night. This small example speaks to a broader shift away from local mediation systems toward state police and courts.

The growth of the market town of Afaf has been integral to the spread of secular government influence. There used to be a marketplace at Ura, on the peninsula, but at some point in the late 1800s the marketplace at Afaf was established. Afaf occupies a patch of clear land at the edge of the Zege forest. One story people tell of its origins is that the fathers of Zege needed a larger place to hold meetings as their numbers expanded, hence *ke af le af,* "from mouth to mouth." The local historian *Mergéta* Worqé offers more detail, saying that the marketplace was opened under the ownership and control of one Fasil, a local landlord, who would extract rent from trading plots.

In Zege, the marketplace also marks the point of crossing from the peninsula (sacred, forested) to the rest of the world: the farmlands around, the city of Bahir Dar, and beyond. In the past, this was where visitors to Zege had to request permission from the monastic leaders to enter the peninsula itself. It was also the site of the *dingay masmereq* (graduating stone), the stone at which church dignitaries would in the past make all announcements and new appointments (according to *Mergéta* Abbi), and so was a major interface between the church associations and the general populace. Abebe told me he has still seen older men stop and pray at the stone when entering and leaving the market. Afaf is where the first government schools were built, and remains the only place with a regular police presence. It was also the locus of the slave trade until the 1930s (Abdussamad 1997). Afaf is the point where the forest ends, and as such plays a crucial intermediary role between the land of the monasteries and the surrounding area, as well as with the government.

SACRIFICE, FEASTING, AND SOCIAL CHANGE

The decline of monastic-landholder authority does not correspond to a decline in Orthodox Christian practice; in fact the opposite might be true. Across Orthodox Ethiopia, the Derg's redistribution of church lands and subjugation of the patriarchate seem to have been met, almost immediately, with a surge of grassroots participation (Clapham 1988, Bonacci 2000, Chaillot 2002). Nominally atheist, the Derg seems to have preferred to appropriate the popular energy around the church, rather than attempt to suppress popular religious practice (Donham 1999: 143).

What we do see is a decline in funerary feasting and similar practices based on the slaughter and redistribution of meat. These semiofficial practices had long coexisted with the Orthodox liturgical orders of the church, and their reduction is described by many, especially higher-status elders, as part of a general disturbance and decline of the moral values of hospitality (and, by implication, a certain kind of hierarchy).

The general idea, as any local priest will tell you, is that the sacrifice of Christ obviated the need for animal sacrifice (meswat).[8] The Eucharist remains, accord-ing to the Orthodox Church, a true sacrifice in itself, but nothing else is necessary (Kaplan 2003b: 15). However, in practice animal sacrifice has been performed in Zege in recent times and may still be during funeral rites (see chapter 6). A notable example is the practice of fel.

Fel was practiced throughout the Haile Selassie era but started much earlier. It always involved the gift and slaughter of an ox. The way it started was that on holidays such as Christmas and Easter, a landlord (balabbat) or wealthy person would slaughter an ox and give it to the monks and the poor people who lived in the church—though at some point, as the economy worsened, they stopped doing this. Another aspect of fel was that, during droughts, groups of people would col-lect money to buy a virgin (dingil) ox, which local dignitaries would sacrifice and then consume together.[9] Importantly, whatever remained of the meat would not be taken home, but buried in the ground at the spot of the slaughter—to pray for rain, people had to give up a part of the consumable meat. They would also bury the skins, which would otherwise be sold in the market. This kind of fel was a form of prayer, and was directed to God, but church scholars including Mergéta Worqé discouraged the practice and refused to attend. But, especially during bad times like the Italian invasion, and whenever the rain was late, people would revive the sacrifice.

There seems to have been a formalization of the fel at some point, with a "fel boss" appointed to collect contributions, which were taxed. Tefera tells me that his mother kept a receipt from 1957 (Ethiopian calendar, 1964/65 European) for one birr contribution toward the fel, including tax. It is not clear, however, whether this was for the redistributive kind of fel or for prayers for rain. The practice has stopped now, but both Tefera and the Mergéta told me that people still thought in these terms, and that if the rains come late now it is quite likely that people will perform the sacrifice again, including the burial of the surplus.

Fel, then, could be a redistributive practice that served to establish the benefi-cent role of the nobles as providers of life or a way to pray for rain. In the first case, it resembles the kind of feasting that has long been opposed by the government as backward and wasteful; in the latter, it is a form of offering that the church has always disapproved of. The proper way to pray and give thanks for rain is to walk the Acts of Saint Betre Maryam around the peninsula—multiple times, if necessary. This returns the responsibility for environmental mediation squarely within the official church purview, and is still regularly practiced today. The final factor that sealed the decline of *fel*, at least for the time being, was the fear of Muslims making claims to land in Zege and the ensuing need to make sure that local practice was recognizable as properly religious. The practice has been discontinued, and the hilltop on which the sacrifice took place renamed *mesqel adebabay*, the square of the Cross.

The decline of sacrifice and hospitality, or their relocation within the aegis of the church, represents massive changes in how status gets figured out. The correct manner of resolving these status questions was through the distribution of food and the shedding of blood. The moral killing and consumption of animals (with Christian prayers, followed by hospitable distribution of the meat) are a key mode by which religious and secular authority become practically associated. To participate in such feasts was to bodily participate in the social order of the church-landlord complex. At such moments, the core model of the Eucharistic feast is never far away.

Narratives of the decline of socioreligious and funerary feasting will continue to emerge throughout this book. They are integral to a particular elite understanding of how proper, moral hierarchy was reproduced in Zege. Within the scope of this narrative, the decline in hospitality signifies a sign of a general decline in trust. As we will see in the next chapter, however, fasting and the observance of calendrical prohibitions are as salient as ever. A productive way to think about this contrast is that fasting, along with the refusal to work on saints' days, distinguishes Orthodox Christians from Muslims, who fast differently, and Protestants, who reject the Orthodox fasts entirely. Fasting also asserts a religious dimension to everyday life in a context where that religious dimension is no longer institutionalized in the apparatus of the state. Traditional feasting practices, by contrast, while closely associated with the saints and the monasteries, were more concerned with organizing hierarchy and class relations within Zege society. From this perspective the shift in Orthodox practice reflects a deep change in the social stakes of religious belonging within wider Ethiopian society.

NOTES

1. *Mislené* (district chief; Kane 1990); literally, "one like me"; see also Bairu 1986: 296, 300).

2. Literally, "leader of the assistants."

3. Before the remapping of Ethiopia along ethnic-federal lines in the early 1990s (Donham 2002), Zege lay in the western part of Gojjam province, and a strong sense of *Gojjamé* cultural and political heritage remains to this day.

4. The question of how and why Judaic and Old Testament influences became established in Ethiopian Orthodoxy is far beyond the scope of this book. Ephraim (2013) and Afework (2014) offer the most detailed recent accounts.

5. As if to demonstrate this point, Paulos's own patriarchate would be marked by conflicts between monasteries and the state and accusations of political complicity

6. The *gult*, or rights to tribute issuing from the land, bestowed by the emperor, were in *Zege* all held by the church (Binayew 2014: 19). *Rist*, hereditary usage rights, could be claimed by anyone who could demonstrate descent from one of the first inhabitants, or *aqni abbat* (Binayew 2014, Teshale 1995: 74). As Alan Hoben (1973) describes in great detail, the Amhara cognatic descent system meant that a very large number of people could theoretically claim any particular plot of land, and actual rights would depend on being physically present and having sufficient influence or litigation skills.

7. Along with drawing on Binayew (2014), information on *mislené* and *líqered* is gathered from interviews with *Mergéta* Worqé, *Mislené* Fantahun, and *Mergéta* Abbi, with the assistance of Tefera Ewnetu.

8. Ephraim Isaac (2013: 37) argues that the concept of *meswat*, along with the importance of sacrificial practice in Ethiopian Orthodoxy, is further evidence of deep Jewish and Christian influence.

9. The virginity of the animal is important for reasons of purity, beyond the usual practical reasons for the castration of oxen.

2

Fasting, Bodies, and the Calendar

CALENDARS, BODIES, AND RELATIONS OF SCALE

Notwithstanding the decline of monastic authority in the past century, it remains the case that everyday Orthodox life in Zege unfolds, to a remarkable extent, within a religious framework. The geography of the land and the movement of people across it, regimes of labor and production, exchange and trade, and the everyday consumption of and abstinence from food are highly coordinated within the Orthodox calendar. In the introduction to this book, I showed that prohibitions around food and labor have a formative influence both on the environment and on the experience of time. In this chapter I broaden my perspective to the Orthodox calendar as a whole, and in particular to how the rhythms of feasts and fasts tie together human bodies, the productive environment, and the seemingly abstract religious calendar. The result is that meaningful, highly structured religious distinctions get sewn into the everyday fabric of experience.

Orthodox Christians in Zege maintain the importance of the calendrical feasts and fasts, in the face of secular governance and fears of Protestant expansion. This is not passive adherence to tradition but the active affirmation of a set of principles about how life should be organized: by the religious structuring of time and space, the discipline of fasting, and the observance of feasts in the names of the saints. The calendar, with its feasts and fasts, is the engine of what I call the ritual regime: that is, a system in which bodies, space, and time are mapped, divided, demarcated, and otherwise experienced in terms of the temporal geography of ritual. This is the system that connects bodies and patterns of work, exchange, and consumption to a much larger schematic vision of the world in which time and experience are comprehensible through their connection to foundational religious events.

While church attendance may be variable, fasting is the means by which the whole community participates in the ritual order. For those not attending church, the minimum requirements on a fasting day are that no animal products be consumed. Sexual activity is also forbidden. Those going to church must not eat or drink anything until the liturgy is finished, and many who do not go to church voluntarily follow the same restrictions. Priests and monks must observe every fast, meaning that for more than 250 days of the year they take no meat at all, and go without food or water for at least part of the day. So while religious labor is unevenly distributed, fasting establishes the minimal participation of every Christian in the Orthodox regime.

Interpersonal moral pressure and the mutual surveillance of neighbors do much to ensure the observance of the fasts. But it must also be said that my acquaintances in Zege describe fasting as a joyous and fulfilling activity that they perform gladly, and I know of many people young and old who sometimes perform extra fasts for specific personal reasons, on the advice of the priests who act as their confessional fathers.

The Orthodox calendar was inherited from Alexandria but developed over time to include a range of monthly saints' feasts and a close association with the seasonal patterns of northern Ethiopia (Fritsch 2001, Ancel 2005). A good deal of its current form, however, is due to the explicit Christianizing project of Emperor Zara Yaqob (r. 1434–68). As Steven Kaplan (2014) puts it, "He demonstrated an intuitive understanding of the routine and habitual in bodily practice. . . . He sought to transform the Christian experience of time so that each week, month and year became imbued with Christian content." The calendar and especially the annual and monthly feasts were developed as a deliberate plan to regulate the lives of imperial subjects as part of a broad project of power. Zara Yaqob's vision of disciplined, devout bodies synchronized in worship (and obedience) provides a template for understanding the importance of the calendar today.

This focus of temporal power at the level of bodily experience recalls Nancy Munn's account of calendrical power: "the construction of cultural governance through reaching into the body time of persons and coordinating it with values embedded in the 'world time' of a wider constructed universe of power" (1992: 109). Calendars, that is, coordinate different scales of existence: between the phenomenological, immediate life of the body and the relations within and among states and world systems.

The Orthodox calendar is the most powerful normative tool in Zege society (and therefore also, as we will see, the object whose violation most effectively demonstrates dissidence). There are twelve thirty-day months, beginning in September by the Gregorian calendar (the end of the rains in Ethiopia, associated with harvest and renewal), followed by the intercalary month of five or six days known as P'agumén. P'agumén is a period of both renewal and preparation

for the new year, an *entre-temps* in which liminal things such as spirit possessions happen.

Each day of the thirty-day month is dedicated to a saint or saintly event, and
which of these is observed depends largely on local tradition. In Zege, Saint
Michael (twelfth of each month), Saint Gabriel (nineteenth), and Saint George
(twenty-third) have special importance, among others, and on these days no
work is permitted—usually this is interpreted as agricultural labor and work on
the land, while shopkeepers and people in town carry on work as normal. The
number of saints' days can add up, and has become one of Ethiopian Orthodox
Christianity's great controversies. That farmers refuse or are forbidden to work for
religious reasons has come to be seen as unmodern, antidevelopmental, and harmful to national productivity. Many urban Orthodox Christians hold this opinion,
as well as critics from outside: I have been told more than once by taxi drivers that
the holy days were a Coptic plot to keep Ethiopia lazy and underdeveloped, and
hence prevent them from fully utilizing the water of the Nile, upstream from Egypt
(dams have become the quintessential, highly divisive symbol of the Ethiopian
developmental state as promoted by the current EPRDF government).

Saints days may stipulate different kinds of action depending on the place,
the church, and the individual. If a person has made a vow *(silet)* to a saint, she
may give commemorative meals *(zikir)* on that saint's annual or monthly day (see
chapter 7); likewise voluntary associations named after a saint will have their
meetings (which also involve a meal consecrated to the saint, in the attendance
of a priest) on these days. Each church has an annual saint's day of special importance, depending on the consecration of its *tabot*. This will be marked by a *zikir*
feast for the community and is the only time, aside from Epiphany, when the *tabot*
leaves the church.

We can start to see already how the Christian calendar specifies when work
happens, and differentiates between work and nonwork days. This differentiation
is the mechanism that produces a qualitative distinction between sacred and profane life across many axes of experience. The distinction comes into closer focus
when we attend to major festivals and fasts.

There are seven major fasts in all.[1] Some fasts are more widely observed than
others. Clergy are expected to keep all fasts; the usual minimum for laypeople is to
keep the Lenten and the Wednesday and Friday fasts along with the three-day fast
of Nineveh that precedes and prepares for Lent. Others, like the fast of *Qwiswam*
commemorating the flight to Egypt, may be observed by the more knowledgeable
and devout—such as those attending Sunday school—while others are less aware
or involved. The clergy tends to consider these fasts optional for the laity (Ephraim
2013). But in a very real sense they also perform the fasts for the laity and on their
behalf. Fasting is a collective practice that allows for different degrees of participation precisely because it is cooperative.

Christmas is celebrated on *Tahsas* 29 (usually January 7), and Easter is calculated according to various formulae, happening usually not far from Gregorian Easter. Each of these is preceded by a fast: fifty-six days for Lent, and forty-two or forty-three days for Advent (*Hidar* 15–*Tahsas* 28). The eves of Christmas and Easter are *gehad*, "vigils," in which more extensive fasting takes place (and there seems to be some disagreement between parishes in Zege as to exactly how these should be observed).

Christmas and Easter are the major feasts of the year, and they are feasts in the strict sense of the term. While some festivals involve public ceremony, Christmas and Easter mostly involve serving and consuming food in the home. They are turning points in the annual cycle of fasting and feasting, and in each case the transition from fast to feast is marked by the performance of the liturgy (itself a ritual model of the progression from fasting to feasting). Parallel to this is a rhythm at a smaller scale, as people move through the seven-day week, in which each Wednesday and Friday is a fasting day. Outside of the major fasts and feasts, then, people are still constantly moving between fasting and nonfasting times.

The calendar conditions and synchronizes bodily experience by stipulating fasts and feasts. At the same time the calendar has, over the centuries, come to mirror the seasonal changes of the solar year. As well as the comparatively obvious fact that the new year occurs straight after the rainy season (early September by the European calendar), the liturgical cycle also marks the passing of local environmental time, creating, as one church scholar described it to me, "a science of the seasons." Fritsch's account of the liturgical year makes this especially clear:

> "Alleluia (twice). The sound of the footsteps of the rain when it rains: the hungry are satisfied. The sound of the footsteps of the rain when it rains: the poor rejoice. The sound of the footsteps of the rain when it rains: he made the *Senbet* (Sabbath) for man's rest" (*Mezmur* chant *dems'e igerí lezinam,* sung in the first week of the rainy season). (Fritsch 2001: 307)

These rain and fertility chants and readings continue throughout the rainy season until the new year and the *Mesqel* festival, which are closely associated (Fritsch 2001: 304). *Mesqel,* the Exaltation of the Cross, has close parallels in non-Christian parts of Ethiopia and appears to be a Christian development of a preexisting festival (Kaplan 2008). Fertility imagery abounds, particularly in the yellow *Mesqel* flower that symbolizes the feast and its designation as the opening of the "Season of Flowers" (Fritsch 2001: 304). The *Mesqel* ritual as currently practiced places huge emphasis on the concept and form of the cross and the new life brought about by the Resurrection. It also draws analogies between the renewal brought by the rains and the spiritual renewal brought by the Crucifixion (Kaplan 2008).

The coordination between the religious calendar and seasonal change has local importance. Because of its coffee Zege is one of the few places in Christian Ethiopia where the harvest does not take place at the end of the rains, but some four months later, in late January. Here the mutual interdependence of the Christian calendar and the seasonal climate is clearest: coffee harvesting happens only after *T'imqet* (Epiphany) on *Tirr* 12 (January 19), regardless of when the coffee ripens. For the most part coffee picking only lasts for a week after that. No picking happens before *T'imqet* partly because tradition dictates, and partly because people are occupied with preparations for the festival and the celebration itself. After this, large numbers of farmers from the surrounding countryside head to the peninsula to pick coffee for a daily wage of twenty-five to thirty birr (USD 2.50 to 3.00) plus lunch. The landowning families pay the wage on an informal and ad hoc basis, usually to people they know. Young men from Afaf town also join in the wage labor, as do all male members of the landowning families and many females. Women also prepare food for the pickers. Many men who live outside Zege return for the picking season.

The weeklong picking season is not the optimum for coffee harvesting. The beans do not all ripen at once, but over a six-week period from mid-January to the end of February. General practice in Zege, however, is to harvest all beans in the week after *T'imqet*, regardless of their level of ripeness. This leads to a reduced quality of coffee, but is the only economical way to do it. This is largely because, one week after *T'imqet*, the day laborers from outside the peninsula need to return to work in their fields. There simply is not more time to spare. Furthermore, it is extremely time-inefficient to comb over the same land multiple times, picking only the ripe beans, and in local markets this would not lead to enough increase in price to justify the extra labor input. So the picking season is determined partially by the timing of religious festivals, partially by seasonal conditions in the peninsula and surrounding area.

The Orthodox calendar also coexists with a simple routine of market days: there are markets in Afaf on Tuesday, Thursday, and Saturday. If one of those falls on a Christian festival, there will be no market, and the preceding market day will serve for people to buy their supplies for the feast. In fact, a great deal of market activity is dictated by the religious calendar, since livestock are one of the main trade goods: the fast, especially in Lent, means long periods of no livestock sales, while each feast, especially Easter, entails a rush of purchase and consumption. Prices rise and fall accordingly, with chicken prices roughly doubling before a feast.

This all makes it difficult to separate the religious calendar from the seasonal time of the environment, or from the local economy. The rhythms of production and those of exchange, as well as those of feasting and those of feasting, are set by a single calendrical regime. The calendar coordinates the temporality of human bodies and of the local environment together, creating a sense of unity among different scales of social existence. In this way the ritual calendar tends toward creating an encompassing, integrated regime of socioenvironmental experience. The primary mechanism of this integration is fasting.

FASTING AND EXPERIENCE

While most people during my time in Zege wanted to know if I was Christian or not, I cannot recall ever being asked about my beliefs or even if I was a regular churchgoer. But everybody wanted to know if I kept the fast—primarily taking no meat on Wednesdays or Fridays or during Lent, but also potentially on a number of other occasions throughout the Christian calendar, amounting, if you were really strict, to more than 250 days of the year spent in either partial or total abstinence from food and drink. In the eyes of most Orthodox Christians I know, certainly in the villages, if you follow the fasts you are a Christian and if you don't you are not, and that's really all there is to it. Communal abstention can shape communities as surely as common consumption (Fortes 1966). While eating produces moral registers of sharing and generosity, fasting affords an even more potent moral distinction, between those who restrain their appetites in the name of higher virtues and those who do not or do not do so correctly (as in the common denigration of the Weyto and other groups as, supposedly, nonfasters; see chapter 5).

Fasting maintains a continuous ritual vibrancy throughout the rhythm of the calendar (cf. Lambek 1992). It changes the physical condition of a collective while also marking the boundaries of that collective as a distinct group—*and* setting terms by which outsiders can be incorporated or related to. In this sense, one thing that Ethiopian Orthodox fasting does is produce Christians; or, better, fasting is a discipline by which Ethiopian Orthodox Christians intersubjectively produce one another. The material form that fasting takes—the refusal of certain or all foods at certain times—is integral to fasting's particular effectiveness because it shapes the very experience of sustenance and nutrition and of the passage of time.

Fasting and the calendar establish Orthodoxy at a prediscursive level. This point is important, since it captures much of the tenor of what daily Orthodox life is actually like in Zege. Fasting is not directly translatable into a single meaning, reason, or doctrinal exegesis. It is very difficult to produce a statement like "Orthodox Christians fast because X." There are, of course, extensive doctrinal and dogmatic explanations for why and when people should fast, although most people are only roughly aware of them. In any given situation a number of reasons could be given for a fast: to remember; for penitence; because it brings joy *(desta)*; because of Mary; because of Our Lord. There is a widespread idea that fasting is necessary to tire the flesh out and so weaken its aggressive and lustful urges (Levine 1965); for others, it constitutes more of an identification with a saint or saintly event. Or one may simply do it because not to do so would attract opprobrium.

The point is that people fast regardless of which of these meanings they may choose to highlight or fix upon. It is not reducible to any of them; fasting is not a form of language. And this helps to account for the comparative lack of focus on creed in popular Orthodoxy: Christians are already doing the work of being Christian, together.

When somebody says that we fast on Fridays because of the Crucifixion, it is therefore not obvious exactly what that "because" is doing. The Amharic *sile* means "because, for, or for the sake of"—the relation it denotes is not directly causal, but describes a commemoration of, identification with, or following of the suffering of Christ, in a subordinate way. One of the things that fasts do is establish an identification between today and the archetypal event, as well as with all previous and subsequent Fridays in which the same identification will be performed. They do so not by commanding you to think of Christ's suffering (though for many this is part of it), but by telling you to reenact a small part of it, to adopt a condition of privation and denial. Fasting performs an act of allegiance and iconic-indexical connection between all those who fast and the person or act for which they fast. It is divine patronage in practice, and it shows popular Orthodox Christianity to be built on conditioned relations of loyalty and repetition.

What precisely fasting entails depends on circumstance and personal conscience. At a minimum, no animal products are to be consumed on fasting days— a rule I have seen broken only once, when a friend beckoned me into a back room and served mutton stew in the middle of the Lenten fast. Never a particularly observant person, he had grown tired of fasting and suspected that I had too, but he had to be secretive or face general disapprobation and perhaps a visit from the priest if word got out. In towns, some restaurants will now serve meat on fasting days, particularly if they have any foreign clientele, but most Orthodox Christians still avoid meat and eggs on these days.

If attending the liturgy, then you may take no food or water between the beginning of the day and the end of the service, which is 3 PM on regular fasting days and 9 AM on weekends. For those taking Communion, a minimum of fifteen or eighteen hours' total fasting is required. On Easter Saturday, the devout will take no food or water for the entire day, not even swallowing their saliva. Note that this does not efface the flesh so much as make one hyperconscious of one's body, both because you have to take care not to swallow, and because of the fatigue and thirst that you feel when performing a big fast. When I asked one young man why he was following the Saturday vigil to its full, exacting extent, he simply replied, *"yasdes-sital"* (It makes one happy).

Thinking about how people describe the feeling of fasting—usually in terms of a combination of tiredness and happiness—reminds us that there is an inward, more individual aspect to the practice. It is important to recognize that fasting is not simply an activity of rote obedience. Not only are there many optional fasts, or fasts of optional intensity; there is also the possibility of performing extra fasts for penance or for other personal reasons.

I have noticed that many of my friends move between periods of more and less intense fasting over the years. There is a stereotype that older people fast more and better as their fleshly urges subside, but it is noticeable that younger people often emphasize their fasting at times when other aspects of their lives are more tumultuous—when leaving school, moving to the city, flirting, or, as Malara's (2017) research shows, doing legally or morally questionable work. Over the time that I knew him, Zebirhan, a young man in his late teens, went through periods of fasting with more intensity than his friends did. None of them would eat meat on fasting days, but Zebirhan would often wait until afternoon before taking any food or water at all. This made him tired and sometimes morose, and this difficulty was part of the point. He never gave me an exact reason for his extra fasting except that he felt that it was the right and proper thing to do.

Fasting, like any religious engagement, unfolds over the trajectory of a life (Schielke & Debevec 2012). Individual Christians may choose to perform extra fasts, or may be recommended to do so by their soul fathers (yenefs abbat), the priest responsible for their pastoral care. This may result from the confession of sins (nessiha) or simply from personal desire. Hannig (2013, 2017) has shown how important this kind of fasting is for women prevented from entering church by physical ailments that make them feel insufficiently pure; similarly in Zege many women who are kept from church by work duties use fasting as a way of maintaining their devotion (see also chapter 8). The play between fasting as intersubjective, world-making discipline and a kind of devotional self-orientation that goes beyond external constraints is a key dynamic. Individual fasts can be simultaneously acts of submission to God and acts of self-mastery, asserting control over one's desires and one's life situation; this potential partially counteracts the normative weight of calendrical fasting.

FAST TO FEAST

Fasting is not really a world-denying or world-hating practice, but rather a way for people to do religious work on and through their bodies. Moreover, most fasts have as their culminating act a feast, and should not be considered without this context. There are a very large number of possible feast days (be'al) in the calendar—nine major feasts of the Lord and nine minor; the thirty-three feasts of Mary instituted by Zara Yaqob, as well as the monthly and annual saints' days, the feast of the Exaltation of the Cross, and others. But the longest and most significant fast-to-feast progression is that from Lent to Easter. Because of the length and intensity of the fast, and its more or less universal observance among Christians, it becomes the event to which shorter fasts get compared. It becomes a model in which each year Orthodox Christians reenact the salvation of the world.

By the time Holy Week arrives, the fast has been going for forty-eight days, with profound effects on the ambience and economic life of Afaf town. The lack of livestock and egg sales combined with people saving for Easter means the market has been slow, and this is compounded by the fact that we are now six or seven months into the dry season. People are tired from not eating, and not much work gets done. No drums are played in church, and priests' chants stick to the mournful register of the *zi'il*, the songs of penitence. The pop songs that usually play on radios and sound systems are replaced by the mournful drone of the *begena*, the ten-string harp said to have been played by David, whose sole purpose is the contemplation of our remorse for our sins. No marriages take place during the fast, and by the end of Lent the livestock will be extremely thin and the grass a uniform shade of yellow brown.

In the final week before Easter the general air of subdued penitence kicks up a notch. Radios begin broadcasting the story of the Crucifixion, focusing on the acts of betrayal and cruelty in the lead-up to Christ's death. Holy week (*himamat*, "suffering") is a time for *sigdet* (prostration, surrender): the performance of repeated prostrations in the churchyard, in penitence, and in commemoration of the Lord's suffering. As one man told me, you should perform 133 prostrations, for the number of times Christ was beaten. Priests are busy all week chanting in the church, but no absolution is given. During this week, especially from Thursday on, people must not shake hands or otherwise greet one another—something people have to constantly remind one another of, since greetings are so habituated.

Holy Week enacts a world without trust or redemption. It does so at the level of the most basic embodied habits, hence its power; it is very strange not to be able to greet people. This must not be underestimated: the feast of humanity's salvation begins with the production of its opposite, a world in which salvation is not possible.

Some people, further, go shoeless, and the most devout will go without food or water for the duration of Easter Saturday, isolating themselves entirely from any kind of conviviality. When asked why they do not greet one another, most people say it is because of the betrayal of Christ by Judas (or by *Ayhud*, "the Jews," although I do not think many people make the connection between the supposed enemies of Christ and any currently existing people). Equally, many perform ritual acts without knowing why, and still others are critical of this degree of ritualism. As one teenage boy told me, pointing to a friend who was barefoot, "What matters is in your heart, and being good to people. It isn't stuff like that."

None of this action would make sense without the transition into the feast, marked by the midnight service. As the young spend the night in church, learning about the Resurrection from deacons and other slightly older Christians, men get ready to slaughter and women to cook the first chicken and sheep for a very long time.

The liturgical service itself reenacts the event of the world's salvation, revolving around the performance of the Eucharist. Starting from slow chants of penitence, over three hours the service builds to the offering and consumption of the sacrament, followed by joyful song, drumming, and hallelujahs.

Easter Sunday itself is a day of lavish feasting. Families that can afford to will slaughter a sheep and a chicken, and groups of men may share the meat of a cow among themselves. Poorer families may make a stew with at least a few pieces of meat in it, and serve cheap liquor in order both to show hospitality and to disguise the quality of the food. Men move from house to house visiting their neighbors, in direct contrast to the practices of holy week, while women cook and serve guests. All who greet one another say, *"inkwan aderresen"* (Rejoice, for he has brought us across). Having fasted for fifty-five days, and intensively in the last week, makes Easter Sunday an overwhelming sensory experience. There is too much to eat and drink, along with music and incense. This excessive quality marks an association between salvation and limitless plenitude—the post-Resurrection world is as abundant as it had been barren before.

The phenomenal intensity of the Easter feast comes from the experience of having fasted. This cannot be understood without an idea of how the whole environment of Zege has been affected by the fast, and so of degree to which the fast is effective beyond the limits of human bodies. It amounts to a form of world-building: collective fasting is an ambient phenomenon and becomes a thing of the environment. Orthodoxy becomes the frame of life.

COUNTERCALENDARS

The intimate relationship between calendars and the exercise of power has been widely noted (Bourdieu 1977: 97–108, Gell 1992, Peters 2013). For Nancy Munn, who views time and sociality as coconstitutive, this power takes on an extremely intimate nature:

> Control over time is not just a strategy of interaction; it is also a medium of hierarchic power and governance. . . . Authority over the annual calendar (the chronological definition, timing, and sequence of daily and seasonal activities), or of other chronological instruments like clock time, not only controls aspects of the everyday lives of persons but also connects this level of control to a more comprehensive universe that entails critical values and potencies in which governance is grounded. Controlling these temporal media variously implies control over this more comprehensive order and its definition, as well as over the capacity to mediate this wider order into the fundamental social being and bodies of persons. (Munn 1992: 109)

Munn's critics respond that there is always a second kind of temporality that is not so dependent on cultural construction (Bloch 2012: 79–116, Hodges 2008: 406). They are probably right, but this should not detract from Munn's demonstration of how deeply social regimes of time become part of the prediscursive, embodied, intersubjective experience of living in an environment—as calendrical practice in Zege shows.

However, calendrical power is not so totalizing or so formative of experience that people cannot see other ways of doing time. The Orthodox calendar currently coexists in a partly integrated way with the government's calendar. The Orthodox dating system is widely used, although the government also works in the international Gregorian calendar. The government's calendar includes recognition both of Muslim festivals and of days of more recent national-historical importance, most notably Adwa day, which celebrates the defeat of the invading Italian armies in 1896. While many people in Zege have a great deal of national pride, they tend to ignore the non-Christian elements of the calendar as not having much importance or gravity in the unfolding of their own lives, and ultimately as being somewhat artificial. This mild incommensurability of calendars was clearest at the Ethiopian Millennium, an event that appeared to mark an inherently Christian temporality, since it referred to the birth of Christ, but was not interpreted that way.

The year 2007–08 CE was Millennium according to the Ethiopian calendar and was marked by various government-sponsored celebrations of unified Ethiopian nationhood (Orlowska 2013). The event was a centerpiece of the EPRDF's efforts to promote their secular, multiethnic (and effectively one-party) vision of modern Ethiopia (Marcus 2008), culminating with a much-publicized performance by Beyoncé at the Sheraton hotel in Addis. But my friends Menilek and Mulugeta were dismissive of the whole concept. Although it did represent two thousand years since Christ's birth, they said, it was not a proper Christian festival (that is, it did not come from Ethiopian canonical tradition) but was just a government creation. Like the celebration of victory at Adwa and the recognition of Muslim festivals, it was part of government attempts to make a unified secular national calendar, but as such it carried no legitimacy for them. Both men were from an old church family; they were not exactly traditionalists, but they had respect for the old ways, which meant especially the church's calendar. Here the EPRDF may simply be following the lead of the Derg in choosing to appropriate, rather than undermine, the Orthodox calendar in the name of modernist developmental projects (Donham 1999: 143).

Perhaps because it is so foundational, the calendar is one way that people in Zege can show dissent against the prevailing cultural order, for example, by proclaiming an alternative calendar that differs from the official one in some way. Until about a generation ago, according to *Mergéta* Worqé, there were a small number of Unctionists (*qibatocch*) in Zege. These were followers of a rival Christology to the mainstream *Tewahido*, who maintained that Christ's divinity was not originary but came from his baptism in the Holy Spirit (Crummey 1972: 14–27, Ayala 1981, Cohen 2009: 132). These people or their descendants have all since joined the mainstream. But as Tefera tells me, what people primarily remember now about the Unctionists, and what marked them as aberrant, was not just their Christology, but also the fact that they did not change the date of Christmas during a leap year, whereas the church calendar moves it back by a day. That simple discrepancy of a day every four years was enough to clearly demonstrate the Unctionists' nonconformism.

A more unusual and extreme case is that of "the Prophet Tesfa" *(nebiyy Tesfa)*, as he is known in slightly mocking fashion. Tesfa is in his fifties, lives in the Zege forest, and follows a calendar entirely of his own invention. It includes forty days of Lent rather than fifty-five, and numerous other discrepancies: he counts the months differently, has an extra thirteen days' fasting for Christmas, and ignores several of the other fasts. He told us that we were currently in the year 31 AD, all time before that having been lost in sin and heresy. In addition, he told me, he eats no animals raised by others, and while he prays to God he rejects entirely the authority of the church, which he describes as built by "whores, thieves, and murderers." He harks back to what he considers an Abrahamic faith, before Christian practice became corrupted. He tried to live in a tent, like Abraham, but his family would usually make him sleep in the house. While he cheerfully explained all this to me and Tefera outside his home in the woods, a small crowd gathered to listen, incredulous and mocking. His description of his calendar was what provoked most affront, though he said plenty of other things that might have. To change the dates of the fasts was plainly ridiculous and was met with laughing disbelief.

People in Zege consider Tesfa mad, and some have told me that Tesfa's father was a *mergéta* (religious expert) who gave him too much brain medicine. It is commonly believed (and probably true) that religious teachers have various herbal medicines for the intellect to aid their deacons in their study of the texts. Tesfa's brothers were all highly intelligent, but something had happened to him. It must be said that much of his discourse was fantastic, disconnected, and occasionally messianic and paranoid. He told us about his mission from God to return Hosni Mubarak to rule over Egypt, and about his collection of secret holy texts from the Sinai, and he recounted a long and obscene story about a woman copulating with a dog, to illustrate the faithlessness of other nations.

But while Tesfa was not always fully coherent (or, at least, was not regarded to be so), he certainly knew which buttons he was pushing by denouncing almost every part of the church's timeframe. Some of his practices, like drinking only water instead of coffee or beer, were minor eccentricities, but it was his calendar that set him apart. He told me that prophets are never recognized in their own country, but that he would ascend to heaven in due course.

The calendar is not arbitrary; precision matters. I began working with Tefera after he read my doctoral thesis and we began to discuss the possibility of future research in Zege. In his reading he showed most interest in making sure I got the precise details of the calendar right. I had, for example, counted the Lenten fast as fifty-six days rather than fifty-five, following another source. (It is easy to make errors, since it is not always obvious whether a fast begins at dawn or midnight.)[2]

Correctness matters very much, because the calendar is one of the bases of the Ethiopian church's authority. Even then, there are certain disputes: in Zege, Tefera tells me, the churches of Mehal Zege and Ura are in disagreement about the start date of the Christmas fast by a matter of a day. Ura, which advocates an extra day of fasting, can thus claim to be more devout, while Mehal Zege claims to be more accurate by official church doctrine.

The calendar frames moral social life in what is supposed to be an immutable and unchallengeable way. This is not an invisible or unquestionable ideological structure, although it is a very powerful one that commands great loyalty. Control over the terms of temporal distinctions does, as Munn says, set the terms of relationship between bodies and the cosmos. But people are quite able to question and think past this framework if they so desire. In fact, because of its very formality, the slightest deviation can become a statement of rebellion. At a larger level, the coexistence of church and government calendars gives an impression of ongoing church-state relations. While governments have over the last several decades succeeded in subordinating the Orthodox Church to the state on a legal level, Christians in places like Zege have simply continued to maintain their calendar as they think right, and have even reasserted the importance of the cycle of the fasts.

TRANSIT OF THE *TABOTS*: MATERIALITY AND THE POWER OF LIFE

As with most ritual calendars, the Orthodox calendar contains within it the symbolic seeds of its own negation: certain times that show us what life is like when sanctity is not bound and contained. This is clearest on the festivals of the Exaltation of the Cross *(Mesqel)*, Epiphany *(T'imqet)*, and the annual local saints' days. These all share one key characteristic: they involve sacred performance in worldly space, temporarily breaking down the domains established by regular calendrical fasting and feasting.

When sacred rituals are performed outside of church bounds—especially in the marketplace—it is an occasion for extreme male exuberance, sometimes turning into violence. My first experience of this connection was *Mesqel* of September 2008 (just after the New Year's celebrations of 2001 by the Ethiopian calendar). On the eve of the festival a wooden bonfire *(demera)* was erected on the main street of the Afaf marketplace with a cross rising some four meters from the kindling. In the late afternoon the clergy gathered in a circle around the cross and began to perform the slow votive chants usually associated with the liturgy. A large crowd gathered around them, and as the prayer chants built up into faster *aqwaqwam*, groups of people began to sing and dance around drummers. The celebration built to a crescendo around sunset, and then stopped. *Abba S'om*, the local expert on exegesis, gave a sermon about the meaning of the cross ("the medicine and salvation of our flesh") and the story of the festival: the finding of the remains of the true cross on Calgary by Empress Helena, the wife of Constantine.

After that, the clergy just left. The anticlimax was palpable; a bonfire had been built but not burnt. The people of Afaf retired to their homes or to the bars to drink, and young men gathered in groups with their drums and went from house to house, dancing raucously and singing until they were paid to go away. I talked to two policemen who were, unusually, on the streets after dark because "the young ones are disturbing everyone." They made no arrests, though, and soon disappeared. As the evening drew on, the boisterousness increased. Teenagers whom I had never seen touch alcohol were drinking at the bar on the main drag, making lewd suggestions to the servant women (which were not taken very seriously). Young adult men chewed *khat* (technically forbidden to Christians but widely used by the youth of the village) while an ex-soldier sang *azmari* songs. The noise was loud enough that one family across the street had to carry an elderly relative, bed and all, to another part of the town. Despite their annoyance, there was no possibility of asking the boys to stop. Their behavior was expected, if not sanctioned. One normally mild-mannered friend of mine headbutted another man in a fight over a cigarette, drawing copious blood on both sides.

The actual lighting of the cross-bonfire felt like a deliberate anticeremony. At around three in the morning, around ten people gathered around the *demera*. All had been drinking. One lit the bonfire with a match; another bummed a cigarette from me and lit it from the flames. We sat around the fire, talking and taking naps. Many families had their own, smaller cross-bonfires that they sat around, most having sensibly gone to sleep and then woken again. There was no special ceremony around the big *demera*, but all present watched carefully to see which way it would fall—it was said that if it fell eastward it would mean good fortune for the coming year, and if westward then bad. It fell southwest, to general groans, but then one boy resourcefully jumped up and pulled the burning cross round to the east, saying that nobody need ever know.

As dawn broke, older and more devout people headed to church for the liturgy. All stopped by the grand *demera* to take some of the warm ash and make crosses on their foreheads. It made quite a contrast to the manner of the burning—I was told that the material of the cross is "our power" *(haylacchin)*. There followed a relatively calm day of feasting, as the real exuberance was finished.

The structure of the *Mesqel* festival as practiced in Zege follows a pattern of the suspension and reassertion of order that is quite similar to that described by Turner (1969). A liminal phase sees the suspension of normal rules and hierarchies, followed by the reconstitution of social hierarchy. Perhaps there is subversive potential; perhaps it is just the letting off of steam and youthful aggression that actually serves the maintenance of structure. Either way, the event sets a contrast to forms of constraint and control that exist the rest of the year. However, while the wildness of young men is tacitly sanctioned during the night, it is not so clear that the burning of the cross is meant to be a reversal of the Christian order.

Shortly after my first *Mesqel* I asked why you would burn a cross, and he told me not to think of the fire as destroying, but as "illuminating" *(mabrat)* the cross. He told me that the cross was our sign *(millikitacchin)* and that, if you destroyed a photograph of me, no harm would come to my person. The idea of illuminating the cross is compelling, and consistent with the use of flame in other ritual forms to mark salvation (the flame in a censer, for example, represents Christ's Incarnation). But as with any ritual exegesis, this explanation cannot exhaust what the ritual is about. We might note that the bonfire form exists in non-Christian rituals around Ethiopia and has been adapted, in quite classic Christian fashion, into the Orthodox calendar—rituals have a history, and no exegesis will quite exhaust their meaningful potential.

This point was made clearer to me by the fact that, along with the performance of *Mesqel* eve in Afaf, Ethiopian state television was broadcasting the same ritual from Meskel Square in Addis Ababa, the central plaza that is named for the festival. Those people who stayed in the bars in Afaf were able to watch the Addis version of the ritual, and the differences are instructive. For one thing, the televised version was far more consciously theatrical. Actors played out the Empress Helena finding the cross, standing on a carnival float festooned with lights. Cameras showed foreign tourists with cameras at the front of the audience, which was separated from the performance by barricades. Dignitaries gave speeches, in English and Amharic, highlighting the depth of Ethiopia's unique culture and tradition. National flags were tied to the staffs of the choristers as they danced the votive chants; a general emphasis was placed on Mesqel as an item of national cultural heritage, which was absent in Afaf. Participatory ritual was on the way to becoming a spectacle, with a strong distinction drawn between performers and audience, rather than a focus on the transformation of the participants themselves, as in Afaf.

The strongest indication of this transformation, for me at least, was the moment when, at sunset and following the speeches of the dignitaries, a senior bishop lit the giant *demera* and the camera lingered on it as it burned. The gap between the ceremony and the lighting, which had precipitated the night of exuberance in Afaf, was gone. *Abba* S'om told me he thought this difference was just a matter of local practice and not doctrine. I would suggest also that the ritual would have made a rather unsatisfying viewing experience stripped of its climactic burning—which, as I have argued, was exactly the point of the performance in Afaf. Where I was, the gap between performance and climax was an important period of suspension. In the ritual on television, this no longer made sense. But the televised version was visible in Afaf, and presumably contributed to a sense of nationhood among those who viewed it. Certainly those I spoke to were happy that Orthodox ritual was being given due priority on state television. But the logic of the televised event was, I suggest, significantly different from that of the ritual in Afaf.

The performance of church ritual in town is not an inversion for inversion's sake. As the local ex-deacon Destaw (now an adult, with a strong church education, but no longer part of the clergy) explained to me, this was an important site for ensuring the generational continuity of Orthodoxy. The children were a major focus. Large numbers of children were present at the singing and dancing, many wearing paper crowns with references to Bible verses (Galatians 3:1: "You foolish Galatians! Who has bewitched you? It was before your eyes that Jesus Christ was publicly exhibited as crucified!"; and Matthew 16:24: "If any want to become my followers, let them deny themselves and take up their cross and follow me"). This was one of the few times I have seen public references to chapter and verse, and was part of an explicit drive to educate children in Orthodoxy, as was *Abba* S'om's sermon, which drove home the importance of the cross as both symbol and source of power.

Sacred things cannot remain totally hidden away, or they risk losing all relevance to the collective. Access is restricted, but connection and communion must be possible; we have seen that the Holy Communion is, in practice, highly restricted. *Mesqel* is an important point of contact and transmission for the young, but it also carries with it the elements of excess that I have described. The importance of sacred contact is made even clearer in those festivals, especially Epiphany, in which the sacred *tabot* leaves its sanctuary in the middle of the church and is taken to bless the waters.

The walls of churchyards mark out a clearly differentiated geography of sacred and profane. Churches are out of town, surrounded by trees, and walled in. In the central sanctum, accessible only to priests, lies the *tabot*, the consecrated replica of the Ark of the Covenant on which communion is prepared. For a woman or a layperson to see the *tabot* is to incur certain and instantaneous divine punishment, and my friend Thomas told many stories of thieves found frozen to the spot in the act of trying to steal one.

At least twice a year, however, the *tabot* leaves the church to be carried, shrouded and with great fanfare, to the water (Lake Tana, in Zege's case). On Epiphany and on the annual day of the saint to which the *tabot* is consecrated, it is taken to the water so that the water will become holy and its blessings will be dispersed to the people. In the case of a *tabot* of Mary, there are thirty-three feasts to choose from; Afaf's Fure Maryam celebrates the Dormition (*Asteriyo Maryam*, Tirr 21). One friend told me that these saints' days are like a "little *T'imqet*," sharing many formal characteristics, but with much more of a local flavor, commemorating religious history appropriate to the area. The monasteries in Mehal Zege, at the tip of the peninsula, have annual feasts for the founder, Betre Maryam; Afaf is consecrated to Mary and so observes one of her many days.

In the morning the priests bring the *tabot* outside—the one who carries it must have fasted, and must be dressed in fine brocaded robes (sacred things carry the symbolism of royalty). The people of Afaf, especially the young, follow the *tabot* on its procession round the church and down to the lake, and sing and shout while the priests sing the votive prayers that will bring the *tabot*'s blessing to the water. They then cast the water at the crowd, using whatever vessels available, and people with plastic containers take as much as they can carry for friends or relatives. The water is especially beneficial for the sick but is of value to all. The *tabot*'s presence, given the proper ritual treatment, empowers the water with divine blessing.

On the eve of Epiphany multiple *tabots* proceed from their separate churches to rest together, overnight, by the lakeside. Priests and deacons escort them, shading each *tabot* with brocaded umbrellas as well as its shroud, and the people follow, singing joyfully. As in the case of *Mesqel*, a certain amount of male aggression is noticeable whenever this happens—groups of "fire age" boys (*fendata*, mid-teens to early twenties) rush around in groups, waving their *dula* staffs in the air and barging into people. As the sun sets two tents are set up, one for the *tabots* under police guard, another for the older people who wish to keep vigil, and people walk round the village carrying candles, an extremely effective marker of the coming of the light, in the relative absence of artificial light sources.

While older people keep vigil by the *tabots*, young men drink, sing, and chew *khat*, much as they did on Mesqel. The *T'imqet* celebrations then proceed to a fête day, with penny amusements on the streets and, formerly, marriage arrangements being negotiated. In an important example of status suspension, Abebe told me that *T'imqet* was *yegered be'al*, "the housemaid's feast," being the one festival that servant women were permitted to participate in rather than having to tend the home or place of business. Maids always come from poorer parts of the countryside and are among the lowest-status people in the village; *T'imqet* is seen as a chance for them to find husbands and, perhaps, a chance of improving their situation. All of this happens, note, while the *tabots* are resting by the lakeside and the inner chambers of the churches lie empty. Over the next two days the *tabots* proceed back to their resting places, accompanied by crowds of jubilant followers, and order is restored. The Afaf festival ends with the accompaniment of the *tabot* of Saint Michael back to Wanjeta village, out in the farmlands, so people trace the geographical movement of the *tabot* from its place in church, to the meeting place at the waters, and back again. They follow the seat of divine power across the land, marking out its religious contours and making clear the relationship among the different churches.

These festivals have associations with both fertility and aggression, which we should probably understand together as aspects of the worldly condition of the flesh, which is most fully expressed feasting. The relationship between repletion and arrogance or aggression is paradigmatic and, in some accounts, one of the main reasons for the importance of fasting (Levine 1965, Malara 2017).

Liminal times are especially important in the relationship between sanctity and the environment. *P'agumén,* the short intercalary month, falls at the end of the rainy season in early September, straight before the renewal of the new year and the harvest festivities that have for centuries been tied into the framework of the Christian calendar. Those five days are neither really in the old year nor yet in the new. On the Zege Peninsula on Lake Tana in northern Ethiopia, it is said that this is one of the few times that *zar* spirits tend to descend, as if the boundaries between human and spirit worlds have been suspended like the boundaries between years and seasons (the other times are at funerals and during the annual feasts of Saint Michael, the subduer of demons).

P'agumén 3 is Archangel Raphael's day. Of the multitude of saints' and angels' days, it is the only one to fall in the intercalary month. On this day and this day only Raphael makes holy the rain and the water of the lake. Children dance naked in the streets of the village of Afaf, absorbing blessing, and adults head to the shallows of Tana to bathe and wash their clothes for the new year.

Holy water is usually associated with churches. Either it is made holy by the prayer of priests, or if a sacred source is found by chance, then a church will be built on that spot (Hermann 2012). But on Raphael's day, the water of the environment itself turns into blessing. This is not normally possible precisely because blessing, that elusive and potentially dangerous quasi-substance, must be contained and regulated within the structures of the church. It takes the authority of angels at the special in-between time to extend this blessing to the wider landscape. In the night, in the privacy of people's homes, *zar* spirits emerge in those they possess. Usually they come only at funerals and on the annuals feasts of Archangel Michael, the angel of mastery over the demonic.

Raphael is not mentioned in the sixty-six-book Bible as used by Protestant Churches, but he appears in Enoch and Tobit, Deuterocanonical texts that are included between New and Old Testaments in the eighty-one-book Bible of the Ethiopian Orthodox Church. An intermediate figure from intermediate books, the archangel links people to blessing, and hence to the power of an encompassing reality, through the local environment and the contact of water on and in bodies. Intermediate times such as *T'imqet* eve and Raphael's day have profound spatial consequences. They temporarily reorder relationships between bodies, environment, and spirits, and so, by way of contrast, make visible the distinctions and divisions that exist the rest of the time.

CONCLUSION

This chapter has aimed to show how pervasively the Orthodox calendar shapes everyday life in Zege, and in particular how it brings bodies, the environment, and Christianity into a single spatiotemporal framework. The calendar stipulates when and where people should fast, feast, and work, and denotes specific fasts and feasts as commemorations of particular events and personages from religious history. This system is remarkable in its pervasiveness, especially because it appears at odds with secular government ways of organizing time and space. This continuing adherence is possible in large part because Orthodox Christians consider fasting so important: as a discipline, as a practice of integration, as a mode of group formation, and as the moral grounding of any kind of religious life. The fast is as meaningful and as available to the wildly unobservant as to the devout, and to marginal people as much as to grandees. It can be practiced with deep and educated reflection, or with the certainty of habit. It can tie one to the church, but also offer a space of independent practice in which to assert control over one's person.

Fasting is also strongly normative. It creates a simple binary of fasting and non-fasting by which whole worlds can be ordered. But this normative force is never quite total, and in Zege we see multiple cases of people resisting or debating the precise terms and time frames of fasting. While the fast is ordinarily associated with the division of space and time into spiritual and worldly, there are moments when blessing spills out into the world, and a less-structured existence briefly becomes palpable. But it is the nature of fasting as abstinence, as a practice that marks and acts out different kinds of body-time, that makes the calendar such an enveloping and immediate presence.

NOTES

1. The seven fasts in chronological order are:

    1. *Qwisqwam,* forty days commemorating the holy family's exile in Egypt.
    2. The fast of the prophets, forty-three days.
    3. The fast of Nineveh, three days preceding Lent.
    4. The great fast, *Abiy Sòm,* fifty-five days of Lent.
    5. The fast of the Apostles.
    6. The fast of salvation: kept by all on every Wednesday and Friday of the year, except from Easter to Pentecost and on Christmas and Epiphany, should they occur on such a day.
    7. The fast of the Assumption *(Filseta).*

Of these the great fast, the fast of Nineveh, the fast of salvation, and the fast of the Assumption are generally compulsory for all, while others are only compulsory for monks and priests (Fritsch 2001: 83–84).

2. The Lenten fast comprises three parts: the fast of Heraclius (seven days), the fast of Christ (forty days), and the Pasch (eight days; Fritsch 2001: 177).

3

Proliferations of Mediators

Prohibitions in Zege produce clear distinctions in social space and time. These distinctions, as I have argued, are most apparent around the performance of the Eucharist *(qurban)*. The Eucharist is prepared in the inner sanctum of a church, surrounded by multiple concentric walls, each marking an increase in the purity and observance required to enter. The sanctum itself and the *tabot* it holds are accessible only to deacons and ordained priests, and only the ordained may actually prepare the sacrament. Those who give communion, *qorabí,* will upon death be buried with a candle to mark their special status.

As we have seen, a practical assumption exists that most Orthodox adults lack the purity to take communion. The real, bodily presence of God does not mix well with the domains of sexuality, feeding, or reproduction, and particularly with bodily fluids (Hannig 2013). Nonetheless, through the sacraments *(mist'irat)* and by God's grace *(s'ega),* God does become available to human consumption.

It seems that prohibitions around the sacred can never be total. A holy *tabot* that nobody could touch or see would be a dead object. Instead, priests, endowed by the sacrament of holy orders, manage relations between *tabot* and community, while at the same time making sure general access is restricted. As the former patriarch *Abune* Paulos (1988: 174) makes quite clear, it is the purity of the Eucharist that necessitates the religious division of labor. This is the basic structure of Ethiopian Orthodox mediation: specialist figures both enable and restrict traffic between humans and divinity. The rules of prohibition and separation go along with the rules of mediation and connection. This produces a social universe of structured, hierarchical relations.

What I find most noticeable about Ethiopian Orthodox religious mediators in Zege is their sheer variety and proliferation: priests, deacons, monks, and nonordained church singers all play parts in the management of human-divine relations, but so do saints, angels, and the Virgin Mary. Saints and angels are also important for the control of demonic agents, but there also exists a substantial demimonde of figures associated with the church (but not approved by it) who mobilize religious knowledge for the suppression, and sometimes the propitiation, of demons. This chapter argues that all of these figures share core symbolic elements of hybridity. They are all construed as embodying split states between human and nonhuman form, and between life and death. These hybrid mediators, I argue, are products of the regime of prohibition that structures Orthodox life.

THE BODIES OF ANGELS

In the course of conversation in the front room of Haregwa's bar, Haregwa and Zebirhan asked me, *"Igzíabhér man yímeslal?"* (Who does God resemble?). Haregwa, a woman of my age who had hosted me for many months with her husband, said that God was definitely a white man (which was largely a way of teasing me). I asked if God was definitely male, and after a moment's thought she replied, *"besim wend new"* (By name he's male). What about the Trinity, I asked—grammatically it sounded like it might be female, as in the term *qiddist selassé,* the Holy (f.) Trinity. Haregwa and Zebirhan thought the Trinity was definitely male if it was anything, but said at this point we ought to ask someone more knowledgeable. She sent Zebirhan to find an ex-deacon friend who was passing through town. The friend told us that this was a matter of divine mystery *(mist'íre melekot),* starting from how the three persons *(akal)* of the Trinity could all be in one.

He then told us that it was similar with angels: we refer to Archangel Gabriel and Archangel Michael in male terms but actually they have no gendered parts. The language available to us does not necessarily reflect the nature of the beings we are discussing. Haregwa asked him if angels urinate (I think I had prompted this by asking her about it earlier), and he replied, "of course not." Nor do they eat like us; while we eat food, they eat only praise *(mesgena).*

I would suggest that the angels' lack of sex, nutrition, or excretion is understood to be integral to their role as messengers (Amh. *mel'ak,* "angel," *melak,* "to send"). In Zege Archangel Michael, Archangel Gabriel, and Archangel Raphael are second only to Mary as recipients and conduits of prayers and vows, while the area of Ura appears to be named for Urael. Each has their own domain: Michael protects from demonic attack and possession (and is generally identified as having dominion over demons); Raphael and Gabriel assist with problems of fertility, disease, and poverty. Their role is explicitly understood, as one elderly told me, as "carrying our prayers to God."

The other place where angels are prominent is painted on the shutters of the holy of holies in the center of the church-monasteries. Michael is often portrayed with a sword; Gabriel saves three children from the fire (see Cowley 1983: 128); Raphael impales a sea monster that threatens an island church. The archangels are warriors and guardians as well as protectors; it is not for nothing that they protect the inner sanctum. They also have wings, highlighting their celestial and nonhuman qualities. In the book of Enoch, which seems to be a key source for much of Ethiopian angelology, and which was only fully preserved in Ge'ez, two of the main roles of the archangels are to plead with God on behalf of humanity and to imprison Azazel, leader of the "Watchers," fallen angels who came to earth and had sexual relations with human women. Azazel has taught humanity how to make tools and weapons and how to beautify their faces and wear jewelry. The angels are gravely punished: Gabriel is commanded to destroy the children of the fallen Watchers and set them to war against one another; Raphael is sent to imprison Azazel; Urael is dispatched to announce the coming flood to Noah; and Michael is ordered to imprison the fallen angels who have "united themselves with women so as to have defiled themselves with them in all their uncleanness" (1 Enoch 11).

Angels must not have sexual relations with humans (implying, of course, that they might desire to do so). The archangels, on the other hand, serve the dual purpose of pleading with God on humanity's behalf and of carrying out his punishments and smiting wrongdoers. In both senses they stand between humans and God. It is the presence of such go-betweens, partly like humans, but also radically different, that is so important in the practical logic of Orthodoxy in Zege. The vital importance of having mediators is greatly enhanced by the expansion of Protestantism into traditionally Orthodox areas.

HOW MEDIATORS MAKE RELIGION

The afternoon trade was dying down in the veterinary pharmacy in Afaf village, on the edge of the Zege peninsula, where my friend Thomas and his teenage factotum Abebe kept shop. A local man popped his head round the door to say hello. His face was familiar; I had seen him in Thomas's bar and knew the two were friends. The man was chatting to Thomas when Abebe, talking to me but intending to be overheard, remarked, "Tom, this guy is *Péntey*"—Pentecostal, though the term now refers colloquially and rather dismissively to any kind of Protestantism (Haustein 2011: 229). He was the only Protestant I would meet in Afaf village or the adjoining peninsula where I conducted my fieldwork, although I knew the religion to be growing in the regional capital nearby.

Our friend smiled and did not deny it. The exchange was light-hearted, and his religion did not seem a great impediment to his friendship with Thomas and Abebe, both, like the majority of the area's residents, Orthodox Christians. But

Abebe was bored and saw an opportunity to use my presence to say things that he normally would not: "Tom, ask him who heals" *(Tom, man yadenal belw)*. Playing my part as the naïve but mostly harmless outsider, I asked.

The man paused, still smiling, but did not respond. As he turned to leave, Thomas said quietly, *Maryam tadenallech* (Mary heals). Their Protestant friend appeared not to hear, but when he reached the door he turned defiantly, raised both arms high, and exclaimed, *Iyesus Kristos yadenal!* (Jesus Christ heals!). Then he walked away, leaving Thomas and Abebe scoffing and shaking their heads.

Abebe's choice of question is instructive: "who heals?" (or "who saves"—the words *medhanít*, "medicine," and *medhaní*, "savior," are cognate). It illustrates not just the importance of Mary as an intercessor in Ethiopian Orthodox cosmology, but the central and defining role of intermediaries in general. The notion of appealing directly to Jesus Christ for healing is, for most Orthodox Christians, rather like a peon addressing an emperor by name. Even the casual use of the name of Jesus clashes to the Orthodox ear; they prefer *Gétacchin* (Our Lord) or *Medhané Alem* (the Savior of the World).

Educated Orthodox Christians in Addis Ababa have made it clear to me that they regard secularism and Protestantism as contiguous. According to one church student, Daniel, for example, secularism (he used the English word) is not a rejection of the eternal like atheism, but an attempt to break down the divisions between the eternal and the realm of worldly things. A religious world was one that observed partitions, a secular one did not, nor did the world of the Protestants as he saw it. This was why Protestantism was opposed to monasticism—it wanted to have Christianity in all things, but in doing so made it excessively worldly. There are echoes between Daniel's argument and Charles Taylor's (2007: 145) in which "the need to make God more fully present in everyday life and all its contexts . . . prepares the ground for an escape from faith, into a purely immanent worlds." Protestantism does not do away with God, but with the elevation and separation that make human-divine relationships legitimate and meaningful. This is more insidious and hence more threatening than outright atheism, which few Ethiopians outside of a small urban elite consider a serious position.

This is not a wholly inaccurate view of the various schools of Protestant practice in Ethiopia. For example, Haustein notes some of the key characteristics that were understood to define the Pentecostal "revivals" of the 1960s: "Bible study, prayer meetings and eventually salvation and Spirit baptism" (2011: 108). These remain key points of contention between Orthodoxy and Pentecostalism. Note that the revival movements do not reject mediation entirely (if that were even possible). Rather, mediation occurs through reading scripture and nonhierarchical prayer groups, alongside more directly embodied techniques of Spirit baptism and speaking in tongues. The hierarchical mediator has been removed, be they priest, monk, saint, angel, or Mary. This was the key point. Pentecostals and other Protestants do not do away with all mediation, but with a specific kind of agent who serves as the go-between of legitimate religious activity.

The rise of Protestantism is not the only challenge Ethiopian Orthodoxy faces. Policies of religious equality enshrined in the 1995 constitution have allowed Muslims to launch new claims to public belonging, and Muslim groups have been happy to cite the principle of state secularism in order to advance their claims (Abbink 2014, Samson 2015). But Protestantism and Islam present different kinds of challenges: while Orthodox Christianity is losing a significant portion of its congregation to Protestant conversion ("stealing sheep"), relations with Islam are based less on competition for followers than on perceptions of political sovereignty and territorial rights (Boylston 2014). We will see this dynamic in chapter 8, in which political claims to Christian centrality are made in opposition to Islam, while thought about what actually constitutes proper Orthodoxy takes Protestantism as its foil.

Orthodox responses to these transformations have been complex but always active. Reformist movements have multiplied, with reform being generally understood as a challenge to hierarchical mediation, but so have powerful antireform sentiment and neotraditionalist movements. Grassroots participation in parish councils started increasing almost immediately upon the dispossessing of the church by the Derg (Larebo 1986, 1988, Clapham 1988, Bonacci 2000, Chaillot 2002), while youth movements, Sunday school organizations, and lay religious societies have become driving forces in the promotion of Orthodoxy, acting semi-independently from the central church. Some of the local developments of these movements are detailed in the next chapter. But this vast increase in lay activism and engagement with religious texts has entailed not a devaluation of the role of specialist priests and monks or of liturgical ritual, but a forceful and conscious reaffirmation of them.

MEDIA, MEDIATION, AND PRESENCE

A series of landmark works in the anthropology of Christianity have identified the search for direct, unmediated contact with God as central to global Protestant projects (Engelke 2007, Keane 2007, Meyer 2011). These works go on to argue that the desired immediacy is a practical impossibility; rather, the impression of directness is produced through material mediations: sincere words, holy honey, the use or abandonment of text, electric sounds and images (Meyer 2011, Stolow 2012). More to the point, they attempt to trace the connections between Protestant notions of semiotic transparency (ironically enabled by print technology) and the development of global colonial and postcolonial *epistemes* in which increasingly sophisticated media technology gives the impression of increasingly unmediated connection. This tendency of media to become invisible—that is, for hypermediated communications to be cast as unmediated or "im-mediate"—has long been identi-fied as a characteristic of modern ideology (McLuhan 1964, Mazzarella 2004).

When Tomas and Abebe insisted that it is Mary who heals, they were perceiv-ing the same apparent trend in Protestantism, and objecting to it as irreligious. Mediators are required; Jesus is God, and God cannot mediate with God. In the words of Roger Cowley: "The work of intercession belongs to created beings. The creator is prayed to, and does not himself pray to another" (1972: 246). What they are saying is that the central problem of human-divine relations is not really how to make God present to humanity; in fact, a certain separation must be maintained.

The animating problem for Ethiopian Orthodoxy is not that of a gulf between humans and God that must be bridged, but rather that the boundary between humans and God (or the environment or one another) is not sufficiently stable. What we see in Zege, as will become clear, is not just an emphasis on mediation, but a proliferation of mediators, far beyond what would seem necessary if the ulti-mate goal were simply to mend a rift between humans and God. This proliferation suggests that a dialectical process is occurring: any attempt to keep domains sepa-rate results in profusions of in-between figures.

THE WORK OF PRIESTS

There is good reason to talk about priests, deacons, and monks along with saints and angels as part of a single analysis. Steven Kaplan (1984: 70) has writ-ten extensively on the angelic capacities of holy men in Ethiopian tradition, as figures between humanity and God, but also as mediators with animals and the environment and in resolving disputes. Saints such as *Abune* Betre Maryam were holy people who later became fully fledged intercessors. And I would suggest that the restrictions surrounding religious work—the clerical observance of all 250-plus fasting days, the need to fast before performing the Eucharist, the celibacy of monks—are parallel to the angels' lack of need for sex or food. But priesthood also involves a great deal of mundane work.

Clerical authority stems from the ability to perform the sacraments—the legiti-mate manifestations of divine grace *(sega)* on earth. This is understood in explicit opposition to Protestantism:

> Some Protestants say that the sacraments are mere symbols and "signs of the new covenant," and that they are mere outward rituals, through the observance of which "the church of Christ confesses her Lord and is visibly distinguished from the world." But our Church believes that there is a real efficacy in the sacraments themselves, and that they truly bring invisible graces to the believers.[1]

The fact that only those empowered by the sacrament of ordination can per-form the other sacraments implies the organizational monopoly of the Orthodox

Church on legitimate mediation. However, institutional control over access to the sacred is only part of the story

The central part of priests' work is the performance of the Divine Liturgy (*qiddasé*), culminating in the Eucharist. Excellent descriptions of the service in all its complexity are given by Ephraim (2013: 85) and Fritsch (2001); as well as the service of the mass itself, there are morning prayers *(mahlet)* and, on the eve of feasts, the vigil *(wazéma)*. The morning prayers often begin with the *Widassé Maryam*, the Praises of Mary, and will begin long before the congregation arrives.

The main body of the liturgy consists in the performance of one of fourteen *anaphora* (a variety of prayer texts, literally "offering") that include Gospel readings and orders of service. The performance of the Eucharist itself, after the carefully regulated prayers of offering, requires a range of paraphernalia: "three candles (made of beeswax, a cross, and other consecrated vessels), the chalice, . . . paten, . . . cross spoon, napkins for wrapping the Eucharistic bread, ciborium, the bread and the wine. . . . Other requisites are the censor, a processional cross, holy water, . . . two crescent circles to be placed over the Host, . . . sanctuary lamp, and a small hand bell," as well as the New Testament, the Missal, and a list of persons to be remembered (Ephraim 2013: 88). The complexity and precision, and the seeming redundancy of equipment, serve a metacommunicative function, showing that the utmost order must be preserved in this space. It also creates a lot of work for the people tasked with providing all of this equipment, who have traditionally held important political roles in Zege (see chapter 1).

Performance of the liturgy requires at least three deacons and two priests, all of whom must have fasted properly. It will be performed every Sunday and on important saints' days and feasts, at a minimum, and the orders of service follow a closely regulated annual progression (Fritsch 2001). The liturgy is performed at dawn on regular days and at noon on fasting days, and is usually followed by *aqwaqwam*, plain chant with dancing performed by priests and *debtera* (discussed below in chapter; Fritsch 2001: 88). There are different *aqwaqwam* for different seasons, and the *aqwaqwam* of fasting days never use drums. The liturgy itself takes around three hours; the total performance required of the priests, including morning prayers, is much longer and is all done without food or water. It is a complex and exacting task.

Monks in Zege tend to live within monastery grounds. Noncelibate priests have only arrived within the last three generations, apparently on request of the people of Mehal Zege from the bishop *Abune* Qerilos.[2] This was due to concern that monks were making families—in this way, some people could become priests, who are allowed to marry once. Priests' and monks' incomes vary quite widely across the peninsula. Clergymen receive fees for performing funerals, weddings, and baptisms, often in the form of food and drink, and in some churches they also receive a monthly stipend. In 2008, I was told, this could range from eighty-five birr per month to a few hundred (roughly eight to fifty US dollars). Fure Maryam, for example, outside Afaf, is quite poor and does not receive tourists. *Abba* S'om, the priest of Fure whom I came to know best, would work as a tailor on market days. He lived in a very humble hut just outside of Afaf town, where he grew a small amount of corn and chillies along with some of the other priests and monks. Near his home were a few even smaller huts where young students would stay.

Abba S'om described ordination to me as conferring "power" *(silt'an)*, understood not as power in the priest's own right, but as the ability to channel the power of God. This power is most visible and tangible in daily life through the priest's hand cross, usually made of wood and nine inches to a foot in length. When a priest walks through any thoroughfare, he will generally be stopped at frequent intervals by men, women, and children who approach him with bowed heads to kiss the cross and receive blessing *(mebrek)*. Because of the cross, the everyday public life of priests (and all clergy) is punctuated by small, regular acts of blessing.

Clerical training effects a permanent but incomplete separation between trainees and fully social worldly life. The path to priesthood begins between the ages of seven and ten years, perhaps twelve at a maximum, when a boy becomes a deacon. As Girma Mohammed points out, church education is ascetic training:

> Students . . . are carefully coached to lead ascetic life in monasteries as opposed to engaging the material world and pursuing innovation. They are encouraged to beg, rather than work, not necessarily because they are needy, but as a part of spiritual discipline and a means of "disowning" their souls from "this world." (Girma 2012a: 118, see also Alemayehu 1973, Chaillot 2002: 97)

Church students are known as *yeqollo temari*, "grain students," in reference to the raw grains on which they are supposed to survive (Cowley 1983: 54). According to Levine (1965: 169) and to some priests in Zege, *yeqollo temari* may refer particularly to a one- or two-year period of absolute mendicancy in which students' social ties are to be cut off. More generally, *yeqollo temari* refers to the whole religious studentship (which may lead to becoming a church assistant or lay scholar instead of to the priesthood), and *yeqollo timhirt bét*, "grain school," to the institution of traditional church education (Young 1975).

Abba S'om, my main contact on exegesis in Fure Maryam church, recalled his period as a *yeqollo temari*, some twenty years before, as one of unrelenting hardship. He told of being perpetually hungry, being cursed and abused by people he begged from, and recalled especially the danger posed by dogs. He described the process as one of being humbled before God. The monk *Abba* Haylemaryam described how he had formed close links with Mary during his period as a *yeqollo temari*. By chanting songs and prayers to Mary he had gained her protection from dogs (every former *yeqollo temarí* I have spoken to mentions dogs) and the other dangers of the mendicant life.

In *Abba* Haylemaryam's account, it was the experience of privation and danger, above all, that formed his relationship with Mary. The relationship between ascetic life and saintly or angelic mediation has often been noted, and is central to Kaplan's work on Ethiopian monasticism:

> By living an "angelic life," the holy men became like angels, divine messengers believed to be capable of both conveying and influencing divine will. . . . Such a mediatory role was of tremendous importance in Ethiopia where a pious Christian was primarily concerned with gaining the favor of an immediate figure such as an angel, Mary, or a holy man, rather than appealing to a remote and unreachable God" (Kaplan 1984: 82; for examples in other Christianities, see Pina-Cabral 1986: 197, Brown 1988: 324).

If priests are simultaneously authoritative and marginal, monks can be even more clearly set apart from daily affairs, and yet have more authority to pronounce on them. The decision to enter monastic service can be chosen by church students at the point of ordination; monks take up the *qob* cap and the requiem for the dead is then sung for them (Paulos 1988: 26). They will remain celibate for life and observe the rigorous hours of the monastery. Because of this, as many Christians in Zege have told me, monks are the only people the populace will really listen to on matters such as whether to allow eucalyptus planting on parts of the peninsula or the proper response to HIV/AIDS. Monks have also long been the only people who could talk back to emperors or other state authorities.

But, as we have seen, mediators are always also buffers or regulators. Priests in Zege are in charge of spatial and temporal boundary maintenance. They must escort every human life in and out of this world, via baptism and funerary prayers. It is the priests who admonish people not to partake in the liturgy after eating food, not to enter the church or take the Eucharist in an impure state, and not to cut trees or plough the land in the vicinity of the church. *Abba* S'om once told me that he regards it as his job to make sure that people do not work the land on holy days and to encourage them to come to church instead. He compared his work to that of the police, and discussed how the worst sanction, at least in theory, would be excommunication *(wigzet)*.

Understandings of church poverty and asceticism have transformed in recent decades. I have been told by theologians in Addis Ababa that the poverty of *yeqollo temarí* now has much to do with the church's lack of resources after having its lands confiscated by the Derg government in the 1970s. Ideally, they say, students would not spend their whole time begging, and priests would not work secondary jobs, and many fundraising efforts among Christians in the city go toward providing better funding for church students who might otherwise be drawn to the opportunities that secular government education provides. The embattlement narrative of dwindling church resources, especially surrounding education (and therefore the future of the priesthood), has proved a potent way of galvanizing middle-class Orthodox Christians in the cities to greater fundraising and support efforts directed at the rural church schools and monasteries. One prominent fundraiser in Addis Ababa told me at length how rural Orthodox Christians were in constant danger of succumbing to Islamic or Protestant propaganda if traditional education was not supported. The amount of resources being poured by Christian organizations into the support of church schools is significant, and shows the degree of importance that people place on the continuation of the priesthood and the traditional education system. But the new context of competition for resources may fundamentally change the grounds on which ascetic training is founded.

ENVIRONMENTAL MEDIATION

Kaplan emphasizes the importance of the role of Ethiopian holy men as mediators between humanity and the environment. Here too we see important recent changes in Zege. A number of semiofficial practices had arisen based on prayer for rain and protection of the peninsula from hailstorms. But even since the beginning of my fieldwork in 2008 there have been moves to replace some of these activities with others more easily reconcilable with church doctrine.

In Zege, the priests and monks are said to mediate between humans and non-human nature via the pact with God, established at the founding of the first church by the Saint Betre Maryam, that no wild animal will harm a human on the peninsula and that no person will be struck by lightning as long as the forest and the churches remain (Cerulli 1946, Bosc-Tiessé 2008). This is consistent with Kaplan's (1984: 87) account of holy men as mediators not just with God but also between humankind and nature.

Hailstorms are an infrequent but serious concern in Zege, having destroyed the peninsula's coffee crop once in the 1960s (Rahel 2002, Binayew 2014). Because of this, every year at the beginning and end of the rainy season, the priests circumambulate the peninsula carrying the book of the Acts (*gedl*) of Saint Betre Maryam, in which his foundational deeds are recorded (Cerulli 1946). In this way they reiterate Zege's devotion to its patron and renew the environmental protection that he affords, where both book and the forested environment itself are markers of the saint's historical presence.

However, there have also existed important nonpriestly mediators between people and environment. Until the last five or six years there was a figure called *yebered tebaqí*, or the "ice guardian." This man was in charge of making prayers, and perhaps magical charms too, for preventing hail, which strikes only rarely in

Zege but can devastate the coffee crop when it does. One charm involved wrapping a certain medicinal plant in grass, carrying it round the peninsula, and then suspending it upside down in the church rafters—a parallel to the more proper practice of carrying the book of the Acts of Saint Betre Maryam around the peninsula, making a sort of divine enclosure.

The guardian would receive money from the community in return for these services. As the *mergéta* explained it, the guardian had to know certain prayers (*s'elete bered*), and would stand on a big stone, never moving, so as to be connected to the land. The *mergéta* himself had performed the role in the past, due to his religious knowledge. However, at least one Muslim man has held the role of *yebered tebaqí* in recent memory, at least in the districts of Ura and Yiganda, which according to some priestly informants is one of the reasons the position was discontinued.

Because of recent concerns that traditional, quasi-Christian practices that had developed in Zege did not reflect the authority of the church, there is currently no *yebered tebaqí*. The community must instead offer coffee to the church, and the church's prayers alone must keep the hail at bay. Tihut (2009: 43) describes this move as an extra act of taxation by the church, saying that each household was required to give two kilograms of coffee to the church for rain and hail prayers. Rahel (1999) describes how households may have been pressured to contribute out of fear of being blamed should a disaster occur.

Likewise the practice of *fel*, described in chapter 1, in which Zege's dignitaries would slaughter an ox on a hilltop at the start of the rainy season in prayer for rain, has been discontinued, and the hilltop renamed *mesqel adebabay*, the square of the Cross. Some priests have told me that this was in response to the building of a new mosque in Afaf village, whereupon it was felt that the Christianity of the peninsula should be marked in more explicit fashion. They also said that the sacrifice of Christ had obviated the need for animal slaughter, and "only the blood of our Lord" could provide protection.

These examples show how an explicit concern with the increasing public visibility of Muslims in Ethiopia has led to a crackdown on mediatory practices that used to be understood as unproblematic parts of local Christian life, and to a new emphasis on the church and the priesthood as the only proper mediators. If the growth of Protestantism has led Orthodox Christians in Zege to reemphasize the importance of mediators, the enhanced status of Islam (a direct result of secularist state policy) has led to a retrenching of legitimate mediation within the organizational boundaries of the church. But this is emphatically not a rejection of the principle of hierarchical mediation, and it is therefore not at all the same kind of thing as Protestant reform.

Popular practices for seeking environmental protection do frequently reemerge regardless of church approval. In April 2014 there was a hailstorm in Zege that threatened the coffee crop. Tefera contacted me to say that some of the coffee farmers in Zege had responded by placing all of their metal objects, such as sickles and axes, outside of the house. His father had told him that putting out the tools was to emphasize the promise that the farmers would not work on the monthly saints' days—a key sign of devotion that would ensure the saints' protection against further hail.

In December of that year when I visited Zege again, Tefera and I went to ask *Mergéta* Worqé about the incident. He told us that this was not an official religious practice but an old tradition *(bahil)*. He said it might well display that farmers were obeying rules about not ploughing, and added that if it did hail, the tools that had been placed outside would ring with sound, which would act as a prayer to Betre Maryam for protection. But the real, important practice was for the clergy to carry the book of Betre Maryam around the land.

In sum, while all agree that God's protection for the environment must be sought via saintly intermediaries, especially Betre Maryam, there has been wide variation in which earthly specialists should take on responsibility for the work of prayer—often quite arduous—that this involves. There is an important political-economic dimension, as major questions also surround the appropriate kinds of contribution from the community for the work of seeking protection. Mediation is a kind of work, and like any form of going-between, it can be a source of power and can be subject to disputes of legitimacy and appropriation.

MEDIATION WITHOUT DISEMBODIMENT IS MAGIC

One final kind of mediator exists in Ethiopian Orthodox societies, who can do much to enlighten the ethics and logics of human-nonhuman contact and the flesh in a place such as Zege. The *debtera* is a term that has caused some confusion in the literature because of its constitutive ambiguity: it may refer either to a church chorister—an adult man who has received training in Ge'ez texts and chants but has not been ordained—or to a sorcerer, a purveyor of healing magic and curses, and a master of demons, capable of flying on clouds and controlling the weather (Young 1975). Many men perform both roles simultaneously, combining licit and illicit techniques of mediation; it is precisely this ambiguity that has come to define the *debtera* in popular discourse.

Ask someone in the village and they will likely be able to point you toward a *debtera*, but two villagers may not agree on who is or is not a *debtera*, and the person indicated may not answer to the term. *Debtera* is not a clearly defined position like a priest, but designates a person with some kind of special knowledge. The *debtera* I knew best was a man in his fifties who lived in Afaf town and performed *aqwaqwam* dance and chants during festivals and church services. He wore the white turban of priests and church servants *(agilgay)* and could read Ge'ez. All of this indicates years of church education. Perhaps because of his education and connection with the church, he was also secretary of a large *iddir* group in the name of Saint Michael, in Afaf. These are funerary associations, where each member pays two birr per month, and the association pays for the mourning tent and for food and drink for mourners and priests when you die. The *debtera*, along with another adult former church student, kept the register of members and payments in a neat ledger book.

He also sold a variety of medicines and charms against demonic possession, and showed me a number of plastic bottles full of potent-looking brown liquid that would be drunk or poured in the nose to get rid of *ganén* spirits that could drive their victims mad and cause them to jump in the lake. This he described to me as *sigawí sira*, "fleshly work" done for a living, and totally distinct from church service. He could also make Ge'ez prayer scrolls and amulets to be worn around the neck for demonic protection, which is a widespread tradition in Orthodox Ethiopia (Mercier 1997). Finally, he was rumored to be a sorcerer *(t'enqway)* of possible slave descent, and to be capable of much more potent and harmful magic than he let on. A pillar of the community, a servant of the church, a skilled practitioner of esoteric arts, and also the object of fear and stigma, this man epitomizes the ambiguity of the *debtera* more generally.

By most people's accounts, *debtera* turn away from the priestly path because they have violated (or wish to violate) the sexual purity rules, having had pre- or extramarital sex. They are widely viewed as epitomizing a state of religious knowledge without religious purity, and so are archetypal boundary-violators; one man told me that you become a *debtera* by urinating on the sacred *tabot* of the church. They have mediatory powers, being able, it is said, to command spirits, but they work, as my friend said, in the service of the flesh. It is, I believe, from this basic paradigm that the local legends of *debtera* as fearsome sorcerers who fly on clouds and summon snakes and hailstorms emerge (with the encouragement of a number of *debtera*-like experts who know the value of cultivating mystique for their line of business). *Debtera* are marginal figures, both feared and respected, and usually operating at a remove from general sociality.

In the minds of many Orthodox Christians in Zege, even deacons, monks, and priests may engage in illicit magic and medicine. One young man, Yilekal, told me that he was sure an elderly local priest in Afaf knew how to make love medicines, but would not give one to him because he had not yet won the priest's trust. He did find information about a priest in Zege who could supply such medicines, but had heard that he was worried about being arrested for practicing traditional medicine without a licence. Disappointed, Yilekal nonetheless gave his baptismal name to the elderly priest so that he could pray for him. I do not think that the priest was actually practicing magic, and this would certainly not be sanctioned by the church, but there remains a widespread popular perception that those educated in the church tradition possess esoteric magical power.

Countless people of Zege have told me about the magical activities of deacons who, I am told, can summon hailstorms (or give the impression of having done so) and curse people with unstoppable flatulence. One man, Addisu, told me that he thought deacons probably cultivated this image, and would throw pebbles on peoples' roofs to pretend that they had summoned hail. The common conflation of *debtera* with priests or deacons suggests that a general category of "mediators" is operative, encompassing any people who have access to powers outside of the visible world.

The esoteric nature of church knowledge plays a part in conflations between the religious and the demonic. It is not just that church knowledge is written in Ge'ez and thus opaque even to most literate people, though this is part of it. It seems that the church's literary tradition has long produced offshoot texts of dubious propriety. In Getatchew Haile's (n.d.) colorful description:

> Some naughty people who have the rudimentary knowledge of Geez compose or translate from other languages prayers against illnesses and for warding off evil spirits, which are said to be the cause of illnesses much like germs and viruses. . . . Interestingly, one finds among these prayers a few for healing what Viagra is supposed to heal. The prayers contain strange names that are supposed to have the power to do the thing for which they are invoked. The church is against turning to them under the threat of excommunication.

Such spells and prayers are widespread, and *debtera* are rumored to trade them with one another in secret. But certain texts have become well established, most notably the *Awde Negest,* the *Circle of Kings.* This book contains various horoscopes, information on numerology, and guides for the treatment of spirit possession (Young 1977).[3] A traditional doctor, Beza, showed a published copy to me and Abebe during one of our visits. He read our horoscopes after working out our star signs from the letters of our names—I was told I would die at age sixty-nine or seventy. Abebe was nonplussed to be told he would go blind at age thirty, and that he would one day kill a man and then become a monk. On the way home we discussed our fortunes, and Abebe suggested we go speak to a priest for clarification.

The priest confided that he had read the *Awde Negest* in detail while a church student. A lively and curious man of around thirty, he had been interested in the book in his youth, before deciding that it was improper and likely fraudulent. He raised an issue that had troubled us—how could the book describe a person's fate in such detail when there was only a limited number of star signs? We couldn't all go blind at thirty and commit a murder. Abebe was much relieved. But the priest's case shows us that students in the church, through their literacy, do gain exposure to esoteric texts as well as more canonical works. Combine this with the wide-spread idea that church students make use of stimulants and other plant-based mind drugs in order to assist their intensive study, and it is easy to see how religious knowledge sometimes appears quite close to more ambivalent, pragmatic, or illicit sources and techniques of authority.

CONCLUSION: MEDIATION AND KNOWLEDGE

Knowledge, especially knowledge of God, has been traditionally treated as problematic and potentially dangerous in Ethiopian Orthodox society (Levine 1965). To seek to know God carried implications of *t'igab:* pride and the illusion of repletion (Messay 1999). But in fact humans are not producers of knowledge. Rather all knowledge is God's. The first time I interviewed *Mergéta* Worqé about local history, he thought it was important to preface any answers he had to my questions: "I am a *mergéta* specialized in *aqwaqwam* (votive dance chants), and also a church painter. God has ordered us to tell the truth. All creativity is from god. If you pray to God angels will support your learning. The world is led by the books of the saints, not the constitution." Human learning is not the production of knowledge, but the submission to angelic and saintly guidance. It follows that religious knowledge has often been the domain of specialists, while for the laity, as we have seen, religious engagement primarily revolves around fasting and calendrical events.

So Orthodox life in Zege is characterized by a large and diverse array of religious and quasi-religious specialists on the Earthly side, and an equally diverse set of saints and angels (and, conversely, demons) on the celestial end. These figures relate to the laity through the calendar of fasts, feasts, and holidays in the names of saints and angels (and calendrical occasions when demons are known to proliferate), and also through personal appeals via prayer, through relationships with one's soul father, and through thanksgiving meals (see chapter 7). Common basic principles of hierarchy and mediation underlie these systemic relationships.

But why so many mediators? In part, this seems to stem from shifts in local authority and relations between landlords, the state, and the church. But I would suggest that symbolic logics of prohibition and the flesh are equally important. We began this chapter by asking why it matter that angels are genderless and do not eat or excrete; we have seen the various restrictions and separations that priests and monks must observe, and the consequences when esoteric knowledge is not subject to such strict purity regulations.

Purity and prohibition, as shown in previous chapters, build boundaries into social time and space. Especially, they place restrictions on the bodily conditions of those who would approach God. But such structured grids are not sufficient for human collectives to live. Each separation produces intermediaries who both enable and restrict traffic across the symbolic divide. In doing so, they must often be marked as partially dead or disembodied, or must embody partway states between humanity and something else.

Some mediators are considered legitimate and authoritative, some immoral and improper; still others occupy zones of ambiguity at the edges of the Orthodox Church hierarchy. The designation of which mediators and methods of mediation are legitimate is demonstrably subject to historical change. But Orthodox Christians in Zege have consistently maintained, against Protestantism as they understand it, that there must be mediators. And to a great extent the history of Zege can be understood in terms of the transformation of what counts as legitimate mediation.

NOTES

1. Taken from the Ethiopian Orthodox Tewahedo Church's English website, www.ethiopianortho-dox.org/english/dogma/sacramentintro.html, accessed June 23, 2017.

2. According to *Mergéta* Worqé.

3. From my field notes: "He insists that holy water can NOT cure *zar*. Rather you revolve a chicken round the patient's head, possibly 3 times, and the zar will enter into the chicken. I ask if the colour of the chicken is important, on a tip from a friend, and he says yes this depends on your '*kokeb*' (star), which is derived numerologically from your name and your mother's name. Mine (slightly dubious as Mum's name is impronouncable in Amharic) is *shert'an wiha*."

4

Blood, Silver, and Coffee

The Material Histories of Sanctity and Slavery

The Zege coffee forest is locally understood as material testimony of the work of the monasteries on the peninsula and of the covenant with which they were founded. Church forests have recently become an object of research interest in conservation research, as part of a wider recognition of the environmental importance of sacred groves in Ethiopia and throughout Africa (Tsehai 2008, Klepeis et al. 2016, Orlowska 2015). But the forest also has a complex and painful labor history associated with the legacy of slavery (Abdussamad 1997, Tihut 2009). Indeed, there are intimate connections between this history of slavery and the official history of the sacred forest, and these linkages are quite fresh in local memory.

It is the two narratives of sanctity and slavery that I want to try to pick apart in this chapter, and in particular how people are able to read these memories from the material landscape. While I have found that Orthodox Christians in Zege present the public history of sanctity in terms of the landscape of the forest and churches, the more troublesome history of labor and production is equally present and tangible in the living, material environment, especially in the coffee trees. Coffee possesses a problematic double quality as both a local medium of hospitality and a long-distance trade commodity. The difference between mediating hospitality relations and mediating trade has tremendous moral and practical significance that helps us understand the dual quality of Zege's history and the way that this dual history is present in the immediate material environment.

This is a discussion of historicity rather than history: not an attempt to construct a narrative of what happened from the sources available (though I do my best), but an investigation into how people in a certain locale live through and understand their existence in time, how they carry the past into the present and future (Lambek 2002, Hirsch & Stewart 2005). This temporal engagement can be with material things that endure through time, like silver coins, or with regulated and organized forms of action, like the ritual cycle. Usually it is a combination of both. People in Zege tend to describe their connections with the past through their churches and monasteries and through the coffee forest, both of which have stood for a long time, but only with continuous human tenure and maintenance. In addition to maintaining their surroundings, Zegeña are able to perceive or infer, in their churches and coffee trees, condensed chains of action and interaction that led to their being here in the present (Ingold 2000). A large part of this history is borne in the environment, and in the ongoing interaction between people, churches, and trees.

RICH MAN, SLAVE, AND SAINT

Official local history traces the presence of the church-monasteries and of the forest alike to a foundational covenant *(kídan)* between God and the holy man *Abune* Betre Maryam, whose name means "The Staff of Mary." This history is recorded in the book of the Acts of Betre Maryam, who lived during the reign of Emperor Amde Sion (r. 1314–44; Cerulli 1946, Bosc-Tiessé 2008). The book is kept in the monastery of Mehal Zege Giyorgis and dates from around 1685 (Derat 2003: 507), but versions of the story are known to most inhabitants of the peninsula. It states that Betre Maryam had been commanded by God to leave farm life in his homeland and become a monk. After various travels he was commanded by God to travel to Zege, whereupon his staff miraculously transported him across Lake Tana, like a boat. There he received a vision in which Gabriel (some accounts say Saint George) told him that God wished him to build a church. With the emperor's blessing he did so, and a monastic community began to gather. Some were local residents who had been miraculously healed by Betre Maryam.

As the community grew, so did the need for sustenance. Betre Maryam divided his staff into three pieces, which he planted into the ground. These grew into hops, coffee, and buckthorn *(ades),* which would support the people.[1] God promised Betre Maryam that those who lived on the peninsula would be saved, and that it would be holy like Jerusalem. They would also be protected from wild animal attacks and natural disasters. But in return, all farming must be done by hand, with no extra tools; and no plough animals were to be kept anywhere on the peninsula. More or less everyone in Zege knows a version of this story, which is commemorated in paintings on the walls of several of the peninsula's churches.

I would later learn a second story, almost as widely known, often repeated, but far less public. It goes like this: The time of Zege's greatest wealth was roughly a hundred years ago, from the time of Emperor Menilek (r. 1889–1913) until the early twentieth century, when many landholder-merchants grew rich from the coffee trade. When a trader got rich, he would need a place to hide his silver thalers, since there were no banks. He would bury the silver in an interior room of his house, and would have a sorcerer *(t'enqway)* place a curse on it by promising it to a demon, so that anyone who took the silver out would die. But when the merchant himself wanted to retrieve his money, he would sacrifice a slave and let their blood fall on the burial place. Then the debt would be paid off and the merchant could take his money.

When people tell this story (which I have cross-checked several times), some are skeptical, while others are absolutely insistent that this took place as reported. I think its frisson, along with the reason for its popularity, apart from the sheer horror, is the moral reversal taking place—or perhaps a moral revelation. Coffee merchants were landowners, usually noble, frequently closely connected to the church (see chapter 1), and some of the most respected and highest-status people on the peninsula. Slaves are and were despised, and bear a shame and stigma that carry on to their descendants today. It is a comment on the dramatic obscenity of power, but one shot through with ambivalence. Showing high-status people doing unconscionable things to low-status people brings out the uncomfortable conjunction of the supposed impurity of slaves with the inescapable recognition of their common humanity—especially given the shared Christianity of master and slave.

The word people have used for killing a slave, when telling me the story, was *mared,* which usually means to slaughter an animal. The slaughter of the slave is an inversion of a positive model of sacrifice, which might be epitomized by the slaughter of a sheep on a person's grave forty days after they die to remember them and assist in the expiation of their sins. At the center of the tale is the absurdity of trading silver for blood, and hence of trying to square market exchange (establishing values of things against one another) with sacrificial transactions (arranging moral relationships among people and God). But behind the blood and the silver lies coffee, the basis of Zege's economy, which is understood as both a commodity and a gift from God.

My argument is not exactly that the first story—of the holiness of the place and the conservation of coffee for the population—is ideology, and the second story counterideology. It is more that people in Zege are well aware of both histories—after all, I got these stories from them—and recognize both stories as their own. Let me start with the sacred story. The forest has significance because Amhara people have paradigmatically been associated with Orthodox Christianity and plough agriculture (Levine 1965, McCann 1995). Cattle and ploughing have been and remain central not only to productive life but to Orthodox Christians' self-understandings and conceptions of civilization, by contrast to the normative roles of Muslims as traders and pagans as artisans. Endless proverbs attest to the deep connection between a man, his lands, and his oxen. This is why it matters that all cattle and ploughing are forbidden throughout the Zege peninsula by church edict. The cattle ban, which Zege people regard as the basis of their distinctiveness, sets them apart from the vast majority of Christians in highland Amhara. Instead, people live on the cultivation of coffee and petty cash crops—hops, chillies, fruit— along with some smallholding and, nowadays, the tourists who come to visit the monasteries and walk in the forest.

There is a widespread tradition in Ethiopia of not clearing the land around churches. Churches are refuges (*deber*, Kane 1990: 1779), and are supposed to exist at a remove from the worldliness of human productive and reproductive work. Ploughing is the curse of Adam, and churches, by some accounts, are supposed to resemble the Garden of Eden. In Zege this trope of the sacred forest has been applied to the entire inhabited peninsula, which locals refer to as *yegedam ager*, "land of monasteries." The centerpiece of the story is this: we have coffee because we are blessed by the covenant of Betre Maryam. Coffee is less labor-intensive than ploughing, and so fits very well into discourses about how to be free from labor is holy. Inhabitants of Zege often take pride in being "forest people" *(yeden sewocch)* and not "peasants" *(get'eré*, Tihut 2009: 48–49)

However, based on regional history, the fourteenth century is far too early for coffee to be present in this part of Ethiopia (Merid 1988).[2] There are hagiographies written in the seventeenth century that Enrico Cerulli (1946) has discussed in which the story of Betre Maryam has the form that people now tell, except that, instead of coffee, the monk is given hops, buckthorn, and fruit by God. Later additions to the text, in Amharic rather than classical Ge'ez, say that the fruit was the fruit of the coffee tree.

It is possible that this is a sincere piece of interpretive work—such annotation of texts was standard practice. The writer may not have been aware that there had not always been coffee. But it is also possible that this was a cynical interpolation by somebody looking to justify large-scale coffee cultivation on church land. In any case, we can deduce that Zege was considered special because of its lack of plough agriculture before the seventeenth century, but that only later did coffee come to the area and get incorporated into the story. There are at least a few people on the peninsula who share this opinion.

What is not in doubt, however, is that the monasteries are important in making sure there is still a coffee forest in Zege, which is a fact of great economic significance. It is the monasteries, and the local administrative hierarchies associated with them, that have enforced the ploughing ban and preserved the forest. Zege people are currently very sensitive to the threat that short-term exigencies can pose to the forest; in the last decade many people have been pressured into cutting the forest for firewood or even some ploughing to address their immediate hardships. There has been some deforestation in Zege largely because of the number of people struggling with their basic subsistence (Rahel 2002, Tihut 2009). In this context people describe the church regulation of the forest as an important guarantor of Zege's future although Tiliut (2009: 6, 15) presents a strong case that the sacred forest narrative has impeded attempts at diversification that might improve livelihoods.

The story of Zege's historic depth is understood as a story of belonging, of holiness, and at least sometimes of prosperity. These days, it is exactly the historic qualities of the churches that draw in tourists and with them vital contributions to Zege's income. In this version of the story, deep religious continuity and economic and environmental life are thoroughly integrated. It is a good story for tourists, and when I was first there in 2008, the abbot was pushing this history quite strongly—he visited me personally to make sure I had the English copy of the pamphlet that explained it.

Material history piles up in churches and monasteries. The inner walls are decorated with murals depicting biblical events and stories from the Ethiopic canon; main themes include angelic protection and the violent deaths of saints. Sometimes they incorporate local dignitaries who have made donations to the church, sometimes local founding events, such as portraits of Betre Maryam in the churches of Mehal Zege. The murals are palimpsests of history from different eras, and are one of the principal attractions that draw tourists to the area, both for their beauty and for the venerability that they index. Around the murals are the gifts that have accrued in the church: the crowns and shields, military regalia, hanging portraits, and royal robes gifted by various dignitaries and fellow churches. Pride of place goes to parchment books, hand-illuminated and claimed to be over a millennium old.

Recent years have seen efforts to build more formal museums and bring these piles of memorabilia into a more formal display. Each amassed item testifies to the consistent attractive power of the monasteries, the gravity they have accumulated in a sort of continuing feedback loop that marks these places as "historic" for foreigners and as pilgrimage spots for Orthodox Christians. The feedback loop that starts from blessing and becomes increasingly layered in material things shows how the monasteries exert a force of their own, having gained an inertia that impels their continuing maintenance (Hodder 2012). As far as Zege's official story goes, this inertia of the monasteries is also the inertia of the coffee forest, which is one more material accrual signifying the blessed status of the land.

Being a holy land has certain benefits, which is another point that local histories emphasize. Bosc-Tiessé (2008) has shown how the monasteries in Zege were very skilled at portraying local leaders praying to the Virgin or to saints in a way that both flattered them and subtly reminded them that they were subject to higher powers. The role of the monasteries in sheltering the population from political power has been quite prominent in local memory; as sacred places they were not just inviolate, but able to project some of that protection to their parishes. Church protection of the forest is presented as continuous with this tradition: the monasteries protect the coffee from short-term factors that would threaten the environment, as a counterbalance to the government-run system of land tenure and the exigencies of the market.

There are multiple stories in which kings and emperors release the people of the peninsula from their tax duties because they wish to receive blessing or healing from the monasteries—the pamphlet mentions Emperor Iyasu the great (r. 1682–1706), and local historians tell me that Emperor Menilek also freed the people from taxes for a period.[3] According to Binayew Tamrat (2014: 21), during the two centuries from Iyasu to Menilek, taxation in Zege was due only to the church, hence the saying *be Zege yellem gibbir, be semay yellem dur* (There are no taxes in Zege, as there is no forest in heaven).[4] In Zege's public memory, the presence of coffee is integral to this story of holy protection.

THE PROBLEM WITH COFFEE

We have established that coffee was not a part of the original founding story of the monasteries. It seems likely that the early monastic communities, and later the lay communities that settled around them, supported themselves by growing hops, buckthorn, and fruit, which was traded with the surrounding population. The mango trade across Lake Tana is still quite important in the area. At some point, probably in the eighteenth or nineteenth century, coffee gets introduced to Zege and starts to become much more important than the other trades (Cheesman 1936, Pankhurst 1968).

This is important because coffee and hops have slightly different ranges of value. Coffee is now an archetypal medium of hospitality for Christians in Ethiopia, and the coffee ceremony has become part of how the country is presented and presents itself abroad. But until the nineteenth century Christians considered coffee a Muslim product and did not partake in it at all (Pankhurst 1997). Hops, however, were always a good hospitality product for Christians because *t'ella*, homebrewed beer, is so well established as a good thing to serve to guests, and because Muslims do not drink it. Coffee, hops, and perfumed leaves are all aromatic substances, which is a part of their use in hospitality—in creating a certain kind of convivial space and a sensory atmosphere that hosts and guests can share in. Nowadays beer and coffee are both good for hospitality in Zege and so there is a small local market in both. But what coffee has that hops do not is long-range commodity value, and this introduces a whole new turbulence to affairs in Zege—and yet, despite this, coffee has fit straight into the foundation narrative of the monasteries so that it is as if it were always there.

Centralization and expansion of the coffee trade in Zege appear to have been most pronounced in the time of King Tekle Haymanot of Gojjam and his son Ras Haylu, who were the local rulers from 1880 until the 1920s or so. In this period, marked by the substantial independence of regional warlords, there was an explosion in the coffee trade throughout Ethiopia, brought about by the presence of British and Italian markets in the area and the birth of Addis Ababa (Crummey 2000: 230).

According to local memory, this was also a time of a sharp increase in the slave trade in the peninsula. Both Tekle Haymanot and Ras Haylu were showing increasing interest in lands to the west as sources of both gold and slaves (Triulzi 1981: 136, Cheesman 1936: 185). Muslim and Agew traders would bring people from what is now South Sudan and the Benishangul Gumuz region of Ethiopia, as Abdussamad (1997, 1999) has documented, and sell them in the local market town. Abdussamad is quite clear that Orthodox priests were major slave owners in this period, though there is cause to wonder whether some of these were in fact parachurch figures such as the *yager líqered* and the *mislené* (see chapter 1). These men may or may not have been drawn from the clergy, but always had relations to the church through education or financial or other kinds of service.

From local testimony and what we know about the slave trade in this region, it seems that many slaves were domestics as much as field laborers (Fernyhough 2010: 68). While slave labor was certainly important for the watering and harvesting of coffee, it seems that slaves were also status symbols and house servants for those who grew rich from the coffee trade. These are the people referred to in the story of the rich man, the silver, and the slave. It is remembered now as a period when the peninsula was much wealthier than it is today, but when both land and wealth were concentrated in few hands.

LEGACIES AND DESCENDANTS

The high period of slavery appears to have been a time when distinctions between "proper" *(ch'ewa)* people and others became more deeply essentialized and propriety come to be seen as a hereditary condition of the body, through metaphors of bone *(at'int)* or blood *(dem)*. In many of the interviews I have conducted, the concepts of slaves *(bariya)* and *mislené* stand for broader categories of clean and unclean. Slave descent carries a hereditary impurity that remains extremely relevant in Zege today. It is described in terms of "seeds" *(zer)*; just as coffee seeds make coffee, *yebariya zer,* "the seed of slaves," makes slaves, and *yemislené zer* makes "proper" people. Abdussamad (1997: 549) reports that priests would often bequeath all their worldly property to their slaves on their deathbeds, but this did not transform them into true free people.

Amhara society, as Allan Hoben's classic study (1973) describes, is cognatic— you can trace descent and land claims through your father or your mother, so there are no great family lineages like those found in other parts of Africa. Instead you get a cloud of relatedness and competing land claims—something that the chronicler of Gojjam, Aläqa Täkle Iyäsus, laments: "That it is a disadvantage not to know how to enumerate ancestral descent has not been learnt yet in Ethiopia" (Täklä Iyäsus 2014: 30).

However, it is also the case that people keep quite careful private genealogical records. Local scholars know the names of the fathers of most people back several generations. Now one reason for this is to prevent incest according to the seventh-generation rule, but a much more important one is to know who is descended from slaves. Indeed, the identity of slave descendants is a public secret. It is not discussed openly, but *chewa* people, especially of older generations, are careful not to eat with slave descendants and especially not to let their children intermarry.

What is visible on the day-to-day level is a certain amount of uncomfortable joking about boys and girls with dark skin. This exists in a context where Amhara people are generally thought to have lighter skin than people from elsewhere in Africa, especially areas from which slaves were taken. The group of teenagers I play football with refer to one of their friends as "Babbi Bariyew"—Baby Slave. This was the sort of joke that actually carries a serious and wounding insult. It does not stop the boys from being friends, but it serves as a permanent reminder of an underlying difference that would become much clearer if questions of marriage or even romance ever came up. The last time I returned to Zege, this young man had left the area after an argument (see next chapter). Such disruptions appear to be quite common in the lives of slave descendants.

Abdussamad (1997: 547) reports that escaped or freed slaves from other areas would actually move to Zege to work as dependents there, because the situation was better, in part because of the coffee boom. So we have to understand the formation of this class of people—both slaves held by landlords in Zege and their descendants, but also slaves from other areas, and various other kinds of landless people, including the *Falasha,* or Beta Israel, of whom there were some in this area. Various different stigmatized people came to be identified in the same class, and could often intermarry, forming quasi-ethnicized and racialized class-caste groups. Today most of these people are Orthodox Christians and attend church together. The church does not recognize slave/nonslave distinctions as legitimate, but there is still a great deal of tension, and racialized class distinctions still have a lot of traction.

Something I have noticed—this is anecdotal but quite striking—is that it is former noble families who tend to have pictures of their sons in graduation gear displayed in their houses. The children of the nobles are more likely to receive education in Bahir Dar and to obtain some of the new paths to some kind of success—tour guide work, and with it the potential of meeting foreign women and starting relationships with them (see chapter 9). Here again there are important overlaps between clergy and nobility. Many tour guides are the sons of priests, and therefore come from literate homes, which provides a number of benefits for future work opportunities.

By contrast, it is extremely difficult to talk directly to slave descendants about slavery. More commonly, people would tell me general, nonspecific stories that later turned out to have specific personal meaning. One young man, who I later heard was a slave descendant, shared with me a story he had heard about how mothers in Gumuz left their children out in the sun, which was what made them so dark—but then hastened to say that he hated all this talk of color and slavery and considered it all illegitimate when everyone was equally Christian. His father was a singer in the church but also a *debtera* who was said to perform esoteric magic (see chapter 3)—both a pillar of the community and a marginal figure at the same time. This kind of ambiguous status, and ambiguous relationship to the past, seems to be very common among people whose descent gets questioned.

On a separate occasion the same friend told me that he hated that people used the word *bariya*, "slave," even in jest, as his friends often did. He did not mind *tiqur* as much, even though he acknowledged that the implication was often the same. While calling someone black (as opposed to "red," the presumptive skin color of Amhara Christians) has generally been a reference to slave descent, among younger people a different understanding of blackness as inclusive of all Ethiopians (vis-à-vis "white" or "red" Europeans) has gained a lot of traction. This is likely due to the influence of Reggae, Rasta, pan-Africanism, and global football, all of which offer different perspectives on skin color. For this young man, it was not blackness itself that was stigmatized, but the slave descent that dark skin was said to indicate.

The only person who ever talked openly about being a slave descendant was Baye Barud, the man in his sixties who unloads the boats when they arrive from Bahir Dar. We sat by the lake and I asked about his family, whereupon he volunteered that his father had been sold to Zege and had married a local woman, but they had later split up. He talked about being separated from his brother in his youth, and about how his father had been betrayed by his own brother. But mainly, he said that he would die in this land, in Zege, by the lake where he had lived and worked all his life. He said that people were never rude to him about his descent, which may be due to widespread affection for a man who had worked hard his whole life, never treated anyone badly, and simply wanted a chance to retire and rest.

The coffee trade brought wealth and slaves to Zege in a way that created lasting social divisions, many of which built on existing, widespread conventions about the difference between landowner-farmers and everyone else. The descendants of those nobles, those slaves, and those coffee trees all remain in Zege today. There is a materiality to the history of labor relations in which the properties of coffee (stimulant and desirable commodity, substance of hospitality, biological species requiring care and maintenance) have played a huge part. Equally important to this material history are notions of when substances become incompatible: refusing to share food with slaves, or, as we shall see, exchanging living beings for silver.

MORALITY AND SILVER COINS

The story about nobles killing slaves gains much of its power from the silver coins involved. These are Marie-Therese thalers, known locally as *t'egera*. The story of thalers is compelling in itself—minted in eighteenth-century Vienna, they later became the currency of long-distance trade around the perimeter of the Indian ocean, long after they had been discontinued in Europe (Kuroda 2007). People in Zege know a lot about thalers because there are still quite a few of them buried in the peninsula. For a while, people would melt them down into crosses, which would sometimes be sold to tourists, but I am told that recently people have realized that the coins have more value in their original form, as collector's items and historical relics.

Thalers in Ethiopia were used for a very specific purpose: the exchange of long-range trade goods by which relationships between kingdoms were arranged—coffee, civet, ivory, slaves, cardamom, and some others (Pankhurst 1968, Fernyhough 2010). Abdussamad (1997: 548) suggests that the slave and coffee trade became a particularly concentrated phenomenon in Zege, as merchants ploughed their profits from coffee back into slavery. And we can find data from various trade posts along the northeast African route that show the changing prices for slaves, always measured in silver thalers (Fernyhough 2010: 126). So when people tell stories about merchants exchanging human lives for silver, it is because that is exactly what they were doing.

When people tell the story of the killing of the slave, they have handled the exact coins that they are referring to, which have themselves become a part of the physical history of the landscape, just as much as the coffee plants that were the center of everything. This point highlights the extent to which both of Zege's histories are embedded in the material environment. When people tell their history, they are telling the stories of the stuff around them, and one of the things that stuff shows is how thoroughly connected Zege has been to the outside world—both the missionary trajectories of the expansion of Christianity and the trade routes that connected Europe, Sudan, Arabia, and the various parts of Ethiopia. The evidence of these connections is very much something that people in Zege think about, as it is something they grow up with.

Buried treasure is a recurring trope in Ethiopia and always has to do with greed and the illegitimate accumulation of wealth. One of the more widely known examples is of the Sheraton hotel—one of the finest hotels in Africa, a place of high business and an extraordinarily incongruous sight from the road that leads to it, along which there are always numerous people sleeping under sacks and rubbish bags. (The bookshop in the hotel also sells the complete works of Ayn Rand.) A commonly told story holds that the Sheraton lies on the site of a cache of gold buried by the Italians in the 1930s, which *Sheikh* Alamoudi, now the richest man in Ethiopia, found, perhaps with the help of Italian soldiers, perhaps assisted by the great jazz singer Tilahun Gessesse. The way the story goes, a great python lives under the Sheraton, which is the demon that guarded the gold, which now haunts the building. I discussed this with a former waiter at the Sheraton who told me he was convinced that the place was haunted, and that this was commonly agreed to be the case.

The point is that buried treasure and precious metals are very potent metonyms of selfish accumulation. Their whole point is to last while other things fade, to retain value; but at the same time they are easily stolen. To protect such valuables, it is assumed, you need to make deals with demons. Compare this to the morally positive crops of Zege—hops and perfume leaves—which are perishable and fragrant, to be consumed by neighbors and among guests. They are the stuff of hospitality, which is locally understood as the basis of morally correct relationship-making.

Graeber's distinction between human economies and commodity economies is useful here: a human economy is one where "the primary focus of economic life is on reconfiguring relations between people, rather than the allocation of commodities" (2012: 411). Of course, it may be that these relationships are configured in steep hierarchical fashion, but the point is that such configurations are taken to be morally proper, at least by the church-agrarian hierarchy that sets the prevailing terms of morality. Hospitality relationships are fairly explicitly set against quantified exchange relationships (see the next chapter on relations between merchant exchange and witchcraft): in retellings of the story of the sacrifice of the slave, people often emphasize that the rich man buries the money in the private chamber of his house, which was accessible only to family, rather than in the main room, where one receives guests.

Coffee is interesting and problematic because it has become a medium of both hospitality and quantified exchange. Initially dismissed as a Muslim drink, it has become accepted as a primary medium of hospitality for all Ethiopians: the symbol of the country in the new millennium. But it is also easily packaged, highly desirable for its stimulant qualities, and difficult to grow in many places where it is desired. Coffee moved along the same trade routes as did slaves and silver; in Zege, it seems that slaves and coffee were at many points the only things that people exchanged thalers for.

The contrast between fragrant products and precious metal resonates with Matthew 26: the woman anoints Jesus's feet with perfume; the disciples question why the perfume was not sold and given to the poor; Christ gives his famous response, "The poor you will always have with you, but you will not always have me; when she poured this perfume on my body, she did it to prepare me for burial," and then Judas, outraged, agrees to hand over Jesus for thirty pieces of silver.

I take the passage to be working with the same kind of opposition that we find in Zege: fragrant products have value in rearranging relations between people. This is morally preferable to things that can be exchanged for accumulating wealth, and doubly so when it is used to make proper preparations for death. When a product, such as the perfume, can also be sold and transformed into money—and not just money, but tasteless, odorless silver—this is a problem, even if you intend to use the coin for good. The problem is that products of hospitality can never be separated from products of exchange and profit, because silver and money are so effective for transforming value. The logical end point of the problem, in the stories of Judas and of the Zege merchant, is the idea of exchanging a human life for silver, an absurdity that happened rather often in practice, and could only be squared by questioning whether the person being sold was really human at all.

CONCLUSION: MORAL SUBSTANCE

I have described life in Zege as built from a set of core prohibitions and mediations. A central concern is the way that materials by which people exchange and connect with one another get organized, controlled, appropriated, and regulated. The correct organization of relationships of blood, reproduction, and feeding, in particular, is a recurrent theme in Zegeña discourses of proper sociality. The church's rules about prohibition and fasting, while central, are only part of the complex dynamics of separation and substance that have emerged from the shared history of the church and the slave trade.

Coffee is a revealing case study for this purpose, because in one product it brings together the church's regulation of labor and production, the moral mediation of local hierarchical relationships, the pact between humanity and God on the part of a founding saint, and the commodity trade relations between Zege and distant areas. Coffee does not remain in a single sphere of exchange, but shifts between hospitality medium, commodity item, and sacred tree. In similar fashion, silver coins can be melted down into crosses, which can then be sold as mementos. It is clearly not the case, then, that the material properties of the medium dictate the sphere in which it will be used. Material things and substances are multifunctional; they exist beyond the uses to which they are put. We can think of these materials as the bearers of history, because it is through them that relationships themselves are made. I would suggest that people in Zege do to a large extent think of history in terms of the substances of mediation and their dissonances.

The stories of *Abune* Betre Maryam and of the merchant sacrificing the slave are "key scenarios" in the social thought of people in Zege (Ortner 1973). There is ample evidence that understanding the role of different material media of sociality, especially as they relate to hierarchy, is necessary if we are to understand why these stories in particular are so gripping. But it is equally important to keep sight of the imaginative work that makes these material media operative.

These are stories about morality and desire, and about the relationship between material life and human imagination, especially our ability to empathize and intuit the feelings and desires of others. Imaginative empathy comes from interacting not just with humans, but with the materials that allow us to infer human intentionality behind them (Gell 1998). Coffee and churches and human bodies make up the tangible, immediate environment of the peninsula, but at the same time they point always to other places and existences beyond themselves—whether it be the trading posts at the Sudanese border, or the waiting gates of heaven and hell.

It is not just contemporaneous worlds that are thinkable; the past accumulates in the soil and the buildings and bodies of Zege (Ingold 2000). Churches stand as evidence of their own centuries of being. Many of the silver coins that used to be traded for people or for coffee are still buried and get unearthed from time to time, and people sell them to tourists who visit the monasteries—tourists who themselves are part of the ongoing connection with far-off places. These connections allow people to imagine a wider world (geographically far, temporally distant, or separated by the difference between flesh and spirit), but also, crucially, to engage with that world, to try to mobilize its resources. This means constantly imagining other people's perspectives, so as to understand what saintly benefactors, trade partners, or demons might want from us. Imagining what others are thinking, in turn, opens up the dual possibility of empathizing with people or manipulating them.

Take the story of the rich man and the slave, which involves a staggering interplay of different levels of empathy and manipulation. First, the tellers of the story understand the motivation of the rich man, to keep his wealth. We infer automatically, of course, that the coins need protecting because other unnamed people covet them. The rich man must be able to understand what demons want and what they are capable of, and must further be able to initiate a pact with them, which is not easy since demons are invisible. When he slaughters the slave (with the connotations of killing an animal), he must presumably sever any sense of empathy or commonality—or perhaps the point is that he must give up something close to him. Finally, the listener cannot help but think about the perspective of the slave, no matter how hard the culture at large works to present slaves and their descendants as polluting, dangerous outcasts. That is a very great deal of imaginative work surrounding a few silver coins.

Blood, on the other hand, evokes a very different kind of imaginative empathy: an almost inescapable idiom of shared life and shared mortality, particularly for anyone who has ever slaughtered an animal (Feeley-Harnik 1995). Carsten (2013: S17) points out a shared potential of blood and money to flow "between domains," although in radically different ways. Here the fact that silver money can be stored, accumulated, kept secret, and used to buy and sell trade goods contrasts with a single-domain transfer of blood, between life and death. In Ethiopian Orthodox thought, blood can be seen both as the vessel of life (Ficquet 2006) and as a source of pollution and fear. As such it epitomizes the conflict between vitality and order that underlies the prohibition system.

Time and again, we will see how the key substances of mediation are those that mark or call into question the boundaries of humanity. At the primary level, the spilling of blood marks the breach of the integrity of an individual's body, either in injury or in reproduction. But at the second level of the imagery of sacrifice, we see a more general questioning of what is human. The archetypal blood sacrifice for Orthodox Christians is the Crucifixion, repeated in the Eucharist, in which the flow of Christ's blood enables the salvation of humankind (Paulos 1988: 171). It is possible because Christ is both human and God.

The sacrifice of the slave inverts the archetype; it is quintessentially immoral, serves the ends of the sacrifice alone rather than the community, and is possible because the slave is human but is treated as an animal. Yet the story absolutely requires the tacit recognition of the slave's humanity; if he were just thought to be an animal, it would not have any interest or moral force.

The link between slavery and sacrifice thus offers a key to understanding religious thought in Zege as premised on the management of the substances of the body and the substances that feed the body. Idioms of sacrifice relate these substances to external powers; they principally relate to the power of God, but they proximally relate to demons. But the moral model of sacrifice built around the Eucharist and around Hebraic traditions cannot quite encompass the history of slavery and the coffee commodity. These present moral dilemmas that are still recounted in terms of the exchange of substance and its regulation, as stories of blood, silver, and hierarchy.

NOTES

1. The arrival date of coffee in this part of Ethiopia is contested. It seems that the original manuscript of the Acts of Betre Maryam said that the three plants were hops, buckthorn, and fruit, and later additions clarify that the fruit was coffee (Cerulli 1946). This would fit with external sources that suggest coffee arrived in this part of Ethiopia in the late eighteenth or early nineteenth century (Merid 1988, Pankhurst 1968).

2. Pankhurst (1968: 202) notes that coffee was flourishing in Zege by 1830.

3. Comparing different accounts and drawing on Binayew and Bosc-Tiessé, I have still not been able to ascertain for certain when taxation was due only to the church, and when residents were relieved of tax entirely. In any case, the narrative of monasteries as bulwarks against state taxation is of clear importance.

4. In the 1940s, by contrast when taxation was enforced on the churches, local officials are said to have replied *Inkwan Zege Eyerusalemim Geberallech* "Let alone Zege, even Jerusalem has paid tribute" (Binayew 2014: 46).

5

The *Buda* Crisis

In early 2009, while walking to an interview, Abebe told me: "Life in Zege has got worse. People are afraid to eat together." The reason, he said, was widely thought to be competition in the Afaf market, which was driving traders to seek the services of sorcerers *(tenqway)* to boost their business by occult means. The problem was that while the sorcerers' medicine was effective, it carried a side effect: it turned the client into a *buda.* This meant that they would make others sick, usually inadvertently, usually by looking at them or their food. Everyone I spoke to agreed that trade was at the center of the problem because of the merchants competing to get ahead. A couple of deaths had been attributed to *buda,* and eventually the crisis became so severe that a town meeting was called and the police were urged to arrest the sorcerers responsible—even though, as we will see, this was not legally permissible. While this was a flashpoint, caused in part by the world food-price crisis that had doubled the price of basic staples, *buda* are an everyday hazard of the environment in Zege. Probably they are the most consistent source of anxiety in daily life, because they are ever present, unpredictable, and potentially fatal. They are also known to be extremely numerous in this particular area (and, by national repute, in the whole of old Gojjam province).

In the light of this story of spirits and the market it is tempting to regard the *buda* crisis as a response to the growth of market capitalism and its attendant inequalities. There is some truth in this, but a moment's attention reveals a more interesting and complex picture. For the notion of merchants becoming *buda* is unusual, and coexists with a much more widely attested association of *buda* with certain marginalized groups: potters, weavers, the Beta Israel, lepers, and in this area, the descendants of slaves (H. Pankhurst 1992, Reminick 1974, Salamon 1999,

Finneran 2003, A. Pankhurst 2003). We have to understand the crisis in the market in the context of these wider associations of *buda*; once we do this, *buda* looks less like a situational response to markets, and more like a key idiom of local historicity (Lambek 2002), a major figure by which people understand and participate in the unfolding of events, especially processes of social differentiation over time.

But *buda* is not just an interpretive idiom or a conceptual tool that people apply in order to make sense of unclear or emergent situations. These are spirits, understood to reside or inhere in people and in the environment. They are unpredictable, dangerous, and exert action beyond anyone's control. *Buda* possess a potency of their own that even a skeptical methodology must acknowledge if it is to have any hope of understanding why people are so concerned about them.

BETWEEN ACTION AND ESSENCE, AT THE BOUNDARIES OF THE HUMAN

One of Abebe's good friends, Zebirhan, gave me an explanation of *buda* that could have been a boilerplate from Africanist literature: "*Buda* is when a person gets rich for no obvious reason, without any special ability." Numerous studies have shown how similar practices have been important as capitalist markets came to Africa, with their power to apparently arbitrarily enrich some at the expense of others (Masquelier 1993, Geschiere 1997: 10, Comaroff & Comaroff 1999). This is undoubtedly part of what we see in Zege, particularly in the market village of Afaf with its substantial trading of foreign-produced commodities. But there are also reasons to be suspicious of attempts to frame spirit illness too narrowly as a response to capitalism and colonialism, or to treat it as if it were only a cipher for politics (Geschiere 1997: 218).

Buda is a constitutively ambiguous phenomenon. It is often unclear whether *buda* act intentionally or not; and it is very unclear whether *buda* is something you are, or something you have. While Ethiopian spirits do not fit into any kind of ordered typology (Aspen 2001), a *buda* is usually a nonhuman spirit, not a type of person. However, in conversation people frequently say, "So-and-so is *buda*." This may mean that so-and-so has visited a sorcerer and become a vector of sickness, or it may mean that they have inherited the condition of *buda*, as some people are known to do. In these cases calling someone *buda* refers less to the morality of their actions than to something essential about them that makes them impure. If a person is *yebuda zer*, the race or seed of the *buda*, then no person of standing will marry them or even share food with them, for fear both of losing social standing and of being physically harmed by the *buda* spirit. At least in this area, this puts *yebuda zer* in the same category as *yebariya zer*, slave descendants, as well as lepers, weavers, tanners, and other outcast craft groups that exist all over Ethiopia.

At the same time, however, it is difficult to discern outwardly who is *yebuda zer* and who is not. In Zege these people are all Orthodox Christians, and very often they are friends and socialize together in all sorts of ways. If non-*buda* refuse to receive food from *buda,* they find subtle and polite ways to do it. The same goes for slave descendants, except that they are frequently teased about their skin color in a semijoking, semiserious way that reveals quite deep underlying rifts. *Buda* articulates, with overlapping spheres of inclusion and exclusion, where we can be together as Christians and as friends, but our substance must remain apart, and it is here that the phenomenon can tell us most that is specific to Zege, and to some extent other parts of Ethiopia. *Buda* operates between action and essentialism, and between the human and the nonhuman, and it is this that makes it most revealing about Ethiopian life. Is *buda* a kind of person or a spirit that inhabits people? Do my neighbors harm me because they are doing bad things, or, and here is the key question in Zege, are they basically different kinds of people from me (Lyons & Freeman 2009, Lyons 2014)?

A CATEGORY THAT VIOLATES CATEGORIES

Because some of the material is controversial, it has taken time to unfold some of the details of local spirit politics, and there undoubtedly remains more that is hidden to me. I have made it a point not to press people on matters that, in my judgment, were likely to be experienced as rude or intrusive. However, as I have got to know people better over the years, I have found that many were willing to discuss this subject matter—nonetheless I have endeavored not to do anything to exacerbate the local tensions described below.

People in Zege are all classified as Amhara. Most are Orthodox Christian, with a Muslim minority living in the market village of Afaf. The broad designations—adopted in both government and local discourse—belie substantial diversity of background and status among Zege's residents, much of which is revealed through the practice and discourse of *buda.*

Almost all of the research that exists on *buda* describes it as a hereditary phenomenon associated with more or less endogamous groups of blacksmiths, potters, or other kinds of craftspeople (Finneran 2003). Special attention has been devoted to the Beta Israel, still known in Ethiopia as *Falasha,* who have suffered particularly visibly from *buda* accusations (see especially Quirin 1992, Kaplan 1995, Salamon 1999, Seeman 2009). Many draw attention to the similarity between *buda* and caste-like artisan groups in other parts of Africa, especially metalworkers (A. Pankhurst 2003, Finneran 2003, Lyons and Freeman 2009). *Buda* is described as a spirit, or a person possessed by a spirit, that harms people by "eating" them, and that may transform into an animal, particularly a hyena, at night (Reminick 1974, Tubiana 1991, H. Pankhurst 1992). Those accused of being *buda* may be forced into humiliating confessions and purifications and are sometimes in real danger of being killed (Rodinson 1967, Salamon 1999). In all cases, non-*buda* will refuse to eat, marry, or have sexual relations with *buda*. Of particular interest for this book, some sources note that *buda* are not just crafts-people, but specifically those who sell their products in the market (Rodinson 1967: 58, Lyons 2014). Related to this, those accused of being *buda* are almost always described as landless people, or at least those who cannot adequately support themselves from the land (see especially Reminick 1974, Pankhurst 2003, Lyons 2014). There is broad recognition of a pervasive class dimension to *buda* ideology, in which the powerful use *buda* accusations to restrain and stigmatize other groups (Reminick 1974, Salamon 1999, Finneran 2003; cf. Galt 1982 for a similar argument about "evil eye" in Italy).

Explanations of the phenomenon fall roughly into two camps, not necessarily mutually exclusive. On the one hand, there are those who emphasize the material-symbolic properties of crafts, especially metalworking, which appear to a settled farming population as occult, even outright evil, since opposed to the principles of the growth and fertility of crops (Finneran 2003, Lyons and Freeman 2009, 2014). The other group focuses on the historical experience of dispossession as generative of stigma, with craft-working being the only profession available for those without access to land (Quirin 1992, Kaplan 1995, Freeman 2003). Quirin and Kaplan both demonstrate that the *Falasha* did not become a stigmatized group, much less a quasi-caste, until they had been stripped of their rights to *rist* land in the fourteenth and fifteenth centuries—and that, even then, it took hundreds of years for a fully stigmatized identity to coalesce. These efforts to show the historical emergence of dispossession and *buda* accusation are persuasive, but they do not explain why the accusations take such strikingly similar form in quite culturally distinct parts of Ethiopia—even in a work such as Pankhurst and Freeman's *Peripheral People*, which considers a wide range of cases. Some part of the symbolic argument must therefore be necessary in order to get at the shared underlying logic of *buda* and related phenomena. In this regard, one element that I will argue has not been given due notice is the association of *buda* with differing ideologies of exchange, particularly the conflict between the values of hospitality and those of the market.

Part of the defining nature of *buda* as a phenomenon is that it is capable of incorporating a great diversity of ideas and practices under a monolithic rubric that is recognized throughout the country. After all, *buda* designates an invisible, inscrutable being. It is powerful precisely because its referent is not well fixed. Even more than this, and critical to understanding the flexibility of the phenomenon, *buda* is always something that violates fundamental, normative social distinctions: male and female (Lyons 2014), human and animal (Salamon 1999), or master and slave (Reminick 1974). This boundary violation may be *buda*'s definitive aspect—a sort of antidefinition that would go some way to explain the variance in the literature (cf. Hannig 2014).

As I have indicated, these interpretive associations do not amount to an exhaustive description of the social phenomenon of *buda;* there is also a very important phenomenological dimension. People feel *buda* as an environmental presence, one that causes pronounced fear and anxiety. This conditions daily experience, particularly the experience of being unwell. It also ties this conditioning of experience to interpersonal relations, thus shaping the contours of society to a remarkable degree.

Buda spirits cannot be seen, as Beza, the local traditional doctor, informs me, even with a microscope—this is the key way in which they differ from bacteria. A good starting point therefore seems to be to ask how people learn that *buda* exist. There is no doubt that they do exist, although some of my friends have questioned whether *buda* eat white people, since they never seem concerned about them. If you grow up in Zege, by a young age you will have heard your parents and other people discussing *buda* and speculating about whether a particular illness was *buda*-related. More strikingly, if your own mother was ever worried about *buda* attacking you, she would have held a gourd of incense and charcoal to your face, so the smoke would drive the spirit away. You might well have seen people collapse on the street, catatonic or in convulsions, as sometimes happens with *buda* attacks. More memorable still, if you did get sick you might have been rushed through the forest by concerned relatives to see the local doctor. When their usually placid child would not stop crying one night, my friends Tomas and Haregwa, worried sick, carried her for over an hour uphill through pitch black forest to find the local doctor. They were convinced this was a *buda* attack and, indeed, a successful remedy was found.

All of this is visceral experience. Yes, you learn about *buda* from talk, but you also experience them in direct fashion, associated with strong smells, cries, emotions of fear, and feelings of sickness. And you see evidence of *buda* all around you, particularly in the case of more vibrant attacks, where the victim may shout and scream or otherwise violently act out. Children have much more experience of *buda* than they do of, say, leopards, of which some may or may not remain in the area. Unlike leopards, *buda* cannot be seen, but also unlike leopards, there are very many *buda* in the village and the forest. The experiential qualities of *buda* also convey a play of uncertainty between humanity and animality. *Buda* victims often growl and grunt and are said to eat ashes or feces. These are striking contradictions of the things that are understood to make humans human—the power of speech and avoiding impure foods—but our initial responses to them is shock and surprise, not (yet) conceptual reflection.

It is only later that a child learns that her neighbors may be causing *buda* attacks in some way. She may have always worn a protective amulet containing a Ge'ez prayer scroll around her neck, which her mother placed on her because the family next door was known to be *yebuda zer*, the race of *buda*. She will start to hear speculation and gossip, and to learn what is generally known about how *buda* behave and which people are responsible for them. Analytically, it is essential to realize that the experience comes before the interpretation—most people have become sick with a *buda* attack long before they really understand what that might mean.

FROM SICKNESS TO HISTORY

As people become socialized they learn quite quickly that *buda* is associated with a range of interpersonal phenomena—status and power being key issues—without necessarily being reducible to them. This section traces some of these associations, both historically and across contemporary Zege, to try to understand how *buda* emerges as an intelligible phenomenon among other relationships, especially those between people, property, and spirits. Foremost among these is the relationship between *buda* and slavery. In the minds of many in Zege, as I will show, the two categories remain closely tied.

I had been in the field for a long time before I worked up the courage to ask direct questions about slavery. When I finally did ask Abebe if there had been slaves in Zege, and what had happened to their descendants, he began reeling off a list of names—many of whom were friends of both of ours—who were *yebariya zer*, seeds of the slaves. Seamlessly, he also began listing people who were *yebuda zer*, seeds of the *buda*. While *buda* and *bariya* were not the same thing to him, he made it clear that they belonged in the same category: they were people that nobody would marry, many would not eat with them either, especially in Abebe's father's generation. I was surprised because I had attended weddings with many of these people, and had never noticed any divisions. Abebe said that, indeed, there were ways to be subtle about which table you ended up at, so that the rejection would not be explicit. I asked him if there had been slaves in his family and he responded, mock indignant, *nes'uh nen*, "we are clean." I conducted a number of further interviews on the topic that elicited the same picture.

He had learned all of this—which families are "pure" and which not—from his father, talking in his home. Establishing purity is not simple, because of the Amhara cognatic descent system, which means that there are no clear lineages or descent groups of any kind. Instead there are clusters of competing land claims and patriarchal households in which slaves, servants, women, and children have historically been subordinate in just about the same way (Hoben 1970, Reminick 1974). People do keep careful patrilineal genealogies, though. Many men, especially local scholars and those from important families, can trace the names of their fathers back eight generations or more. These genealogies have traditionally served to prevent incest according to the seventh-generation rule (Hoben 1973) but also to exclude impurities of slave or *buda* from the line. But the genealogies are not explicit; they are not displayed in corporate social groups, but are kept in the home and in people's memories. They play a key role in structuring relations of inclusion and exclusion, but as with the food at the wedding, they do so largely below the surface of social interaction. This helps to explain why descendants of the "pure" are frequently on openly friendly terms with slave or *buda* descendants, even when profound rifts exist between them.

An outcome of this system of reckoning descent is that, rather than a set of lineages or segmentary kin-based groups, you have just two categories: "clean" and "unclean." It is part of their semi-implicit nature that there is not an institutionalized term for either category. These categories are not relevant to every social context. In relations of trade, of daily conversation, or of friendship, they can be negligible; in sharing food and in marriage they can be absolute. These different levels of inclusion and exclusion are defining mechanisms of Amhara life.

The idea that slave descent renders you impure and hence unfit for marriage is a common one, for example, in Madagascar, as described in the work of Denis Regnier (2012). It is easy enough to speculate on why this might be—in order to morally justify owning a person, you probably need to tell yourself a story in which they are different from you in some basic way. Regnier's argument revolves around the way that people essentialize historically contingent differences. Mine, on the other hand, is that *buda* discourse in Zege blurs the lines between what is due to your essence and what is due to your actions.

Recall the explanation of *buda* given to me by Zebirhan: *buda* is suspected when people become wealthy through no obvious legitimate means. This definition is especially prevalent in the market village rather than the surrounding forest. Most of the gossip I have heard about people in the village who were *buda* having visiting sorcerers has revolved around some of the wealthier merchants—not coffee merchants, but shopkeepers, bar owners, and other businessmen. That is, these are people who have become wealthy, but not from the land. This landlessness is the obvious thing that merchants share with slaves, but also with the numerous other caste-like groups that experience forms of social exclusion in Ethiopia.

Ethnographic literature from other parts of Amhara describes *buda* as almost exclusively a descent model, with some even describing *buda* as an ethnicity distinct from Amhara (Reminick 1974, H. Pankhurst 1992). In Addis Ababa, according to Diego Malara's (pers. comm.) research, certain neighborhoods are known to be *buda*, in that people from these excluded quasi-ethnic groups have settled there. The taint of *buda* is remarkably broad in scope—it is difficult to shed by moving to new places, and has very much survived the process of urban migration.

The phenomenon of outcaste, landless craftspeople is known across Ethiopia, far beyond Amhara Christian areas (A. Pankhurst 2003). In most cases such people are regarded as possessing harmful spirits akin, if not identical, to *buda* itself.

In the Lake Tana region and around Zege, the most prominent such group is the Weyto, possibly the original inhabitants of the area, who are mostly canoe makers, and who endure comprehensive discrimination (Gamst 1979). For the past century the Weyto have almost all been Muslim and have claimed to have always been so (Cheesman 1936: 92), but find comparable difficulties integrating into Muslim communities as into Christian ones, because of the prevalence of the stigma against them.

There are, finally, numerous instances of *buda* being associated with slavery. In the southern kingdom of Kaffa, for example, during a period of particularly high demand for slaves in the nineteenth century, the government hired sorcerers to identify people as *buda,* and on these grounds they and their families were seized and sold into slavery (Fernyhough 2010: 87). This era was also a high-water mark of slavery in Zege, as British and Italian interest in coffee as a commodity stimulated rapid increases in production.

There is a curious, revealing reversal of the story of *buda* being slaves, which Reminick (1974: 283) reports from the 1960s and which I have heard in the same form in Zege, in which a *buda* could enslave the soul of the recently deceased and turn it into a domestic slave. When any visitor came, the enslaved person would be bewitched to look like a household ornament. Reminick's interpretation of the story is persuasive: a landed man's status was designated by the number of dependents in his household, including, at that time, the descendants of his or his family's slaves. It stands to reason that a *buda* should desire the same status, but having no land to support such dependents, he of course achieved this by occult means. *Buda,* then, are a projection of an agrarian landed people's nightmare of the agency of the landless. Slave owners anywhere tend to become dependent on their slaves and to resent this fact; *buda* articulates the near-universal fear on the part of dominant people about the desires and the potency of those they dominate; it seems to speak to anxieties inherent in the property system itself—or at least, the property system of nineteenth- and twentieth-century Ethiopia, with its extractive aristocracy and long-distance trade markets.

Landlessness does seem to be the common factor in Zege as well, or at least the common factor is anxieties about production that does not come from the land. Certainly desire is central: slaves are dangerous because it is assumed that they desire the possessions of their masters; the marketplace is dangerous as a whole because it is a field of competitive desire. At the same time, it was exactly strong, long-distance markets for coffee that created the demand for slaves in Zege in the first place. Slavery brought in foreigners in large numbers and made them subordinate, in conditions of maximal desire and competition in Zege society at large.

The duality of *buda* imagination, in which oppressors imagine themselves as the spiritually oppressed, is reminiscent of Lambek's (2002) account of witchcraft as projection in Mayotte. *Buda* has been used as grounds for enslavement and dehumanization, and imagined as one who enslaves the souls of the dead and turns people into objects. A horrific reciprocity is imagined, which plays into a wider mistrust of exchange relationships as opposed to the hospitality that the dominant society holds as its paramount value.

OTHER STORIES

Most anyone who gets called *buda* would contest the term, of course—though not that *buda* spirits exist, which is undeniable. The label is shameful and humiliating, and crucially, unlike a group designation, it is isolating. There is no possibility of *buda* getting together and joining an ethnic or class movement or solidarity group, because no person could possibly want to be associated with the concept. This is why it is always incorrect to describe *buda* as an ethnicity. *Buda* is an antiethnicity, it dissolves solidarity. It is an appellation of mistrust and exclusion; it casts people as antisocial agents. Precisely because it blurs the line between individual actions of sorcery and polluting essence, *buda* can never become a unifying identity. By contrast, people who were called *Falasha* have in many parts of Ethiopia been able to organize themselves as a corporate group and to redefine themselves as Beta Israel, their own preferred designation, although many have converted to Orthodoxy in an attempt to escape stigmatization, and have found themselves caught between the two groups (Seeman 2009).

If it is difficult to interview slave descendants about being slave descendants, it is outright impossible to ask people about being accused of being *buda*. Because of the moral connotations of the term, it would be deeply insulting, akin to calling them a murderer. But I have made efforts to find acceptable ways to talk to people on several trips subsequent to my initial fieldwork. Sometimes we can talk about the subject, and sometimes we can talk around it in illuminating ways.

The stories that emerge have a fragmented quality to them. One young man I used to play football with, whose friends had jokingly called him Baby Slave, never letting him forget it, had got into an argument with a local merchant. Ironically, and significantly, he had accused the man of being *buda* and, facing likely legal and social trouble, had left Zege for another part of the country. The last rumor I heard was that he was serving in the army. Another young man was said to have been extremely talented, but to have gone slightly crazy *(ibd)* after being forced to break up with his girlfriend because of his weaver descent.

Those Weyto I have spoken to, mostly in Bahir Dar, have likewise emphasized their Muslim identity; when I tried to talk to one of the few Weyto men in Zege, we were joined by a group of young men who started asking him, if he was a Muslim, why he didn't go to mosque. In the main, this shows the limits of appealing to religious belonging to overcome stigma. Muslims, the vast majority of the time, still do not marry Weyto, who go to their own mosque in Bahir Dar, and noble

Christian families do not marry weavers, though some people have told me that this may be changing slowly, and that the younger generation was not quite so concerned with this.

One part of the story that emerges is of fragmentation—lives narrated in terms of disruption and broken relationships. These people are excluded from the mechanisms by which coherent-seeming narratives and interpersonal belonging get produced. But at the same time people move beyond the disjuncture and build relationships with the land and the church, make a living, have families, and build respect. Shared Christianity does not obviate the fragmenting discourse of *buda*. But the church is a powerful agency of continuity, and the universalism that lies at its heart always exists, at least in potential.

HOSPITALITY AND EXCHANGE

The fact of shared Orthodox Christianity is incommensurable with the discourse of exclusion that surrounds *buda*. Lambek (1993: 12) points out that incommensurability is often a central feature of social life, but here the disjuncture is particularly intense. In the era of slavery, a Christian had to baptize his slaves. For one thing, it is commanded in one of the key Christian law books, the Fetha Negest, which also forbids Christians from selling slaves to others (Paulos 2009: 175). Christians would buy from Muslim traders and then the slaves would eventually be set free, or pass to their owners' descendants and become dependent retainers (Reminick 1974, Abdussamad 1997). For another, slaves prepared food for the household, and so they had to be Christian. This immediately causes problems, because you need to bring the slave close enough into circles of commensality that they cook for you, but keep them distant enough that you can claim complete superiority. This dilemma highlights the perennial tension between parochialism and universalism that runs throughout Ethiopian Orthodox history. According to my research assistant Tefera, one solution was to tell slaves that they were accursed, and that any fine meat would give them leprosy, so as to stop them from stealing food while they cooked it. The way Tefera tells it, slaves would have to eat rats, thus marking them as substantially inferior and morally compromised.

Likewise, those who remain of the *Falasha* people in Zege have not kept their distinct religion, but converted to Christianity a generation ago. Nonetheless they, too, retain the taint of *buda*, which means that their hospitality is always potentially poisonous, and their children are unmarriageable. The merchants who are suspected of being *buda*, too, are almost always Christians. This is why they are so troublesome—you are supposed to eat with them, but the spirit within them, because of its greed, threatens this commensality.

Abebe's comment that "people are afraid to eat together" summarized what for many people is the major trend in Zege in recent years. While conducting interviews in the forest with Tefera, one of our most frequent topics was the decline in hospitality because of economic hardship. The elders we spoke to framed Zege's history as one of collective feasting, as described in the next chapter, in which all proper relationships were defined by acts of eating together, either in the great funerary *tezkar* feasts or in the clerical dining rooms *(mefraq)* that organized church-lay hierarchies. The church dining room epitomizes proper hospitality, with its dignitaries sitting in prescribed order under the blessed authority of the church. Now, as Tefera told me, people would rarely offer food to nonrelated visitors or ask it of their hosts. There are two overlapping reasons for this: one is consideration, not wanting to compel people to part with their very limited supplies. The other is fear of *buda*: because of an atmosphere of competition, hardship, and envy, there is always a danger that people who serve you food may inadvertently harm you by means of the *buda*. These fears are particularly pronounced when people go to areas slightly poorer or less central than their own, which is not unusual—people in a hierarchy frequently attribute occult powers to those less central to them. Fortunately there are ways to offer hospitality without serving food: homebrewed beer and coffee are relatively safe and can always be served to guests.

Eating together is how Amhara act out who belongs and who is excluded, but *buda* are not only threatening because they disrupt hospitality; they actually eat you. This is the point where we are reminded that *buda* is both a kind of person and a kind of spirit. I remember a friend asking me in the course of discussion what the English word *cannibal* meant. I said it was a person who ate people and he replied, "Oh, you mean *buda*."

In many parts of Africa eating is a trope of dominance (Mbembe 1992). In Ethiopia the word *meblat*, "to eat," is used for when one wins a game: the winner eats and the loser is eaten. To some extent we can read this, again, as a projection of the dominant onto those they dominate: we are more successful than them materially, so they must take their revenge spiritually. This only goes so far, however, since the market traders who are called *buda* are hardly disadvantaged. More significant is the concern of a hierarchical relationship turning into an exchange. You may eat the *buda*'s food, but rather than this acting to arrange a relationship between you, as hospitality normally does, the *buda* exacts direct repayment in the form of your own vitality. Again, *buda* looks like a projection of the powerful relating to desires and ways of making value outside of the landed agrarian hierarchy.

At the same time, the trope of eating calls into question the dividing lines between humans and animals. Countless people have told me in interviews that *buda* are animal spirits, as distinct from *zar*, which are human-like. And yet, as this chapter demonstrates, people continually talk about *buda* as if it were an essential quality of certain kinds of people. In many parts of Ethiopia, the archetype of *buda* is that it transforms from a person into a hyena at night. Since the hyena eats carrion, the *buda* therefore steps out of the realm of proper personhood. Its predatory and gustatory habits are then unpredictable and it lacks the repression or suppression of the appetites that makes people moral. *Buda* are both animal spirits that roam the village and the forest and people who live among others. The conflation of one with the other is central to the logic of *buda*, and plays a key role in deciding what counts as a proper human.

RESPONSIBILITY

One of the major practical consequences of these uncertainties about what is human is the difficulty in establishing personal and legal responsibility. Although harm caused by *buda* is understood to be due to some aspect of interpersonal relationships and to the emotions of other people—principally desire, envy, and greed—those people are usually not thought to deliberately cause harm or eat their victims. The *buda*, as agentive spirit, is malevolent, but the person might not be, and I have witnessed numerous cases of people maintaining close, friendly relations with others whom they later told me were *buda*. There are ways of ascertaining the party responsible for a *buda* attack, mainly by inducing the spirit, through the mouth of the victim, to say the attacker's name.

This accusatory practice has led to violence and ostracism in the past and in other parts of Ethiopia. I was once asked to consult on an asylum case involving people who had had to leave Ethiopia because of persistent persecution on the grounds of being *buda*. However, in Zege, during the time I worked there, there were no overt *buda* accusations. The reason has to do with legal definitions of reality, as Haregwa explained to me. She told me that after baby Christina's attack, Tomas had also been attacked by *buda*. Haregwa had administered incense and the *buda* had spoken the name of a local merchant whom we knew quite well. Tomas had been cured with holy water, but I wanted to know if they had tried to openly accuse the merchant. Haregwa replied that they could not because "He would have us arrested" (*yasassern neber*). It was no longer permissible to make *buda* accusations because *Mengist sew sew aybellam yilal* (The government says people do not eat people). There is gossip and resentment about *buda*, but it is almost impossible for this to turn into overt conflict.

I suspect that this is a large part of the reason why so many people described 2008–09 as a time of *buda* crisis. Following up on my interview with Haregwa, I asked a friend (from the Zege forest, of quite high birth) about the legality of accusation. He confirmed that *buda* accusation was forbidden because it was "not scientific." He told me that *buda* had multiplied in recent years, partly because of coffee traders traveling to more dangerous parts of the countryside, but that it was increasingly difficult to "remove them from the society." Somewhat alarmed, having heard enough tales of the violent ostracism of *buda* accusees, I asked what he meant, and he said that it was difficult to get suspected *buda* out of *mahber* associations, church groups, and other positions of local influence. It remained, of course, ambiguous whether he meant that the bad spirits had to be removed, or the people possessed by them.

The question that had disturbed me was still present, and underlined that there was a genuine ontological disagreement between us. For my friend and others like him, *buda* were a present and general threat to the well-being of the society and individuals alike. For the government, which still works from a broadly Marxist materialist definition of reality, this was pure superstition and a prime example of harmful traditional practice (cf. Marsland 2015). In this case I find it hard to disagree with the government's position, which has undoubtedly prevented some grave injustices. But the experience of *buda* crisis during my years of fieldwork shows how deep the effects of such contestations over the definition of reality can run.

As an anthropologist, the point that strikes me is this: it is easy enough to gloss over significant differences in ontology, culture, or cosmology (however you prefer to cast it) until actual situations of justice and punishment arise. It is when action is called for, action that has real effects on people's lives, that we all discover how much we "mean" our ideas. Which is to say that questions of ontology or belief cannot be understood without attention to the consequential moments, and sometimes matters of life or death, in which they are put to the test.

During that same conversation Haregwa explained to me how the stigma or suspicion of *buda* can follow people from place to place. When she had married Tomas, people had been suspicious because he came from elsewhere, and therefore his *zer* (seed, race) could not be known. But, she told me, if she had married a local weaver's son, it would have been even worse, and her family would have asked her why she was spoiling her seed. She also said she felt this *zer*-thinking was on the way out *(iyyeqerre new)*, whereas her father's generation had been very strict.

What makes *buda* sometimes seem like an ethnic or caste designation is that, if you divide the world up into pure and impure people, you create two de facto endogamous moieties. Those who are likely to get called *buda*, whether because of slave descent, or because of being *Falasha*, or because of their profession, are likely to marry others in a similar position. Anecdotal evidence suggests that this is the case in Zege, with marriages between slave descendants and tanner's descendants, for example, being acceptable. By these means a general opposition between pure people and impure people, opposed to each other as honor is to shame *(kibur/hifret)*, is preserved and transmitted. The two groups, however, are not symmetrical. One part has all the cultural attributes and institutions that anyone can aspire to; the other is acknowledged only in gossip and innuendo, and has no grounds for solidarity.

LAND, TRADE, CRAFT, AND CREATIVITY: MODES OF VALUE PRODUCTION

We can now return to the original problem that sparked this discussion: the *buda* crisis in the Afaf market in 2008–09. As we have seen, there was broad public consensus that the cause of the crisis was traders visiting sorcerers and accidentally becoming *buda* in the process. This interpretation resonates with a wider distrust of trade in the predominantly agrarian heartlands of Ethiopian Orthodoxy (Levine 1965, McCann 1995).

A large part of this distrust exists because the accumulation of power and money through trade is unpredictable and difficult to regulate through the normative social conventions that distinguish good power from bad. We have already seen a paradigmatic example of this in the story of the merchant and the slave (in the previous chapter). Like that merchant, today's traders are thought to be dealing with demons in order to get rich at others' expense—except that the lines of intention and responsibility are more blurred, because these events are unfolding in time rather than being retold in hindsight. The last few years have seen significant volatility in the Afaf market, with new businesses (veterinary pharmacies, bar/hotels, general stores) opening up while others have gone under or moved location several times, and a general increase in food prices has intensified a sense of competition.

I have heard gossip about at least three of Afaf's most successful businessmen being *buda*. Much of this gossip, so far as I can gather without being rude, derives from their nonnoble backgrounds. People are becoming (comparatively) rich who should not have under the old system, at least as people remember it. The key turning point here is the land reforms after 1974 carried out by the Derg government, which redistributed the lands of the church and nobles (Rahel 2002). The old system was upheld by feasting—to be a legitimate wealthy person you had to feed your neighbors—whereas now to be a legitimate landholder you just have to be registered. At the same time, nobles lost control of taxation rights on plots in the Afaf market, which now went to the state.

Another factor that makes the accumulation of wealth unpredictable, and trade seem mysterious and threatening, is the dependence on commodities that come from outside, and on relations with the traders and companies that supply them. Barkeepers need fridges and a good supplier of bottled St. George's and Dashen beer, while veterinary pharmacists need to source their medicine and general storekeepers need industrially produced goods such as jerry cans, plastic shoes, and flashlights. These things come proximally from Bahir Dar, an hour away by bus, but originally from all over the world—much of the stuff on sale in Afaf is Chinese-made. This means that trade depends both on good relations with outsiders and on mysterious physical processes. Neither I nor many people in Zege know how plastic is made, for example. How crops grow may be mysterious enough in itself, but that is a mystery of God, and furthermore the whole process from sowing to harvest is locally visible, meaning that crops are not alienated in quite the same way.

There is now a substantial literature on witchcraft and sorcery discourse as a way of engaging and critiquing "modernity" or capitalism in Africa (e.g., Masquelier 1993, Geschiere 1997, Comaroff & Comaroff 1999). A common theme is that witchcraft discourse, since it has long had to do with selfishness, secrecy, antisocial action, and power exerted at a distance, becomes a potent framework for understanding and acting out the effects of colonialism and increasing incorporation into global markets. Sorcery often stands also for any kind of creative force that appears to exist beyond normal channels of social control. Because these discourses, like *buda*, tend to involve engagements with the foreign or external, they become key idioms of history-as-culture (Sahlins 2004): products of the conjuncture of unexpected events, established local symbolic traditions, and the human imaginative capacity.

The challenge in analyses of witchcraft-and-capitalism or witchcraft-and-colonialism is to avoid falling into a Manichean picture of a harmonious precapitalist or precolonial world in which mutuality was a shared value and witchcraft the opposite of that value. Precolonial cultures were not unified, insular entities suddenly cast out of Eden by the disruption of the world capitalist system. That disruption is real enough, as the experience of the Afaf market shows, but its historical context is a situation already (a) deeply embedded in state affairs and long-distance trade routes, and (b) divided by various sociopolitical tensions and competing value systems. A comparative and historical account of *buda* shows that the relationship of *buda* with greedy merchants is part of a much wider politics of value. The landed nobility, which regards hospitality as the hallmark of moral sociality, is deeply mistrustful of other forms of value creation such as craft and trade, especially insofar as they involve exchange transactions. Commodities are here understood as opposed not to gifts, but to hospitality and hierarchy.

The idea that commodities are often morally suspect because they create little or no long-term obligation between people, and because the circumstances of their production are concealed, is nothing new (see, e.g., Gudeman 2008, Graeber 2011 for recent accounts). We can add to this by relating the *buda* crisis of market traders to the wider use of *buda* as a term of shame and exclusion. Market traders share with slaves, potters, and tanners the fact that they do not make a living from the land. Because of this, they are thought of as avaricious—merchants because of the nature of their occupation, slaves because of their envy of their masters. This perceived lack of control over the appetites in turn opens up the whole symbolic repertoire of *buda* as indicating animality, the failure to fast, the lack of autonomy and honor, and the propensity to make spirit attacks due to either malice or a deeply shameful lack of control. What makes *buda* such an effective and persistent phenomenon is the allusive flexibility with which it evokes some or all of these clustered referents to describe individuals or whole categories of people.

ANATOMY AND ENVIRONMENT

The challenge for an adequate ethnography of *buda* is to describe the incredibly condensed semantic range of the concept and the history it carries, while some-how accounting for the fact that *buda* is not just an interpretive notion, a sort of local genre of political history. People experience *buda* as an ever-present threat, constituted in a loaded sensory and emotional field of fear, anxiety, sickness, the inhuman noises of the victims, and the smokes and smells of the various remedies. *Buda* has an independent existence that is not fully described by its conceptual use; however, I do not understand this existence in the same way that my infor-mants do. From my standpoint of methodological atheism, I maintain that *buda* is a partially imaginary phenomenon, constituted through uniquely human faculties for projecting and inferring the desires and intentions of others. Much of the hor-ror and even violence that surrounds *buda* discourse is due to fear, especially the fear that you or your children will be killed, deliberately or not, by the actions of your neighbors. This entails a significant imaginative dimension—both conceiv-ing of possible future suffering and inferring the desires and intentions of others. Indeed, the conviction that those who are like slaves will enslave their masters is entirely dependent upon the ability to imagine and project fear and desire.

But to say something is partly imaginary (that it could not exist without its imaginative component) is not to say that it is not real (Bialecki 2014). An anatomy of *buda* shows that they are constituted not solely in people's heads—if anything can be—but in the conjunction of imagination with the human production of symbols and discourses, *and* in the return of those discourses as something alien to us, *and* in the unfolding of events in history.

As we have seen, people in Zege would in any case agree with me that *buda* is an inherently interpersonal phenomenon, driven by human desires both con-scious and unconscious. We just disagree on whether they can actually eat and kill a person. This disagreement has significant consequences for our ideas of how to trace responsibility for events and actions, but it cannot be phrased as "they believe *buda* exist and I do not." Nor are people the uncritical pawns of their own concepts. Many of my friends in Zege are well aware that *buda* discourse gets used to unfairly stigmatize people, but that does not imply that they think *buda* do not exist or are not dangerous.

Buda cannot be just an idea, because that idea is always externalized. It can-not just be a symbol, because that symbol always has means of transmission or figuration, which is furthermore beyond the control of any individual or group. Even if we think *buda* is "just" a concept, it is one that gains tangible persistence through its instantiation and repetition—in acts of discussion, interpretation, and treatment—and through its emergence from real human relationships (Hacking 1999: 34). The concept *buda* has an object, but one that remains constitutively indeterminate. For this reason, the most intransigent social constructivist or the most ardent rationalist skeptic alike would have to agree that *buda* has a tenacity and a resistance, which is to say, an existence of its own. My friends and I tend to disagree on the nature of that existence, though it is always something that we can discuss and perhaps learn more about. And if we shift attention to how *buda* are knowable and how their actions are intelligible, there is much more in common, and a far richer picture of the interaction between human intentions and relations and the lived environment emerges. Pinpointing exactly where we agree or disagree seems to be an extremely valuable exercise for understanding the level at which cultural differences operate and how deep they run.

Some friends have told me that I need not worry because *buda* do not eat white people. Others warned that I must take medicine home with me, because doctors there would not recognize *buda*, and might give me an injection, which would kill me. These speculations bring home the fact that the nature of *buda* is always open to question. But they also point to its local and environmental quality. *Buda* is something that is around, on paths and in houses, though invisible. *Buda* are part of the lived environment in the same way that other people and their productions are: an environment that is always already social, and in which the boundaries of the human are a defining, troubled concern. Capturing this environmental quality offers hope of understanding *buda*'s social, historical, and conceptual density without losing sight of the critical dimension of what it feels like to live in a place where such things are active.

6

Concrete, Bones, and Feasts

A predominant narrative in Zege identifies the decline of nobility and their hospitality mores as the most tangible local outcome of the past several decades of political change. For many, funeral feasts known as *tezkar* were the emblematic practice of this old social regime and the primary means of establishing morally recognizable status over generations. Feasting for the dead was the chief means of reconstituting moral hierarchy (by establishing the deceased and their relatives as hosts and benevolent feeders of others, with the implicit or explicit imprimatur of the church) as well as of managing relations between the living and the dead.

Memories of *tezkar* feasting contrast with a recent trend in Zege of building concrete tombs for the deceased. The rise of concrete graves happened more or less in parallel with the decline of *tezkar,* starting from the late Haile Selassie era, until the practice was forbidden in 2006. The reason given for the ban, issued by the local churches, was that the concrete graves were filling up the churchyards, and leading to disputes over graveyard plots. This chapter will show how these disputes over material memorials represent wider questions about the material remains of the dead and the use of these remains to advance the status of the living. Concrete graves brought deep-seated dilemmas to a head: about the relationship between body and soul, but also between universal Christian salvation and the earthly political presence of the church.

The old practices of *tezkar* feasting had come under concerted attack by successive modernizing governments as irrational and backward, and indeed their competitive nature could be ruinous, as a local church scholar *Mergéta* Abbi explained to me (see also Messing 1957, Mersha 2010). The concrete graves represent a shift in the material register of memory and status, but they were an innovation that raised their own significant political-spiritual problems: they were too durable and emphasized the material remains of the deceased instead of the soul's progression to heaven. Their rise and fall offer invaluable insight into transforming relations among churches, people, and land as they have played out in material history.

A society's relations with its dead go a long way toward defining its relations with its past and its land; in particular, remembrance and death ritual tend to be integral to the reproduction (or transformation) of hierarchy (Bloch & Parry 1982). In this light, the comparative weakness of ancestors and lineages in Orthodox Ethiopia is striking, and creates rather different contours of memory and political reproduction than are found elsewhere in Africa. There is a case for saying that the Orthodox Church takes over much of the organization of death and spatiotemporal continuity that elsewhere in Africa is the province of kin groups (Hoben 1970, 1973). This is not to say that kinship lacks importance in Amhara social relations; it is a primary concern for everybody in Zege. Rather, kinship relations and relations to the church exist in a state of often uneasy compromise between universalistic doctrine and the reproduction of class divisions. Many of these tensions come to prominence in the graveyard and in disputes about what constitutes legitimate mediation between life and death.

THE *TEZKAR* DYNAMIC (SACRIFICE, HOSPITALITY, STATUS)

A poor man's tezkar, a drunken leper.
(Both are equally unappealing.)
—ETHIOPIAN SAYING,
RECORDED BY ROGER COWLEY

With the caveat in mind that this is a study of how *tezkar* is remembered now, not of the historical specifics of its practice, it is at least possible to say that *tezkar* feasts have become, for many of the men whom others recognize as authoritative commentators, a condensed symbol of the way things were before the Derg, before Federalism, and before the police and the *qebellé* office came to Zege. The place of feasting in local memory is doubly significant because the word *tezkar* itself describes a way of remembering, from the same root as *zikir* (memorial fests for a saint; see chapter 7). The *tezkar* was a memorial practice, closely associated with the funeral services performed by the church, as we will see. To associate *tezkar* with a disappeared past is to say that we remember differently than we used to; our very means of knowing life and death and time are not what they were.

One of the threads of continuity between Ethiopia's Imperial, Derg, and Federal regimes since the start of the twentieth century has been the drive toward modernization, understood to be embodied in the more effective aspects of Euro-American techniques of science and governance (Clapham 1969, Donham

1999, Andreas 2012). For Orthodox Christians in Zege one of the most notice-able aspects of this modernist ideology has been the consistent pressure against funeral feasts on the grounds that these were backward, extravagant, economi-cally irrational, and potentially ruinous. The *tezkar* has special importance across Orthodox Ethiopia and has traditionally entailed the bereaved giving a large feast for their neighbors on the fortieth day after death (Mersha 2010: 881–82). Messing (1957: 485–86) reports that the fortieth day was considered the first on which the soul could be released from purgatory, and describes the feast as "the greatest sin-gle economic consumption in the life cycle."

As a result of this concerted government opposition, *tezkar* feasts today are small affairs for family and neighbors, nothing like the immense tournaments of value described by Messing in which a feast-giver could easily bankrupt himself. The decline of *tezkar* provides for many people in Zege a narrative of the transi-tion from Haile Selassie's time to the present. This narrative expresses a decline in traditional authority, hierarchy, and values, and their replacement by something as yet uncertain. Many people in Zege, particularly but not only elites, associate the resulting decline in funeral feasting with a broader decay of hospitality as the basis for morally legitimate sociality.

This narrative of loss provides the context for the *buda* crises described in the previous chapter: the decline of the feasts that were the received media for the per-petuation of status meant that new status uncertainties were experienced in terms of hospitality and the serving of food itself became dangerous. These days, people say, you do not want to accept food from your neighbors in case they are *buda* (at worst, this could kill you). Serving *t'ella* beer, so Tefera tells me, is considered relatively safe, since it arouses less jealousy. We can understand this narrative as indicative of a broader decoupling of ritual legitimacy from political power. But what has declined is not Orthodox liturgical ritual itself, which remains integral to life in Zege, but the degree of integration between Christian ritual and local political-moral hierarchies.

According to Tefera and to the recollections of *Mergéta* Worqé and *Memhir* Abbi, in Haile Selassie's time any man of any standing at all had to throw a *tez-kar* feast at least once in his life, usually upon the death of his father. If he lacked the resources at the time of death, he might wait years until he had gathered enough to hold a sufficiently splendid feast. Such events could involve the slaugh-ter of fifty cattle or more, and one elder told me of feasts that would serve every one of the several thousand people in Zege. A feast of that size would be referred to as *neguse tezkar*, "the *tezkar* of kings," after the idea that the death of an emperor should be followed by a feast to feed the whole country. This imperial compari-son, which *Mergéta* Worqé makes explicitly, helps to clarify the logic of *tezkar*: the political ruler feeds his dependents, and so shows the benevolence and generosity proper to a powerful man. Or actually, his successor feeds them, and so claims the legitimacy of the one in whose name he hosts the feast. Today it remains vitally important to feed guests at a funeral, but these events are now much more modest, and the expenses are in many cases covered by *iddir* mutual aid groups (see below), which exist for that purpose.

Tezkar entailed the slaughter of cattle: at least one, but as many as possible. What people remember about the *tezkar* of old is their lavishness. Even the most destitute people on the peninsula, Tefera tells me, would be fed from the final morsels of the feast. On a larger scale, when an emperor died, his *tezkar* was supposed to feed the entire country. Tefera, who is the son of a church dignitary, describes *tezkar* as a sort of noblesse oblige, emphasizing how even the scraps of the feast would not go to waste but would be fed to the beggars and other poorest and meekest people of Zege. *Tezkar* meant that one could not legitimately become rich without performing at least one great act of generosity and feeding—basically, it declared that the powerful were subject to the code of hospitality and generosity.

It matters very much that the medium of this generosity is food, because this establishes the accepted medium for morally appropriate hierarchical social relations. Much of this logic remains in place—a moderately successful merchant friend of mine complained to me about the burdens of laying on his daughter's christening feast because of the weight of social expectation—particularly since this man was an outsider and had to work doubly hard to establish himself as a good Zegeña and a father of children.

These funeral feasts, especially in their lavishness, closely resemble similar practices from any number of other societies in which a degree of hierarchy is present (Hayden 2009). The dispersal of vast amounts of surplus wealth in the name of status or glory is a phenomenon often remarked on (Bataille 1991), and funerals seem to be a particularly significant occasion for these events. Maurice Bloch's explanation is that these feasts serve to transform the mortality of powerful individuals into transcendent forms of power—dynasties, lineages, and eventually states (Bloch & Parry 1982, Bloch 2008). To eat in the name of a dead man (it is usually a man) is quite different than accepting hospitality from a living person, because the object of the feast, stripped of his biological qualities, is an identity, potentially stable over time: something like a god (in Orthodox society every memorial feast resonates strongly with the Eucharist). Hence the excessiveness of the feast: it celebrates something that tends toward eternity (see chapter 7, Feuchtwang 2010).

This theoretical generalization gives a useful starting point for thinking about why funeral feasts are important for turning temporal power into something more established and transcendental. However, in the cases described by Bloch (Madagascar) and Feuchtwang (China), funeral feasts contribute to a system in which ancestors have paramount authority and are thought to actively participate in the lives of the living. Here Amhara is quite different. The descent system is cognatic (inheritance can be traced through the mother or father), meaning that it is almost impossible to delineate clear descent groups (Täklä Iyäsus 2014: 30).

Rather than ancestors, the only people who can approach sacred postmortem status are holy people and saints, beatified by their good works, by their extreme acts of devotion and asceticism, and especially by their defense of the faith. Other humans cannot involve themselves in the affairs of the living after they die, but pass on to the next world. This would seem to indicate that, in contrast with Madagascar and many other parts of Eurasia, it is the church and not kinship that decides how the status of the dead can shape and authorize the affairs of the living. However, the importance of *tezkar* feasting shows that powerful families have consistently attempted to legitimize their own status through mortuary and remembrance practices. As this chapter will show, the tension between church remembrance practices and the wishes of families remains a key issue today, although the terms and media of remembrance practice have shifted away from funerary feasting and toward the politics of gravestones.

Zege adds an extra element to the *tezkar* feasting, which I have not seen attested elsewhere: the family may slaughter a sheep upon the grave of the deceased, allowing its blood to fall on the burial earth. Consistent with other interpretations of death, this was explained to me as a way to help the soul away from this world, as a form of atonement. The ensuing communal consumption of the sheep then re-forms community bonds in a manner consistent with the practice for remembering saints (Kaplan 1986: 8). The practice also contains clear analogical links to the salvific power of the blood of Christ. This is understood as further effecting the separation of the soul from this world, and trying to make sure that it is free from sin as it leaves. But any memorial sacrifice in this area is still understood to demonstrate the status of the man who makes it. It demarcates him as having wealth but also as putting that wealth to moral use. Zege's *tezkar* sheep-sacrifice indicates the depth of association between local sacrificial practices as tools for the reproduction of status and mainline Christian ritual. At least as it is understood in Zege, *tezkar* has everything to do with the expiation of sin as well as the competition for status.

Tezkar and related sacrificial practices are marked as morally positive—and, I would suggest, capable of mitigating the sins of the deceased—because they are socially productive. They have their clear counterparts in examples of "bad sacrifice" that invert the principle of generosity. One example would be the sacrifice of the slave described in chapter 4. Another, as told to me by Tefera, is that rich households sometimes, as part of the *tezkar*, slaughtered an ox in their own house, so that the blood ran across the threshold. This was said to enhance their own longevity rather than sustaining the community in helping the soul of the deceased. These "inverted" sacrifices are selfish, and by opposition they declare what a sacrifice ought to be: generous, community-minded, and outwardly connective.

Another key memorial mode, which continues today, is the use of *fukera* (bragging, praise songs) to praise the deceased and sing their accomplishments. *Fukera* is understood to have no religious significance, but to be something that wealthy people can do to enhance their status. *Fukera* is performed by hired specialists, and if done well makes for an entertaining theatrical performance. But it is also, in my experience, often treated with a degree of ironic cynicism from the audience. *Fukera* can be performed during a funeral, before the corpse is buried (or sometimes at weddings and christenings to sing the praises of the families involved). After the most recent funeral performance I witnessed in Zege, a friend commented to me as we were leaving, "That guy was a huge *buda*. The family just hired the *fukera* because he was rich."

This criticism does not seem to be confined to recent events. *Mergéta* Worqé volunteered to Tefera and me that he could remember many examples of men who were slave traders in life hiring people to sing songs of their greatness and generosity. He told us that some people even stole parts from saints' hagiographies and had them presented as their own stories or those of their family.

Fukera is a display for the community but does not leave any lasting mark on the landscape. Likewise, *tezkar* did not require monuments or other lasting physical memorials to the dead. The feasts produced continuity of hierarchy through feeding, which would have lasting effects in the memories of the attendants, but would leave no lasting mark on the landscape. As such, they did not bring powerful men into open conflict with the church's monopoly on the treatment of the dead and the intergenerational continuity of the landscape. After the fall of the Derg, a new fashion for concrete graves would bring quite new and problematic questions of memorialization and legitimacy.

THROWING OUT THE BONES: HUMAN REMAINS AS DUST, AND THE SOUL'S JOURNEY TO HEAVEN

You bury a new corpse by digging up an old one.
—ETHIOPIAN POPULAR SAYING,
RECORDED BY ROGER COWLEY.

Two months or so into fieldwork, my friend Tomas had learned enough about the sort of work I was trying to do that, when an elderly neighbor of ours died, he knew that I would want to attend the funeral. To do so would also be an unequivocally good act on my part; attending funerals is the key marker of social participation and belonging in Amhara Orthodox society. Participation, in turn, and attempting to act like the people around you, not only by conforming to custom but also by engaging in local social networks, were the surest way for me to gain people's approval. This becomes paramount in moments of loss, as people emphasize their remaining social ties ever more strongly, so attending funerals becomes the most significant indicator, for locals, that a person is a member of their group (A. Pankhurst 1992: 188, Kaplan 2003a: 645). Attendance is ensured by *iddir* funerary associations, which I describe in more detail below.

People were gathering in the town center to carry the corpse, shrouded in patterned cloth, to church. There was a noticeable divide in mood: while close family members, especially women, were wailing and dancing around the body, making ostentatious displays of grief, the rest of the crowd was casual, chatting and joking as if this were any ordinary social event—which, in a sense, it was, for I would attend six more funerals in the next three months.

The funeral party arrived at the church, and the priests and monks assembled around the body to begin the mortuary rites (*fithat*). I was called away from the ritual with the nonrelated men to another part of the churchyard to dig the grave. The mood around the new grave was light. There was one shovel, and men were sharing the work according to no particular prescription. When we were about two feet down into the earth, one of the younger men pulled out a bone and asked, "Does this happen in your country?" We had hit upon a previous grave, about twenty years old by my amateur reckoning. His tone was casual, and he nonchalantly tossed the bone away, but the question and his manner of asking indicated that this was not an entirely unremarkable or unproblematic situation. Further bones were simply thrown away like the first as we came to them, including some fragments of skull, until the grave was eventually deep enough to receive its new tenant. I would frequently think back to this moment throughout the rest of my fieldwork as people's attitudes to death and loss became more apparent to me. Their blasé treatment of the human bones now seems to me an instance of a much wider discourse of death and absence. Above all, it indicates that the remains had been deindividuated: whatever there was of a person in them before, it resided there no longer.

The lack of solemnity among the gravediggers is significant. Attendees' behavior is far less important than the fact of their presence. Richard Pankhurst (1990: 195) confirms that it has historically been the case that what counts at funerals is presence. The presence of the living is particularly important in light of the absence of the deceased, and the gravediggers' treatment of the bones they unearthed is a stark demonstration of that absence. In tossing away the bones, the men were behaving in a manner perfectly in line with Ethiopian Orthodox doctrine as expressed to me by the priests who disapproved of concrete graves. They treated the bones, and the site of the earlier grave, as if they were nothing special; or at least, they nearly did. For one man did at least consider it notable and worth asking me what we did in such circumstances in my own country. I have since found out that at least some of my friends feel that, given the choice, they would rather not have someone else buried where their bones lie, and that concrete tombs would be a good way of ensuring this did not happen.

As the funeral drew to a close, the body was brought to the grave and placed inside as the priests continued to chant. The men who dug the grave refilled it, and then placed a ring of rocks, fist- to head-sized, around the grave. Looking around, I thought it was hard to tell which of the nearby rocks marked previous graves and were now disarranged, and which were strewn randomly. Aside from the ring of rocks, no marker was placed on the grave.

Finally, on a signal from one of the priests, the entire congregation sat or squatted for a moment in silence. This, I was told, is called *igzío,* and is the moment that the soul leaves the body, the first step of a journey to heaven that requires seven further ritual services to complete—after three, seven, twelve, twenty, thirty, forty, and eighty days. This was a striking and profound moment, the only point of silence in the whole ceremony, and the only time at which all in attendance acted in unison. My questions at the time revealed that everyone present understood this as the moment of the soul leaving, and found the *igzío* to be a potent marking of this event.

After the funeral the entire party retired to a tent set up in the compound of the bereaved family. This would stand for three days and allow mourners, friends, and well-wishers to gather and pay their respects and express their grief, but most importantly to demonstrate their presence: nonattendance at the funeral tent, unless one is absolutely unable to, will often be taken as a severance of friendship. As with the burial, while close family members, especially women, displayed their grief, much of the atmosphere was jocular. Men chatted and played cards, respectful but not overly somber. What mattered was that they were there.

The term for mortuary rites, *fit'hat,* is cognate with the Amharic *fetta,* to release (A. Pankhurst 1992: 191), and is understood as such by people in Zege: in the sense both of releasing the deceased from her sins and of releasing the soul from this world and from its bodily confines (Merawi 2005). The rite separates bodily things, which are tangible but will decompose, from spirit, which is permanent but elsewhere. For each *fithat* service the family of the deceased must make a payment to the clergy—in Zege, usually an amount of *injera* bread or *t'ella* beer, specified according to the occasion, which accounts for a vital part of the livelihood of the clergy. (According to *Mislené* Fantahun, the *Mes'hafe Ginzet* [Book of Remembrance] stipulates three jugs of *t'ella* and thirty *injera* to the church *mahber* association on day thirty, with one jug of *t'ella* and ten *injera* to those who perform the memorial liturgy; on day forty, it is four jugs of *t'ella* and forty *injera* to the *mahber,* and again one and ten to the liturgists.) Here is also where the much-reduced *tezkar* feast comes in, associated with the fortieth-day *fithat.* The exchange of food and drink for funeral services makes remembrance a public, shared affair. It connects the family's grief and remembrance with the process of stripping the soul of its burdens and assisting it to heaven, and makes salvation a shared enterprise.

TECHNOLOGIES OF REMEMBRANCE AND
GRAVEYARD POLITICS

Every funeral I attended in Zege ended with the deceased being buried in a grave marked only by a ring of stones. All baptized people are buried in the church-yard, although there is no single area designated for graves, and priests tell me that unbaptized children are buried just outside the church walls. The markers used are volcanic rocks from a volcanic lake, and so graves built in this manner soon become indistinguishable from surrounding areas. The stones are no more than twenty centimeters in diameter, and the churchyards see rapid vegetation growth every year in the rainy season. The result is that graves, which already lack identify-ing markers of the occupant's identity, merge quite quickly into their surroundings.

While I was surveying graves in the Ura Kidane Mihret churchyard, Abebe pointed out to me the rough area where his young mother had been buried some five years before. He had no idea of the exact location. It was a poignant moment, as we had discussed his mother several times in the previous years. He told me he would have liked to see the grave, although I must have partially influenced this by asking in depth about burial practices, and taking him with me to catalogue the graves.

My main reason for examining the churchyards was the presence, in each of the church-monasteries of Zege, of a significant number of concrete graves. These took the form of raised oblong blocks, with the deceased's name, birth date, and death date scratched in by hand while the concrete was still wet. They often also had some kind of metal cross embedded at the head. I found thirty of these graves in the yard of Fure Maryam, the nearest church to the local market town, a similar number in Ura Kidane Mihret in Zege proper, and ascertained that there were also several concrete graves as far as the Mehal Zege monasteries on the tip of the peninsula. Most of these graves were constructed between 1991 and 2006 by the European calendar, from the downfall of Communism until a local church edict was passed forbidding any further construction.

There are obvious practical grounds for outlawing concrete graves. Churchyard space is limited and the graves would quickly choke the church lands if allowed to proliferate. According to some interlocutors in Afaf, the problem came to a head when people began trying to stake out plots for graves in advance, causing wide-spread conflict, and the situation became unmanageable. But there is a separate discourse against the graves. As Abebe explained to me, the priests of Ura Kidane Mihret had turned against concrete graves "so that it does not become modern" *(zemenawi indayhon)*. The traditional quality of the churches—their similarity to their past selves—is a key part of their status. As a priest explained to me in Mehal Zege, the most remote part of the peninsula, concrete graves are "what they do in town. It is not done here." This was an appeal to propriety, and to a pervasive local understanding that in Zege the traditional and the holy are isomorphic. Zege has retained its holy status, and the income that derives from tourism and pilgrimage, by preserving its church traditions.

Finally, his companion, an older priest who had been listening to us, made reference to the Bible, "Dust you are, and to dust you will return" (Genesis 3:19), for a theological explanation of the impropriety of concrete graves. Bodily dissolution, not physical permanence, was the proper end of a Christian life. Pankhurst and Aspen (2005: 873) attest that this is generally true of Christian Ethiopia: "According to an old Christian custom, the graves are deprived of inscriptions or other signs identifying the defuntes. In the case of important persons, including emperors and high ecclesiastics, the identity of remains is usually preserved by the local tradition only. . . . Devout Christians, both nobles and commoners, were completely 'depersonified' in their corporal death (this being 'balanced' by the hope for eternal life of the soul)."

Mergéta Worqé provides key insight on the value of the body and burial site after death. As well as saying that concrete graves contradict the *Mes'hafe Ginzet*, the Book of Remembrance, he told me that bodies were to be buried wrapped in a rough palm mat with its sharp edges toward the corpse; a symbol of penitence and of the fact that the body does not travel with the soul after death. In addition, it was not Orthodox for families to mark out burial spaces for their members, as this would emphasize the remains. However, there was strong demand for family members to be buried together, and this stricture was usually relaxed.

There are examples in Ethiopia of graves and human remains given high public importance. One is the history of saints' relics (Kaplan 1986), which I discuss below, and another is the practice of building mausoleums or elaborate tombs for emperors and for wealthy and famous people, which is most noticeable in Addis Ababa. Haile Selassie has a magnificent tomb within his eponymous cathedral in Addis, and the graveyard contains monuments for the resting places of a number of major figures from twentieth-century Ethiopia, including the singer Tilahun Gessesse and the former prime minister Meles Zenawi. Emperor Menilek has his own grand mausoleum under Bata Maryam monastery in Addis. The practice of building mausolea for emperors dates to the 1600s but substantial grave building seems to have been restricted to emperors and some holy people (Pankhurst & Aspen 2005: 873). In the largest church of Bahir Dar, near Zege, there are marble statues and tombs for some of revered monks who were associated with the church. As a friend in Bahir Dar told me, "only rich people and heroes" receive such monuments in the key churches, highlighting the inequality among the dead that material monuments can produce. What is more, many people I have spoken to in both Addis and Bahir Dar have been highly critical of these inequalities in burial practice. The priests in Zege certainly considered tomb-building a distinctly urban, and hence suspect, practice.

As far as I have been able to establish by counting graves and recording the dates inscribed on them, concrete graves proliferated in all seven churches in Zege after the fall of the Derg in 1991, although there are occasional examples extant from the late Haile Selassie era. From this time until the outlawing of concrete graves in 2006, I estimate that one-fifth to one-seventh of the people who died in Zege were buried in such graves. This demonstrates a widespread desire for these kinds of graves as opposed to the standard unmarked ring of rocks. I have been told by Abebe and by priests that some people now mark graves by planting a tree, but it was difficult to find many examples of such trees. That they thought of this detail, however, does indicate an assumption that people desire some kind of indicator of the place in which the remains of the deceased lie. As my friend Addisu put it, "you know how we carry photographs of each other? Well it's just like that, so you have something to remember with, if you have the money."

A gravestone points to the actual remains of the deceased. It declares that they have some significant physical remnant in the environment. Because it bears the occupant's name, it states that something of the unique identity of that person persists in their bodily remains. Yet the priest's citation, "Dust thou art, and unto dust shalt thou return," describes a disavowal of human remains as a legitimate medium of proximity. The standard practice of unmarked graves enacts and reinforces this position, as graves, and hence the remains they contain, quickly devolve into indistinction. Where *tezkar* used to provide a form of intergenerational transmission of status—a kind of living memorialization mediated by food to the bodies of the living—the concrete grave operates in a whole different register of physical-symbolic continuity, external to the circles of food and feeding that constitute legitimate hospitality and power, and so external to the cycles of transmission of life. Gravestones introduce massive nonorganic elements into the life of remembrance, and so completely change the temporality of life and death—if nothing else, by hanging around and blocking up the graveyard.

The durability and individuation of gravestones contrast with *tezkar* as a mode of transmitting status. At the same time, it sits uneasily with the more properly religious side of funeral ritual, which focuses on effecting the separation of body and soul and the denaturing of the body so as to assist the soul on its journey to heaven. When a person dies, a family member will block all orifices of the corpse with material, tie the big toes together, and wrap the body in fine white cloth (Kaplan 2003a: 645). Stopping up the body effects a closure analogous to the bodily restrictions surrounding the Eucharist (Hannig 2013); it is only in death that the separation of spirit from the world of organic continuity can be achieved. The burial is held as soon as possible after death, and friends who asked me about English funeral practice were shocked to hear that we might preserve the body for a week or more before burial, and even leave it open for viewings by the mourners. As the next section shows, funeral practice aims at a complete denaturing of the remains of the body, in the name of establishing proper separations between the worlds of the living and the dead.

As important as the treatment of the deceased is the way that the living anticipate their own deaths and funerals as part of their imagination of a fulfilled life. Both aspects are served in important ways by funerary associations. In Zege as elsewhere in Amhara the institution of *iddir* funerary associations is critical to the arrangement of proper funerals (Pankhurst and Damen 2000, Solomon 2010). Members make a monthly contribution to the pot, which is used to pay for funerary expenses incurred by any member. Just as important, *iddir* members attend the funerals of their fellows. *Iddir* ensures that priests are paid, food is served to mourners, and mourners will attend, the crucial aspects of any funeral. Tomas explained to me that to be too poor to be a member of an *iddir* would be one of the worst things imaginable, since it would mean that nobody would attend your funeral. It would also mean that priests would perform only minimal rites, but he made it clear that it was people's attendance that mattered.

To have an unattended funeral is to live a life unrecognized and unsocialized. It means you have established no meaningful connections and none of the status or respect that would compel people to attend and commemorate you. What people seek in their own funerals, and what the *iddir* ensures, is not just that their soul will be assisted to heaven, but that they will be recognized as having lived as part of the community. Often, indeed, people emphasize this recognition more than their salvation.

The *iddir* pays for food to serve to guests at the tent, which ensures that they will come, and establishes the deceased as host and therefore a person of honor and a feeder of others. Since *iddir* membership is inexpensive, this ensures that most people can be mourned with enough hospitality to establish basic respectability. Alula Pankhurst and Solomon Dejene present *iddir* as having originally been a response among Gurage migrants to urbanization—a form of solidarity to replace kinship ties in situations of alienation. Informants in Zege now regard *iddir* as an institution of perennial importance and of social continuity, in the face not of urban diffusion but of the dissolution of hierarchies based on *tezkar*. *Iddir* organizations participate to some extent in the logic of *tezkar*, which says that funeral recognition is the basis of good social life, and that feeding mourners is the proper way to ensure this recognition. *Iddir* societies make at least a portion of this recognition—and, thus, a foundational level of dignity—available to all but the poorest and most marginal. In this it reflects a key dynamic of the functioning of hospitality ideology: there may be bigger hosts and smaller hosts, but so long as most people can be a host in their own domain, they are able to experience their place in society as nonhumiliating (see chapter 7).

SAINTHOOD, ANCESTRY, AND THE REMAINS OF
THE PAST

We have identified two foci of memorial mediation: that of hosting and feeding, and that of the treatment of remains. Each plays a part in the work of long-term habitation and legitimacy, especially in competing attempts to establish inter-generational status. To a large degree, these are questions of ancestry, which for a number of reasons play out in quite distinct fashion in Orthodox Ethiopia. A major reason for this is the role of saints and other powerful figures as exemplary forebears (Bandak 2015). I have said that most exceptions to the disregard for human remains are in cases of heroism, especially emperors and holy men. Such figures can become key connectors to the past, and Kaplan (1986: 2–5) recounts several stories from hagiographies of a saint's bones being fought over by communities seeking the status and legitimacy those remains would confer.

In many parts of Africa, the burial places of ancestors' bones are central to how social collectives establish claims to autochthony and to a sense of continuous inhabitation of the land over successive generations (Bloch 1971, Cole 2001, Fontein 2011). Bones here stand metonymically for all that is most permanent in the person and, by extension, the lineage. They are physical remnants of the past that people can relate to and venerate, and that indicate how the living can expect to one day be absorbed into a wider whole after their death.

In Orthodox Amhara, by contrast, not only is there no ancestor veneration; there are no lineages. There is no sense that the ghosts of the dead return to haunt the living—the work of *fithat,* if successful, makes sure of that. Descent is cognatic, reckoned through the father and the mother, which prevents the emergence of distinct lineage groups, meaning that no particular group of people has exclusive claim to any one forebear (Hoben 1973). And while descent is crucial for the transmission of land and property rights, the Orthodox Church performs many of the functions that elsewhere would be performed by descent groups: establishing social continuity beyond the lifespan of the individual, and denoting legitimate occupation of the land. For the people of Zege, it is the antiquity and continuity of their churches—as physical structures, and not just as institutions—that make their land special and grant them their sacred right to reside there. According to Kaplan, saints' bones have at various times in Ethiopia served similar purposes as ancestors' bones have elsewhere, of establishing autochthony and legitimacy. Saints, then, sometimes overcome the general tradition of depersonalizing the remains of the dead. However, Kaplan (1986: 6–7) makes clear that the locus of devotional practice was not parts of the saint's body—unlike in Europe, these were never circulated—but at the burial place of his or her remains and, by extension, in the monastery that housed them.

In Zege, at least, it is more often in church buildings themselves that memory is materialized. The ultimate indexes of belonging for inhabitants are the monasteries, especially the first two to be founded, those of Mehal Zege Giyorgis and Betre Maryam. When I asked priests in Mehal Zege what one could do if one wanted to be commemorated, they responded that one could arrange (including payment) for monks to recite prayers in one's name and, by building a temporary shelter in the churchyard, ensure that they would use it for your commemorative prayer. They then took me to the main external gate of the monastery, a large and sturdy structure built from local stone. Built into the gate above the entrance is a small cell where prayers for the dead can take place in seclusion. They told me that an abbot had had this gate built as his memorial gift to the monastery, and was now buried by the entrance. His bones were not treated as unimportant, but they were subsumed into the church, and they were not marked by his written name or his image.

A list of the names of deceased persons is also kept in the church and must be present when the Eucharist is performed for the purposes of remembrance (Aymro & Motovu 1970: 53). Like the Bede-roll in pre-Reformation England, this produces an important sense of permanence in the parish community (Duffy 1992: 334)—and also establishes the church building itself as the legitimate locus of memory. There are also many cases of wealthy patrons having their likeness painted into church murals. They are often seen giving offerings to Mary and followed, in the earlier paintings, by their slaves. In some churches outside Zege men in modern suits have been included in the paintings, although this is no longer allowed on the peninsula itself due to the churches' historic status. With the exception of the list of the parish dead, the common theme is that to be commemorated individually in the traditional idiom requires either wealth or a very high religious status.

This prerogative is illustrated by the one concrete grave I found that had been built after they were forbidden. This was the finest grave I have seen, made of stone, with birth and death dates neatly inscribed and displaying, uniquely, a small painted portrait of the deceased. This woman had become a nun a year or so before her death, and one of her sons had moved to Texas and become quite rich, and so had paid for her grave to be built. Still, it was quite discreetly placed in an unobtrusive corner of the churchyard, since it was technically illegal. Abebe explained that the son must have paid quite a significant amount to the church in order to persuade them to flout the law, which might nonetheless have been unacceptable had the woman not been a respected nun.

The Orthodox Church is the institutional locus of continuity between past and present, much more than any kinship-based form of ancestry. But only certain kinds of memorial are possible within this institutional framework, and the strong overall trend is to impersonal graves. The use of concrete graves in Zege in the 1990s and early 2000s was an attempt to broaden the possibilities of material memorialization of distinct individuals, but one that raised serious practical and religious questions about making permanent additions to the church landscape.

CONCLUSION: MEMORY, MEDIATION, HISTORY

Descendants of the nobility remember *tezkar* as an epitome of moral relationships and of a good society, but many others agree. Funeral feasts present a potent ideological account of power, not as domination but as protection and generosity. From the perspective of early-twenty-first-century Zege, they stand for a past in which power and wealth were understood to serve a moral hierarchy rather than being an end in themselves—or at least could be convincingly presented as if they did. *Tezkar* stands, retrospectively, for what Graeber (2012) calls a human economy: one in which the purpose of wealth is understood to be the rearrangement of relationships between people. The accrual of wealth could not be an end in itself, or at least it could not appear to be so, and therefore the only way to keep one's property was to destroy or redistribute it. Like any other historically oriented memory, this narrative of *tezkar* and the old morality of Zege coexists with counterstories about the rich trying to appropriate sacrificial power and church practice for their own ends.

This provides a useful point for thinking about the relationship between Christianity and culture (Chua 2011). Was the *tezkar* feast a Christian event? It was performed by Christians, with the assistance of churchmen, but it was separate to the burial in the churchyard, and its recession does not seem to have altered people's sense of being Christians as the loss of the liturgy would. Because Orthodoxy is built around the calendar, and because so much that is basic to life happens either in church or in relation to it, many practices and ethical positionings exist within the aegis of Christianity that are nonetheless not integral to Christianity. Serving coffee to one's neighbors, for example, is central to people's ideas of good behavior, but while this can be understood in a Christian framework, it is not necessarily so. Muslims observe much the same practices of neighborliness.

But *tezkar* participated in a number of idioms that tied it to a Christian framework. The slaughter of cattle ties *tezkar* to the feasts of Christmas and Easter and to a dynamic, which I discuss in the next chapter, of feasting for God. To do so at a funeral redoubles the religious associations, not just because it necessarily involves the clergy, but because it means that the feast is being carried out for nonliving beings. There are also practices local to Zege of spilling an animal's blood for the penance of the departed soul, often as part of the *tezkar* feast. Those practices that concern the salvation of the soul of the departed and those that arrange relationships among the living are closely related.

Political circumstances have changed, and while the church-associated dignitaries—the contemporary *mislené* and *liqered*—still command respect, they have much less control over resources or labor. Since the land reforms of the 1970s, land is apportioned by the governmental bureaucracy, and as of the last decade disputes and disturbances in Zege are the province of the police and the government courts, and many people lament the decline of hospitality as the primary mode of arranging human relationships. In the past decade the market town of Afaf gained a government school and then electricity, while the monasteries of the peninsula have become significant attractions for tourists and pilgrims, creating employment opportunities for young men with a command of English. Education holds the key to advancement, and the churches' museums draw as much attention as their altars. And yet ritual remains central to the life of Zege, to people's ethics and their experiences of their bodies and their environment. Zege's environment is still a ritual environment, and is in some ways more strongly effected by the presence of churches than it was in the past.

We can learn much about this transition from looking at the media of remembrance. Gravestones do not establish continuity in the way that funeral feasts do, and each practice has its own symbolic associations that decide its legitimacy or otherwise. Feasts are, at least retrospectively, associated with a range of morally potent sacrificial practices and the asymmetric ethics of care and hospitality. Concrete graves are associated with construction, with an external kind of production and signification that does not sit well with the narrative of Zege as a holy, set-apart place.

The media of remembrance, once established as legitimate, are always in some sense up for grabs, and subject to attempts at appropriation. *Tezkar* and funeral practices are effective means to arrange authoritative relations among people, with reference to external power. They achieve this arrangement through the slaughtering of animals, the giving of food and drink, the correct treatment of bodies, the construction of buildings or monuments, and the use of words. Each of these techniques is a tool of mediation that can be reappropriated or repurposed. This makes it quite difficult to divide mediatory practices into those that are authentically Christian and those that are not; it is also what gives Christianity in Zege, or anywhere, its sense of belonging to a place. But the negation of human remains achieved through Orthodox ritual sets limits on this localization and attempts to maintain the transcendental or universal aspects of Christianity. It is only by looking at the material means of commemoration that we can understand how these two processes can coexist.

Echoes of the Host

The narrative of the decline of hospitality recurs throughout this book, as it did in my conversations with Orthodox Christians in Zege. The fact that changes in hospitality practice have become an idiom for general social decline reflects two key points. One is the ethical importance attached to feeding and eating together as the primary act that allows us to share our existence with others. The second is the religious significance, by analogy with the Eucharist, of any act of hosting. These two points are not unrelated; each speaks to a basic conception of feeding as the sharing of life. Both hospitality and the Eucharist entail hierarchical relations between feeder and fed, but the element of commensality means that there is always a sharing of existence and not simply a relation of command.

I would like to sketch how we might understand everyday acts of feeding and hospitality in relation to the Eucharistic feast. While the Eucharist itself is closely restricted, I will show that a series of practices serve as "echoes"—smaller versions of the same pattern, which allow for everyday relationship-making among people and in the names of saints. My first example is the feast most closely associated with the Eucharist.

Easter Sunday 2009, we rose at dawn to eat meat. We had had none for fifty-four days and were about to make up for it. We began in the home of my hosts, Thomas and Haregwa, with chicken that Haregwa and her servant, Kassaye, had been cooking through the night. Then Thomas and I killed a sheep and passed some of the meat to Haregwa to fry up quickly for us, eating small chunks of liver and rump meat cut straight from the corpse while we waited. We washed it down with a little beer and then Thomas and I went our separate ways. We each had a lot of houses to visit and to receive food, and if we missed any we risked offending our hosts. I was still in the position, common to ethnographers, of slightly odd, lingering, honored guest, and plenty of people were waiting to see if I would fulfill my obligations to honor my hosts by receiving their food and drink. The women would stay in the house and serve meat and beer to the steady stream of people who would visit in their turn.

My first engagement was with Abebe's aunt. This was important because Abebe had been helping me conduct interviews for some time and both he and his aunt wanted to establish a properly respectful relationship—that is, one that was not purely commercial, and that involved a degree of autonomy and dignity on both sides. Hosting me at Easter would be a great way to do this, except that they had almost no money and I had quite a lot. Abebe's father wasn't around much at the time, and his mother had died some years before. His aunt had just moved into a rather bare and run-down place, and they were worried that it didn't look very impressive. So they borrowed a TV from neighbors and played some music videos to liven things up as they served me food. There were only a couple of strips of gristly meat, but with enough thin sauce you could make it look like more. I ate, and as we chatted Abebe's aunt brought me a glass of *araqí*, very strong and very cheap liquor, which she pressed on me, followed by several refills. My field notes say this was 8:30 AM. I left a while later for a sleep, to recover before I made any more visits, and in no way could I say that my host had skimped or held back on me.

Excess is a theme of Easter and of hospitality in general, as we will see. It is part of the strange yet semiuniversal power play of hospitality, in which we dominate one another with a generosity that unites and differentiates us at the same time. Relationships are established not as equal but as alternating, spatiotemporally circumscribed periods of dominance and dependence, all in an atmosphere of utmost conviviality (Pitt-Rivers 1977, Stewart 1991: 48). Within Abebe's aunt's house she was a sovereign and would feast me as a queen feasts her subjects, and while that same relationship would not persist outside the bounds of her house, something had been altered, and a certain honor, dignity, and perhaps sense of obligation on my part had been established. I was a much wealthier person who was employing her nephew, but her act of hospitality had helped to offset that asymmetry, at least a little.

Endalew, a young student, and his friends once asked me what I thought was most distinctive about Zege. I had mentioned the forest, and they replied yes, but most of all it was hospitality and visiting. In Zege you should feed guests, and visit neighbors. This goes together with the number of complaints I have heard that hospitality and visiting were under threat due to fear of poisoning and poverty. This is particularly concerning because of the religious and moral implications of eating together: hospitality is a technique for drawing saints and other mediators into interpersonal relations.

A simple example would be Ginbot Lideta, the celebration of Mary's birthday. It is local tradition that groups of family and neighbors get together to eat, and to promise what contribution they will make to the food in a year's time. Everyone contributes, and everyone indicates the desire to be reunited in a year. The event is inclusive; in the morning I saw priests together with their deacons and church students eating a rare meal of *injera* with butter. After that I joined Haregwa and Thomas with our neighbors to eat corn and drink *t'ella* and coffee. Promises for contributions for next year ranged from a chicken or a box of wine to fifty birr, ten *injera*, or a bag of onions. The housemaid, Kassaye, also promised a bottle of wine, marking her as a cocontributor with her employers. This is an important suspension of hierarchy, and seems to mark the equality of all when it comes to the love of Mary. And here is the point: feeding one another, along with promising to keep doing so in the future, is done for and in the name of the Virgin. Which is to say, you do not just pray to Mary; you feed others in her name and under her protection. If we make one another, in a physical and substantial sense, through relational acts of eating and feeding (Strathern 2012), then in Zege eating and feeding also constitute Mary as a part of these relations.

STRANGERS AND GUESTS

My experience with Abebe's aunt is a reminder that ethnographers usually work with people who have already developed techniques for dealing with strangers. Most often, the feeder-fed relationship is the initial template into which outsiders can be incorporated. Amharic renders both the English *stranger* and *guest* by a single word, *ingida*; a stranger was one who had to be hosted. In Ethiopia before the twentieth century, taverns were unheard of. An old story has it that when the first hotel in the country, the Taitu, was built in 1898, guests came to eat the food and use the facilities and were then stunned to be presented with a bill (Binns n.d.). The very notion of a guest paying for a meal seemed faintly obscene, a violation of the basic principles of honor.

These days the commercial hospitality industry is familiar enough, and the first call of a newcomer in a village like Afaf, who does not have other business, is likely to be one of the taverns along the two main streets. Every traveler needs food and drink, and these spaces also serve as grounds for figuring out who newcomers are, as the houses of hosts did in the past. However, unlike private houses, here food is served to which not every person present is really entitled. If a stranger buys a meal, it would be poor form for everyone in the bar to descend on them and eat it. After all, they have paid a set price for a set amount of food.

In any other situation there would be hierarchy—men eating before women and children—but everyone present could expect to eat. And yet cherished norms hold that one should never eat alone, and as a result complex and implicit codes of behavior arise around tavern food. If one has food, it is ethically proper to say to anyone present, *innibla* (let's eat). It is also prudent, because one never knows if a *buda* will see your food and make you sick. When I lived in Thomas's tavern he would often bring me food in my bedroom rather than the guest area, so as to protect me from dangerous glances. My personal experience was that when someone said *innibla* to me, they would often follow by saying, "This is our culture."

Sometimes if someone says *innibla* to you in a tavern, you should refuse. I noticed that only close friends and boys much younger than me would accept my invitations, for example. Anyone else would refuse, I am fairly sure because I belonged permanently in the category of guest, and should therefore have been an accepter of food except from people much junior to me. Additionally, if someone from elsewhere sits down to what is obviously his lunch, you should politely reject his offer. But if an older man were to offer you food, you might politely take a bite or, if he were obviously making a display of providing a communal meal, join him and eat. But in every case, the offer must be made. As Pitt-Rivers (1977) notes, it is often the very pretense of generosity, commensality, or equality that makes hospitality function, even though it is decidedly not egalitarian. There is a sort of mutual contract that host and guest will play along with their roles.

The case of the tavern offers an interesting test of how hospitality logics adapt to new situations. But it also describes my own entry into the field and my positioning throughout my work, in which I usually ate in a tavern once or twice a day. The first day I arrived in Afaf, I was taken to Thomas's tavern, where, over food, I slowly asked about the possibility of finding a place to live and doing field research in Zege. Eating food—even food I had bought—offered the first chance of finding commonality from which we could try to figure out relationships, which for people in Zege often involved working out whether my presence was likely to advantage or inconvenience them, or at least prove diverting. (The second medium that would ease my integration was playing and watching football.)

An outsider who enters a community such as Zege will be judged largely by whether they eat with people, visit their neighbors' houses, and attend their funerals. These acts of copresence are the basis of social life at the local level. While eating at Thomas's daughter's christening feast, my friend Antihun said to me, "If you eat alone, you die alone, isn't that right?" I asked if that meant that if we ate together we would die together, and he replied, "No, but I'll come to your funeral." To be alone is always bad, and much of village life revolves around making sure to show others that you are present to them, in life and in death. Eating together is, as Antihun describes it, the strongest form of copresence.

There are also those strangers with whom nearness is denied, and to whom the rules of hospitality therefore do not apply—not every outsider is a guest, whatever the language might tell you. The classic example is that of slaves; recall Tefera's story of how masters would deny meat to their slaves even while eating the meals that they served. This appears to be an inherently problematic situation, and one that people would prefer to gloss over. A comparable situation exists today in the case of servants, who are almost always from outside the community. Every tavern has at least one woman employed, and sometimes a few boys, who arrive in arrangements of quasi-fostering. The solution for such people—outsiders who are not guests—is almost always to incorporate them structurally as very junior members of the family. These are the people who frequently get omitted from accounts of hospitality: the ones who actually cook and serve the food (whom we might call disappearing mediators). While you should not accept food from a person junior to you, this does not apply to the woman or child who actually serves you the meal, who is understood to represent the master of the house. This is consistent with the logic of the patriarchal household described in the classic literature on Imperial-era Amhara society (Hoben 1973, Reminick 1974).

THE EUCHARISTIC HOST

There is, as numerous commentators have noticed, a distinctively sacral or cosmic element to hospitality (Hocart 2004: 78, Candea & da Col 2012). As we will see, both hospitality and ritual involve complex relationships of reciprocal honoring (guest honors host, host honors guest) whose end result is not equality but hierarchy. Likewise, a common thread of eating together in the name of a sacred other links overt acts of ritual to more mundane commensality.

The relationship between hospitality and sacrifice is especially explicit in the Eucharist as practiced by those Christianities that, like Ethiopian Orthodoxy, still insist that the rite effects the complete transubstantiation of bread and wine into God. The Ethiopian Orthodox Church states that the Eucharist is not just a commemoration of Christ's sacrifice, but a full repetition of it (Paulos 1988: 171). As *Abba* S'om, the priest widely recognized as the local expert on exegesis, explained to me, at the Last Supper Christ said, "This *is* my flesh"; he did not say that it was a *sign (millikit)* of his flesh. He drew the comparison between the burning of the Mesqel cross (see chapter 2), which was a *sign,* and the actual transformation of the bread and wine.

The English term *host,* referring to the Eucharistic bread, comes form the Latin *hostia,* "sacrificial victim." The Amharic *qurban,* "Eucharist," derives from an Arabic term also meaning sacrificial offering and implying closeness (Amh. *qirb,* Kaplan 2003b: 15, see Heo 2015: 58), and the Greek *anaphora,* describing the Eucharistic prayers, also means offering. The Eucharist begins as an offering to God, and turns into the reception of God. It is offered with ritual prayers, transformed and sanctified, returned, and then consumed. And this is the key point of any sacrificial ritual: we consume the very same thing that we offer, although transformed. It is worth dwelling on this point.

Consuming the gifts that one has given is not so unusual at any kind of feast. As Marsland (2015) notes, for example, in Nyakyusa, one of the problems with feastings is that people bring contributions, but actually eat and drink far more than they bring. Contemporary Western middle-class practices of bringing a bottle of wine to a dinner party are not so different. As with the sacrifice, we consume what we gave, and much more besides. For Stephan Feuchtwang (2010), the very excessiveness of the return indicates that we are communing with a God. It is a special quality of the Eucharist that, however much is consumed, there is always more (Simmel 1997). The Eucharist can be performed at any place and time where a church and priests are present, and so enacts the universal omnipresence of God. This surpassing, overabundant quality of the Eucharist is mirrored, I would suggest, in the Easter feasting that I have described, which also draws directly on the Resurrection of Christ.

Feuchtwang's analysis of ritual as "excessive hospitality" or communicative excess hinges on a special reversal that takes place in the process of offering and return: the invitation of the guest to be host. In performing the offering (oblation, *qurban*) we invite a being that is immeasurably strange and external to us. The "sleight-of-ritual" (Rappaport 1999: 108) reverses the roles and turns the worshipers into guests receiving the newly sanctified (and therefore immeasurably greater) meal. The performers enact both invitation and response. But ritual is not the same as hospitality: "the performance mimics but also makes itself different from the ritual of hospitality by markers such as the camphor flame" (Feuchtwang 2010: 60). Ritual is not just a communication but "a performance of invitation, communication, and seeing off. It is the marking out of an inside, which an outside of greater power, authority, and scale is invited to enter into, respond within, and depart from. The entrance is not just a crossing of the threshold, but an entering into the host position" (2010: 70). This reversal and displacement are a key difference between ritual and everyday hospitality.

Innumerable markers serve to differentiate the Eucharist from everyday hospitality. The practice of communion—of enabling direct physical contact between humans and God—is therefore not just a matter of taking something distant and bringing it close. It requires first the alienation or setting apart of what is familiar. The rite can only be performed by priests and deacons after years of special training, and every piece of equipment (for which there is an extensive formal list)[1] must be specially consecrated. The communion bread and wine, once consecrated, can be handled only by priests. Eucharistic bread is made from wheat or sorghum rather than the staple *t'eff*, and the wine is made from unfermented dried grapes never used outside church (Fritsch 2011: 276). Prior to the liturgy the priests prepare the Communion bread and mark each piece with the imprint of thirteen crosses in commemoration of the last supper, and then the ceremony and prayer of the Anaphora effect the miraculous transformation of the Host. The celebrant priest washes his hands twice and announces that he is free of the sin of anyone who takes the Communion in an unworthy state; once his hands are washed, he touches only the bread and the chalice. The priest gives pieces of bread to the communicants, one at a time, and a deacon serves them wine from a ladle. After the Communion, deacons dispense holy water for communicants to ensure nothing of the host remains in their mouths, and for anyone else in the congregation to take. The service finishes with celebratory prayers and, on nonfasting days, singing and dancing.

As for the people receiving Communion, they must have abstained from all food and water for at least eighteen hours beforehand,[2] and from sexual activity for longer. Communicants must have no open wounds, no illnesses or runny noses; a fly entering your mouth renders you ineligible. Menstruating and postpartum women cannot even enter the church, and it is expected that people who have begun puberty but not married will also not take the rite.

The irony of the Eucharist as practiced in most parts of Ethiopia is that, while it is the sacramental core of the religion, most people for most of their lives do not partake in it. This appears more to be a matter of custom than church edict. Numerous priests in Addis Ababa have explained to me that any adult Christian has only to undergo confession before taking the sacrament. To most in Zege this idea is horrifying, however, and it is standard for men and women to stop taking communion on reaching puberty, and only consider recommencing in old age, often after a spouse dies. But the extreme proscription of the Eucharist also coexists with a number of equally embodied practices by which the general Christian population can maintain their religious engagement.

First among these is fasting. We have seen how fasting is an especially important lynchpin for those whose work duties or fears of physical impurity keep them from going to church. Fasting is a portable discipline that affords people, especially women, a degree of control over their religious engagement that can circumvent other authorities and restrictions (Bynum 1987). The same goes for young men whose sexual lifestyles and drinking habits are most at odds with Christian ideals, many of whom are extremely diligent keepers of the fasts. As one young man described to me, this gives him a way of always feeling in touch with his faith, and feeling that there is hope for him no matter what.

I would suggest that there is a model or diagram (Bialecki 2017) of Orthodox practice that allows for participation at different scales or levels of engagement. Not everyone takes the Eucharist, but more or less everyone takes part in the Lenten fast and Easter feast, and the one can be understood as an echo of the other: it repeats key formal aspects in indexical or iconic fashion, but is understood to have diminished (and hence more accessible) potency.

The Christian Eucharist is an explicit echo of the Last Supper, and intimately tied with the Easter passion from Crucifixion and Resurrection. The passage from fast to feast, described in this and the last chapter, takes very similar form to the practice of the Eucharist, which also requires a progression from fasting to celebratory consumption. The plenitude of the Eucharistic feast—ever-present and all-encompassing—resonates with the excess of Easter hosting, whether with meat or alcohol. In both cases, powerful sensory effects are produced by a period of abstinence followed by a sudden overabundance. This iterative movement from fast to feast and from suffering to joy is one of the core rhythms of Ethiopian Orthodox life, as we saw in the last chapter. It is a means by which people participate in life at a scale beyond their immediate bodily surroundings.

Other important echoes of the Eucharist exist in the form of holy water (s'ebel) and the dark Sabbath bread consumed after church services. These have to a large extent become the popular equivalent of the Eucharistic bread and wine (Lee, pers. comm.), and form perhaps the most commonly used media of popular engagement with divine power. Ethiopian Orthodox holy water has been covered extensively in other studies (Hermann 2010, 2012, Malara 2017) and has become famous for the healing sites that exist around the country and attract large numbers of patients suffering from HIV/AIDS, demonic affliction, and any number of other maladies. At these sites, taking holy water carries purity rules similar to those of the Eucharist, although less extreme. It has been described as having "God's power on it" (Malara 2017) or as indexing the water that issued from Christ's wounds while on the cross (this is especially so of the holy water given out at the Eucharist). So while not exactly the blood of Christ, holy water is a material vehicle of God's blessing that is intimately—iconically and indexically—connected with the Crucifixion and Christ's body.

Malara notes that holy water has another key property, however: it is transportable. On saints' days in Zege, worshipers do not just receive splashes of holy water on their bodies; they bring bottles and jerry cans, and carry the water back to friends and relatives who cannot make it, especially those who are sick in bed. I have been gently teased by friends for not thinking to do so when I have visited holy water sites. This transportability and capacity for being shared are crucial to the ethico-spiritual potency of holy water (cf. Keane 2014). It does not just entail an encounter between the individual, priests, and God, but a much more dispersed interpersonal sharing of blessing, one absolutely vital for showing kindness and care to others.

I think I am justified in describing holy water as an echo of the Eucharist (though this may not be the only way to conceive it). At least, it reiterates the pattern of progression from solemnity to exuberance that, I am arguing, continually reenacts and repeats the narrative of the salvation of the world in multiple, nested microcosms. But as Malara's work shows, this does not mean that each "echo" is an identical copy. The different material and symbolic properties of holy water, the Host, the fast, and the Easter feast offer different affordances, and are available to different people at different times.

Put in other words, the "diagram" of a progression from solemnity to exuberance, mediated by consumption, is not a "scale-free abstraction" (Candea 2012), but one whose repetition and transformation weave certain themes into the experiential fabric of shared life. The Eucharistic host is manifestly not the same as the hosting of a guest in one's home, but they draw on the same patterns and techniques—especially those of feeding—in order to produce organized, meaningful, morally charged power relations.

ZIKIR: MEALS OF MEMORY, PRESENCE, AND PATRONAGE

Local saints' days provide another example of religious echoing, following Epiphany (T'imqet) in the passage of the *tabot* to water and its exuberant blessing, but on a smaller scale; the *tabot* does not spend the night outside, which shortens the vigil and the festival considerably. The blessings by holy water, both on Epiphany and the smaller saints' days, are often colloquially referred to as "baptism" (t'imqet), which led some early European observers to label the Orthodox degenerate practitioners of multiple baptisms. In fact there is no evidence that people mix up the sacrament of baptism taken shortly after birth with the blessing of crowds with holy water—calling this "baptism" points rather to the indexical and metaphoric quality that invokes a portion of the blessing produced by the actual sacrament. This is a recurring pattern in Ethiopian Orthodoxy's religious division of labor: sacramental practices that are the province of the clergy alone have their echoes, rhymes, and resonances through different domains of more accessible and, crucially, shareable practices. This diffusion of sacred form does much to give the feeling of living in a ritual community.

The other defining aspect of a saint's day festival, aside from the transit of the *tabot* and the exuberant blessing of water, is the holding of a *zikir* feast. *Zikir* is a key concept for understanding the relationship between commensality, religious relations, and memory, so it is worth dwelling on it a moment. Meaning "food given in remembrance of the dead" (Cowley 1972: 246), it is cognate with the Arabic *dhikr,* described in Sufi traditions as a communal worship event in which "the devotees are imagined more fully present before God than in regular activities" (Newby in Setargew 2011). Where *dhikr* in Islamic traditions refers to acts of speaking the name of God though, in Amharic Christian culture it tends to indicate a commemorative meal, and to be aimed at saints or Mary. Key resonances remain with the Arabic term: *zikir* is a collective act of commemoration, and it denotes not just remembrance as in bringing to mind, but a re-membering, or a constituting of the object of memory as actually present. Like "remembrance," *zikir* also denotes thanks. My friend Menilek described a *zikir* to me as a meal that you held for your neighbors in order to thank a saint for a vow/request *(silet)* that had been granted;

Haregwa, for example, had a *zikir* for Selassie (the Trinity), which meant that she would host a meal each year on Trinity day, in thanks for an unnamed vow that had been granted.³ *Abba* Som, in turn, told me that all associational meals *(mahber)* were essentially *zikir* in the name of a saint.

In each case, the *zikir* involves people getting together and eating in the name of a saint. This mode of remembrance recalls Christ's words at the Last Supper, "This is my body given for you: do this in remembrance of me" (Luke 22:19), which recall in turn the Jewish Passover commemoration (Feeley-Harnik 1995: 567). Aside from the semiotic echoes of food as commemoration, the crucial factor is that eating is, as we have seen, a shared act, and food a shared medium.

Note the pattern of sacred exchange implied in the *zikir* as vow. When you ask something of a saint and it is granted, you do not repay the gift directly, by returning something to them. Instead, the repayment refracts outward, onto the community; you give the saint shared commemoration, and make them a benefactor of all (see Malara 2017). Like the Eucharist, the host of the meal invites a greater being to be the real host, displacing her or him. Relationships with saints are not dyadic: it is a trope of saintly histories that a person who displays great devotion is rewarded not just by entry into heaven but by a promise that others who pray in her or his name will also be saved (Taddesse 1972b: 2).

The archetype of this promise in Ethiopic tradition is the Kidane Mihret, the Covenant of Mercy (also the name of a monastery in Zege), in which Christ promises to Mary that all who pray in her name will be saved. One might almost say that the essence of sainthood is becoming a benefactor who can save others, and its reward is to be remembered in the shared meal.

The *zikir* feast held on a saint's day operates at a larger scale, and commemorates the saint in a more general way, usually because the local church was consecrated to that saint. This can result from a vow just as much as individual *zikir,* for example, if a church's founder established the church as repayment of a promise—again, the saint becomes a medium for the salvation of others. I visited the church of Wanjeta Mikael (which is consecrated to both Michael and Gabriel) on St. Gabriel's day in 2008 with Beschew, a local vagabond and odd-job man in his forties. A number of people from Afaf were headed to the church, some forty minutes' walk into the countryside, but my usual interview companions could not go, so Abebe enlisted Beschew to show me around, since he was at a loose end. We had got to know each other while sneaking out of wedding parties to smoke, and he would often come around the village in the evening asking for bits of leftover food. He would tell me about how he slept on the verandah of Abbi's hotel, where I often ate, and children would throw rocks at him. He was, suffice to say, extremely poor, but also totally indomitable, and prepared to do undignified things to get by. At one wedding feast, while the *mizé* (groomsmen) cooked a sheep, Beschew took the guts and testicles and ran off into the woods to eat them. Another time I saw him walk barefoot into a swamp. He returned with his feet and ankles covered in leeches, which he carefully picked off and placed in a plastic bag to sell to fishermen as bait.

Beschew, as a likeable outsider, was a great person to visit a festival with. We arrived at the church mid-morning to find the inner sanctum already empty and the feast in progress (food provided by local parishioners, and vegetarian only, since we were in the advent fast, *Tahsas* 19 [December 28]). One rarely sees the inner chamber of the church, guarded by vast doors depicting towering, heavily armed angels, so Beschew grabbed the opportunity to have a look inside (still making sure to take his shoes off before entering the church). We attracted some disapproving looks, but since the *tabot* wasn't there it wasn't actually a sacrilege. We then headed just outside the churchyard to have our food and *t'ella* beer. Beschew ate enthusiastically, because he didn't often get meals so good, but he was also careful to remind me not to smoke this close to the church. Between us we made a slightly strange part of the congregation, but we were part of it, eating in Gabriel's name. Once full, we went down to the water to see the *tabot* and get splashed with holy water.

Beschew showed me that while we were taking part in the church feast, we should pay due respect. We were entering into codes of conduct that he usually had little time for and that had even less time for him. It is easy to forget how potent large, inclusive feasts are when plenty of people are genuinely hungry. We had our point of unity, where a rather larger and more diverse group ate together than is usual, before going our separate ways, and we did so in the name of Gabriel, our host for the period that the *tabot* remained outside the church. Beschew taking part in the *zikir* did not change his status afterward, but it was a point of engagement, at which everyone had to acknowledge that he was not entirely outside the community either, and that he too was a guest of Gabriel for the duration of the feast, rather than eating the things that others discarded. In the same way, on the celebration of Mary's birthday, servants had to be acknowledged as being as much a part of the saintly community as anyone else.

CONCLUSION: BREAD AND SPIRIT

This is my body given for you . . . . This cup is the new covenant in my blood, which is poured out for you.
—LUKE 22: 19–20, CITED IN PAULOS 1988: 175

There is a case for saying that the concept of covenant *(kidan)* is the foundation of Ethiopian Orthodox social thought (Girma 2012, Antohin 2014). Two points stand out: a covenant is a pact between a saint and a community, not an individual; and in Ethiopia the covenant is created and commemorated through commensality.

Feeding is the basic relational act by which a collective of people and divine agents is brought into being. It is not just a joining of constituent parts to form a larger whole, but it actively makes those who participate. I have described the Eucharist as the core (or perhaps climactic) activity of Orthodox life, but the Eucharist can only coexist with the other acts of eating and feeding for saints that I have described. Moments of saintly commensality, such as the *zikir* or *Ginbot Lideta*, can prove inclusive in ways that everyday life is not.

It is not too strong to say that feeding and commensality have been the most important means of relationship-making throughout Zege's history. The focal point of church-landlord hierarchies was the *mefraq* dining room, in which the leaders of church and community ate together but in clearly marked hierarchical order. Meanwhile, lasting status, virtue, and memorialization were established through the feasts of *tezkar*. Today these meals do not define the social makeup of Zege, to the regret of some. But *zikir* meals and Easter and Christmas feasting remain at the heart of human-divine community formation, and the consumption of the body and blood of God remains at the heart of everything.

NOTES

1. See Aymro and Motovu 1970.
2. According to Tefera, the norm in Zege is actually half a day.
3. Of course, the Trinity is not technically a saint, but in practical terms it is often treated in the same way, as a recipient of vows with a monthly commemorative day.

8

The Media Landscape

One of the themes of this book has been how prohibition and mediation create a fabric of religious practice that is deeply embedded in environmental, embodied, and material life, while also maintaining relations with an encompassing divine realm. The mediations I have discussed have operated through sacrifice, through eating in the company of divine others, and through the careful management of bodily and environmental states and relations. This is mediation in the broad sense (Debray 1991, Boyer 2012), the study of the networked, material relations and extensions of the temporal and the sacred.

Media in the more familiar, narrow sense, as the technologies of communication, remain a relevant part of this story. We have seen (chapter 3) how written text has been integral to the operation of the church in Zege, but in a quite restricted way, available to those trained in Ge'ez. Writing was a means of sanctifying as much as transmitting information (Orlowska 2006); a key function of the book of the Acts of Betre Maryam was to be walked around the peninsula and so to reaffirm the saint's protection. Recording or producing information (and, as we will see in the next chapter, making images) required a person to fast and pray to become a vessel for the creative power of God.

The media landscape of Zege is changing rapidly, especially due to mobile phones, 3G internet, stereo systems, televisions, radios, and loudspeakers. As will become clear, this alters how information flows through society. But it also has significant ambient, environmental effects.

This chapter asks how Zege Orthodox Christians' sense of their relation to wider global and religious spheres is transforming with the spread of mass media.

As we will see, flesh and food remain central concerns in Orthodox engagements with the Internet and with religious audio and visual materials.

The literature of religion and media over the past two decades has often amounted to an exploration of what happens when we collapse together our concepts of "technological" and "religious" communication into a single sphere of theo-techno-politics (e.g., Debray 1991, Vries 2001, Stolow 2012, Eisenlohr 2012). As productive as I have found this, I have wanted to preserve a sense of the special status of organic mediation—hospitality, sacrifice, food, work bodies, and blood—that has been the focus of much of this book so far. Or, at least, I have wanted to recognize that the organic has a special problematic status in Zege's Orthodoxy and, I suspect, in most ritual systems.

And yet, the divide between the organic and the technological, like that between the religious and the technological, is nowhere clear-cut. Better to think, perhaps, of the interface between human body (or self) and world not as an obvious fact but as a focal problem that religious action tries to work through. But there is no doubt that the possibilities for engaging with the world are changing, with significant ramifications for every other mode of connection and imagination. In particular I want to focus on Debray's (1996: 28) "properly mediative functions of territoriality." The environmental, spatial, and temporal aspects of religious mediation have been demonstrated throughout this book, but I have not yet explored how this territoriality relates to the claims of other groups sharing the same space, in this case the Muslim community living in Afaf and Fure. It is through this territorial dimension that we need to understand recent changes in interreligious relations.

Regular electricity came to Afaf three or four years before the start of my fieldwork. By the time I arrived, every bar-hotel was in possession of a refrigerator, television, and sound system, and many private homes had radios at the very least. As we will see, local churches and the mosque had also begun to use electric amplification, with a major impact on the shared experience of public space. These changes drastically altered Afaf's soundscapes and sightscapes, while increasing the amount of information coming in to Zege, much of it of a religious nature. On my return visits after 2009, I have found many younger people using the Internet via 3G networks, mainly to access Facebook. This chapter examines the specifically religious aspects of the new media technologies, especially as they affect the sense of spatial connection and political belonging of Orthodox Christians in Zege. The next chapter will turn to other forms of world imagination and aspiration among young people in Zege as they attempt to mobilize the resources that the world around them affords. In each case, it will quickly become clear that the interface between human bodies and the world—in a recognizably Orthodox idiom—remains a critical concern even as its imaginative and technological parameters are shifting.

CHRISTIANS AND MUSLIMS IN LOCAL, NATIONAL, AND CYBER SPACE

The local Muslim community lives in the town of Afaf and in Fure, a forested area on the mainland that abuts Afaf, just southwest of the peninsula itself. The pattern of Christians inhabiting the countryside and Muslims mainly living in towns conforms to a broad normative association of Christians with farming and Muslims with trade, and in local Christian understandings the peninsula proper, as a land of monasteries, is for Orthodox inhabitation only. The dominant narrative of the area as a whole has long been that it is an Orthodox heartland, a land of monasteries, whose Muslim population was depicted as largely incidental and secondary.

While relations between Orthodoxy and Islam in Ethiopia have been experiencing a moment of increasing tension (Abbink 2011, Samson 2015), there is also a well-established and much-touted tradition of mutual tolerance and cooperation. As we have seen, Christians and Muslims do not share meat (some have told me, significantly, that this is because different prayers are said during the slaughter). However, they will always make sure to serve some nonmeat dishes at feasts, so as to be able to host their neighbors. Personal relations among Christians and Muslims in town have generally been cordial and cooperative, accompanied by mutual recognition of the meat separation as proper on both sides.

I have not conducted extensive research with Muslims in Afaf, but have relied mainly on informal conversations with friends in Afaf. The Muslim community traces its presence in Zege to the reign of Emperor Yohannes IV (1871–89), and have historically had a large degree of autonomy through their community head, the *negedras* (chief of trade; Binayew 2014: 16). My Muslim friends would generally uphold the public narrative of tolerance and cooperation between Christians and Muslims, and highlight the importance of shared hospitality without meat or alcohol. Chewing *khat* was an important site of interreligious sociality among young men; while traditionally associated with Islam, social and recreational *khat* use has become increasingly popular among young Orthodox men. As a result, *khat* has become an important local cash crop, though Abebe told me that farmers with an eye to propriety would usually hide their *khat* fields among taller, more respectable crops.

I am told by older Christians that *khat* used to be part of a reciprocal arrangement in Zege: farmers would supply the plant to the Muslim community, who had no land, while Muslims would weave clothes for the Orthodox. Older Muslims, on the other hand, might point to the fact that they were not allowed to hold land (Binayew 2014: 57). But today young men who chew *khat* in bars and teahouses are part of the daily social scene in Afaf. Shared schooling, too, means that Christian and Muslim children grow up together, while Christian-Muslim business relations in the marketplace are also normal. Nonetheless there are occasional signs that the Muslim community feels its historic disadvantage quite strongly, and that Orthodox Christians worry about increasing Muslim influence in the country.

In 2008, when I began fieldwork, there were occasional signs of unacknowledged tension. Most surrounded the small mosque that lay in the center of town. It had a rather powerful loudspeaker, and would broadcast the call to prayer at a volume that would often wake the whole town in the small hours of the night. I would occasionally hear Christian friends complain of tiredness, but there was never any open acknowledgment of a problem: ethics of neighborly respect for religious activity, combined with an aversion to provoking conflict, meant that nobody wanted to speak out. Most people actively denied that anything was wrong. That this was not entirely true became clear when, about a year into my fieldwork, somebody stole the mosque's amplifier.

The traditional rural-urban divide between Christians and Muslims is significant here. At this time there were seven churches in Zege to one small mosque, and most had amplifiers of their own. But all were situated outside of town, as is usual, to maintain proper separation between worldly and sacred space. For those living in town, the churches just weren't very loud, if they could be heard at all. Nonetheless, aside from the theft of the amplifier, things were peaceful when I left the field in 2009.

Village religious politics would become much more fraught over the next few years (my most recent visit was in December 2014). The most obvious point of contention was the reconstruction of the mosque, from a nondescript mud house to a vast painted concrete structure with a minaret tower that dwarfs any other building in the area. In a town of one-storey houses of mud and straw with corrugated iron roofs, the new mosque stands out.

From a Muslim perspective, this was an assertion of legitimate and long-standing presence; many had clearly felt unrecognized and unrepresented for some time. The mosque was one of many similar construction projects across the country, as Ethiopian Muslims are seeking to assert their equal status in the Federal era. Chatting to Christians, on the other hand, I heard two sorts of responses. In public they once again downplayed any kind of tension, saying that there was "no problem." But privately I heard complaints that the construction was inappropriate in a place of such historic Christian importance, and that local officials had been bribed.

At the same time, local Christian organizations moved to counter the mosque construction in kind, and so reestablish their claims to primacy on the peninsula. Raising money from their own national connections, they built two new churches in the peninsula: Medhane Alem, in the forest close to Afaf, and Rufael, near the northern shore of the peninsula on the site of a previous church that had been dismantled during the Italian occupation, its stones used to make a military camp whose remains are still visible. Neither of these churches has anything like the visual presence of the mosque. They are low single-storey buildings situated in the forest, not like the much larger and more elaborate structures now found in towns. This is in line with established practice: churches have not traditionally been built to dominate space; they are supposed to be sheltered, in line with their role as refuges. The monasteries of Zege are known for their murals, the treasures they house, their histories, and the power of their holy water, not for their architectural majesty. By comparison, Orthodox churches in cities have become much more visually imposing in the last century, and in the last two years the façade of St. George's church in Bahir Dar has been renovated to include a vast and eye-catching bas-relief of George and the dragon. These developments seem to derive initially from the influence of European architectural styles, and lately from the need to produce structures that match the Islamic occupation of space (Boylston 2014).

The churches in Zege do other than compete for visual presence. For one thing, they emphasize the Christian argument that the peninsula is Orthodox: there are now nine churches rather than seven to the one mosque. But perhaps more importantly, the Orthodox demonstrated that they could call on their own support networks in the form of Christian voluntary associations (mahber) that are supporting church construction across the country (Ancel & Ficquet 2015). These associations support church building but also provide funds for the training of church students, in an age of great concern that their numbers are diminishing. By 2013 Zege hosted a number of boys entering church training, with new robes and books to work with and some support for food. Building the churches includes making investments in the future of the church as a whole and so combats perceived threats to Orthodoxy's preeminence.

The wranglings over religious construction have led to a sharply increased consciousness that the local churches and mosque are instances of a highly politicized struggle of national and international proportions. Both the mosque regeneration and the new churches were realized by calling upon large-scale support networks, whose financial support had direct and tangible effects in Afaf town and on the peninsula. The presence of the new buildings and the political wrangles that surround them supply evidence of the broader interests behind them—the churches and the mosques are understood to stand for something much bigger that lies just out of sight. People feel these developments acutely because they entail massive transformations in the experience of sensory space, due to both the visual and tangible presence of religious buildings and the greatly enhanced sonic range of religious ritual.

We have already seen how informal but well-established local traditions such as fel sacrifice and yebered tebaqí have been abandoned (see chapter 3), partly as a response to a concern that such nonstandard practice did not provide a firm bulwark against Islamic attempts, real or imagined, to gain ground on the peninsula. The mosque construction brought many of these concerns to a head. One of the more disheartening signs of this development was a handwritten sign on the gate of Fure Maryam church (which lies in an area where many Muslims live) that read: "Orthodox Christians only." I was told that this was due to fear that Muslims might try to desecrate the church in some way, possibly as part of some wider national plot. But, as seen in chapter 6, the importance of shared funeral attendance as the very basis of mutual cohabitation and the suggestion that Muslims may not attend Christian funerals suggest the possibility of deep local ruptures quite contrary to the sentiments of shared belonging that both Christians and Muslims had expressed to me at funerals in the past.

Another key development that has changed local Christian and Muslim conceptions of their interrelationships has been the spread of polemical discourse through public media (Abbink 2011). As Samson Bezabeh (2015) shows, sermons from both Christian and Muslim speakers, which circulate on CDs and video, draw heavily on international discourses of religious conflict, invoking a clash of global forces of Christianity, Islam, and secular modernity. These circulations may not reflect the subtler realities of coexistence and cooperation on the ground, but they are powerful enough to gain a reality of their own, and begin to produce the conflict they describe. It seems at the moment that the rapid development of media technology for circulating religious material has intensified a sense of conflict rather than cooperation. We will see, however, that religious conflict is not the only register of discourse, and that strong notions of a shared Ethiopian national identity frequently take precedence.

The rapid growth of Facebook use among young people in Zege has provided a striking instance of this phenomenon, particularly potent because of the way that Facebook allows users to share images and slogans at the press of a button. In 2008 nobody in Zege had a Facebook profile (or much use for the Internet at all); by 2010 I had a couple dozen "friends" from Zege, and the number has continued to grow. When I returned to the field, I happened to ask some friends about a mutual Muslim acquaintance. My friend told me that they didn't really talk anymore—the man had moved to Bahir Dar, and now "he only posts about Islam." I did not remember him having discussed Islam much at all when I had known him, but through Facebook there was suddenly a steady stream of prayers, exhortations, and macros (images with text edited in) that he could "share" simply with a click and so declare his agreement with them and develop a new kind of public identity, one that some of his Christian friends found irksome—although they were doing much the same thing with the sharing of Christian images and slogans, and perhaps more so. Most of his posts were fairly innocuous statements like "I am a Sufi and I love my prophet," written on a football shirt, or a picture of the Quran that said, "We love Al-Quran," along with pictures of cute children in Muslim garb.

The most recent and shocking example of Christian outrage at the time of writing has been the response to the Islamic State releasing a video purporting to show the beheading and shooting of some thirty Ethiopian Orthodox Christians in Libya. Images from the video, some extremely graphic, have been shared by many of my Zege friends on Facebook (which, of course, is exactly the purpose of releasing such videos) alongside expressions of outrage and prayers for the victims, for example, "To die in the name of the cross is an honour," "They will know my faith by the cross around my neck," each accompanied with a gruesome picture of a beheaded man. My friends now feel personally, viscerally affected by world political events in a way that was not evident before, and galvanized to affirm their Christian loyalty, though they often do so not in their own words but in those provided along with the images that are circulating. In another example of a polarizing event that could never have happened in the pre-Facebook era, one of my friends shared a Photoshopped image of a giant Caucasian woman defecating on the Mecca Kaaba. It is hard to think of a more inflammatory gesture, but I do not think this person harbors any significant anti-Islamic feelings beyond a certain reactionary Facebook tribalism. He would certainly never show such an image to anybody face to face, or make any other similarly outrageous statement. But on Facebook it was easy, something you could click on as a joke, and end up causing extreme anger, which of course it did. An on-screen shouting match predictably broke out, though I do not know of any further ramifications.

A number of things are happening here. First, Facebook blurs lines between what is public and what is among friends and even what it means to say something publicly, resulting in statements that one would never make face to face (boyd 2007). Second, the ability to circulate posts made by others makes it much easier to repeat a discourse originating elsewhere. This means both that the user feels connected to a much wider debate—they know the things they post come from a wider group of people who share some interest—and that they may publicly make statements that they would not in other circumstances have even formulated.

It is tempting to draw a comparison between the graphic photos of murdered Christians and the paintings of the martyrs that adorn the inner walls of Zege's churches. These, too, show people being burned, beheaded, and otherwise brutally mutilated and bathed in blood. In the process of re-presenting and re-mediating images of violent deaths, a new story emerges in which their blood and their deaths are meaningful for the wider body (religious) politic (Shenoda 2013, Heo 2015: 53). Similar processes are familiar from the anthropologies of sacrifice and nationhood (e.g., Bloch & Parry 1982, Verdery 2000, Lomnitz 2005). The spread of saints' legends and of the Libya images works in radically different temporalities, but it reminds us that the imagery of warfare and suffering, and of the murderous nature of Christianity's enemies, is hardly a new story, but one to which people have always made periodic recourse.

The online response to the Libya and South Africa killings did not only take the form of Christian-Muslim opposition, however. Many of the image macros and statements that people were sharing appealed instead to a shared national identity, opposing the Ethiopian tradition of interreligious cooperation to the foreign organization of extremist Islam. Abebe also shared a picture of Muslims in Egypt linking hands to protect a Coptic church. In this same week, Ethiopians had been killed in xenophobic mob violence in South Africa, spurring more general declarations of Ethiopian solidarity on Facebook. Some people responded to all of these events simply with prayers and petitions to Mary to protect the country. John Dulin (2016, 2017) has shown how Christians and Muslims in Gondar responded to the same event with avowals of peaceful solidarity, and not just with mistrust.

Add to this the public connections that Facebook enables with those outside the country. Selam, a woman in her early twenties who has been working as a maid in Saudi Arabia for the last two years, posts a steady stream of macros containing either prayers or laments about missing Ethiopia. In the week of the Libya and South Africa killings, she posted even more prayers, some in very topical forms. In one example, a photo of a man being burned in front of South African police officers is superimposed with an Amharic prayer that reads:

> My heart bleeds
> And my eyes cry
> When my brother burns
> While the police laugh.
> To whom shall I say it?
> Who will hear me?
> Best if I talk to
> Omnipotent God:
> Creator, please
> Say enough of
> My brothers' blood
> And my sisters' tears.
> Please, if not by our sins
> Then by your mercy
> Guide us, Amen.

Selam had shared this from another friend, and forty people have commented beneath at the time of writing, most simply saying, "Amen amen amen," or adding macros with further prayers and images.

The combination of righteous anger, mutual support, and public prayer (along with a fair amount of spurious gossip) that met the Libyan and South African episodes epitomizes much of the circulation of image macros on Facebook among young people in Zege. It is not all anger and conflict; pictures of icons and prayer slogans are equally easy to share, and quite popular. And while nobody would mistake a digitally shared photo of a picture of Mary for a spiritually empowered icon, that is no reason for them not to act as personal reminders and public indicators of deference and allegiance.

The growth of Facebook and the construction of the Afaf mosque happened at around the same time. For people in Zege, especially the young, these two factors combined to produce a vastly increased sense of being part of translocal religious-political factions. This developing sense has clear material foundations: the building of the mosque and churches, but also the networks of money that funded them, and the improving Internet infrastructure that allowed people from Zege to access the Internet, first in the regional capital nearby, and then from their phones in Zege. This does not mean that developing media technology always increases factional conflict. It does show, however, that changes in the media of public prayer have significant effects on how people experience their religious allegiances, connections, and claims to shared space. Public religious activity, I have argued, has always involved a division of labor and the formation of public allegiances under the divine aegis through shared media of prayer. And while these changes in the mediation of religion, whether through buildings, loudspeakers, or the Internet, are enabling rapid transformations in the fabric of that allegiance, they are doing so within a recognizably Orthodox idiom.

NEW AFFORDANCES OF SPACE AND BODY

The circulation of Facebook prayers gives an indication of new possibilities afforded by media technologies, and the consciousness of new kinds of connection that they may provide. But Facebook emerged at a time when mass media technologies had already begun to have significant effects on the contours of religious practice in Zege, since electricity came to Afaf town a decade ago. We have already seen an indication of this in the theft of the mosque's amplifier, and I now turn my attention to the broader ramifications of the electrified religious soundscape, produced by loudspeakers but also by radio and, especially, the circulation of recorded preaching and religious music on CD and Video CD. In particular, we will see how these technologies are leading to a refiguring of the religious experience of space.

Loudspeakers have been used to broadcast the call to prayer in the Muslim world since at least the 1950s, and have been regarded with ambivalence and controversy, by Muslims and non-Muslims alike, for just as long (Khan 2011). In Ethiopia churches and mosques now use loudspeakers as a matter of course. While debates within Islam revolved around the propriety of mediating the voice in prayer, and so stripping it of its sacred status (Khan 2011: 576), Orthodox Christians have been concerned about the projection of the sacred liturgy beyond the walls of the church, where it is heard by Christians who have not fasted and are not in the proper reflective state. One theologian in Addis Ababa told me that, while he saw the value of loudspeakers in the city, he was concerned about the consequences of hearing the holy liturgy while sitting outside the church, perhaps in a cafe, not having fasted, perhaps while quarrelling. The projection of the liturgy over distance was causing problems for him precisely because the grounds of church services are supposed to be restricted, attended only by those in proper bodily states.

But as we have seen, if the liturgy is restricted, Ethiopian Orthodox Christians have always found other means of engagement when unable to attend church. This is especially important for junior women, who are often kept from going to church by housekeeping duties, especially the servant women who work in Afaf's bars, most of whom hail from poorer and more rural areas than Zege. These women tend to stay in Zege for a few months to a year before moving on to work in hotels in Bahir Dar, returning home, or heading to other employers in the countryside.

One of the more significant restrictions on serving women, as they see it, is their inability to attend church on anything like a regular basis. One classic way for servants to engage with their religion is to fast, and they can arrange with their soul fathers to observe extra fasts in lieu of going to church. What media make possible is for servant women, via recorded hymns, to make their spaces of work into temporary religious zones.

The availability of Amharic hymns in digital formats adds a whole new dimension to domestic religious life, especially in the bars. It allows serving women, and others too, to use their employers' stereo systems to play religious music from the moment they wake and start work until the first customers arrive. The place of business becomes a devotional space, at least for a while.

The vernacular Amharic hymns are of recent composition (they were produced after 1991) but use only traditional instruments. However, unlike the traditional classical Ge'ez hymns of the church, they are often performed by women (Shelemay 2012), as well as in a language everyone can understand. They are slow, devotional songs of reflection and penitence, particularly suitable for the morning, before one has breakfasted or done other worldly things. I remember a friend once scolding her husband for singing a vernacular hymn while eating, showing that here, as with official church ceremony, a proper separation was necessary.

The slow, irregular drumbeat and sparse traditional instrumentation set the hymns clearly apart from any other kind of music. This is not music you can dance to, although the singers in the accompanying video perform a slow swaying of upturned hands—video versions of the songs are as easily available as audio versions, copied and distributed by vendors near churches in Bahir Dar.

It is not just servants, and not just women, who listen to hymns in the morning. Anyone with the requisite technology can do so, but it is especially important for the servants given the restrictions on their movement and the nature of the space they inhabit. As they cook the day's food and clean the premises, they can assert a form of control over their surroundings and develop their devotional lives in ways that would not otherwise be possible. When I ask women why they listen to the hymns, they almost always answer quite simply that it makes them happy to do so.

If fasting has always enabled people to engage in devotion no matter where they were—in the space of their bodies, as it were—recorded hymns allow for the creation of new kinds of devotional spaces in homes and places of business, which for servants are the same thing. They also enable new partitions of time, in which each day starts in a religious mode until breakfast is eaten, and this time is clearly differentiated from the rest of the day and its worldly affairs. Since hymns are usually played loud enough to be audible beyond the building's walls, these listening practices begin to shape the shared soundscape of the town, especially in the early mornings. In cities, it has become common to hear hymns played in cafes during the day (under the control of the waitresses), especially during fasting times, further pushing devotional sound into the public, shared sphere.

There are other ways of bringing religiosity into the home, many based on print. While icons do not have quite the prominence of other Orthodox traditions, and most icons are to be found inside the church, many people at least hang a religious picture or two on their walls. The most common are an image of Gabriel saving the three boys from the fires of Nebuchadnezzar and printed posters of Christ or of the virgin and child from Greece or Russia that many people hang across corners of their house (where demons are known to hide), perhaps shrouded with a lacy veil.

These are not consecrated and so are not technically icons, but I do know of cases of them being used for personal prayer. Prayer books are also becoming more common, available cheaply from the same vendors who sell the recorded hymns. Especially in cities, large parts of the congregation may now be found reading in the churchyard during the liturgy. But prayer books also facilitate prayer in the home. In Afaf, too, a man called Temesgen told me about how he liked to start each day reading a section of the Widdasé Maryam, the Praises of Mary, before breakfast. With printed posters and books as with audio recordings, mass reproduction allows people to bring a certain Orthodox sensibility into the home, at least as a way to begin the day, which is important for those whose work lives make churchgoing difficult.

The significance of aural media and religious soundscapes for creating spaces of ethical formation and deliberation has been widely discussed (Hirschkind 2006, Schulz 2008, Oosterbaan 2008). Part of this is due to transportability of media, which "move practices and experiences related to the aural perception of spiritual presence into new arenas of daily life, beyond the immediate sphere of ritual action to which these aural forms of spiritual experience used to be restricted" (Schulz 2008: 175). But just as much has to do with the capacity of sound to cross boundaries in ways that more solid modes of mediation do not (although large buildings may have similar effects, to the extent that they dominate lines of sight, as in the case of the Afaf mosque). A soundscape, as Oosterbaan shows, is a shared living space inhabited by multiple overlapping noise sources. Sound is integral to creating ethically charged environments but, because of its quality of being shared whether we like it or not, a soundscape always has political and territorial dimensions at the same time.

THE AUTHORITY QUESTION

Religious sound and information have become more pervasive in Zege, and Facebook and recorded hymns have opened up new sites for religious engagement. Yet this does not seem to have led to a reduction in the authority of the clergy, as the traditional managers of religious information. Instead, increased engagement by Orthodox Christians in the public sphere brings with it a reaffirmation of the importance of the priesthood and the institutional Church. In this case it seems that new media channels do not necessarily circumvent and undercut established religious authority (Eickelman & Anderson 2003).

One reason for this might be that Orthodox Christians already possess a developed and fairly explicit "theology of mediation" (Eisenlohr 2012) that helps to shape how new media affordances will be taken up—through public prayer, modes of repetition, and the sharing of various icon-like digital images, for example. Furthermore, as we have seen, the institutional recognizability of the church makes it an effective rallying point for appeals to collective Orthodox belonging.

The new importance of church construction and the use of loudspeakers serve to amplify, quite literally, the voice of priests. *Abba* S'om, for example, uses a microphone and loudspeakers to preach to the public on major festival days, and so makes interpretations of ritual activity much more widely available than they had been before.

The emphasis, evident all over Ethiopia, on larger and more numerous churches and mosques indicates a reaffirmation of the importance of traditional authority, bolstered by technologies of amplification, and with enhanced projection over soundscapes and sightlines. We can also look to where ordinary people are putting their money. Both the evidence from Zege and my interviews with Orthodox donors in Addis Ababa show a clear emphasis on two fronts: building and rehabilitating churches, and providing for the upkeep of church schools and trainee priests. Orthodox activists regard the continuation of the specialist priesthood as integral to the survival of the religion. The two newly built churches in Zege serve another purpose, beyond reestablishing a territorial claim: they are bases for church students, funded by the same revenue streams that built the churches. Architectural renovation goes along with the renewal of the specialist priesthood.

Images that circulate on Facebook, as well as many of the recorded sermons that have recently become popular, may stray far beyond the authorized doctrine of the Orthodox Church. There are still widespread debates about whether the new Amharic hymns are appropriate, or whether they constitute deviations from tradition. To this extent, media enable diversions from centrally controlled Orthodoxy. However, Orthodox Christians are expressly and actively returning to the authority of the church and the priests as the public instantiation of Orthodox belonging. The apparent paradox, of increasingly heterodox ideas combined with increasingly vocal loyalty to Orthodox institutions, tells us that there is more at stake here than doctrinal questions of content. Prayer is public, and its media of instantiation, the allegiances it forms, and the institutional basis of its authority are all widely recognized as being integral.

We should also note that, to the extent that media technologies contribute to politicized interreligious conflict, or at least discomfort, it is usually not just in the circulation of images, but in the affective ways that media articulate with the occupation of lived space through churches, mosques, and loudspeakers. Equally, the effects of media are contingent on the material infrastructures and financial networks that underpin them (Boyer 2012, Larkin 2013). In the case of the new churches and mosques, these constructions may be taken as indexical evidence of the political-religious networks and interests that underlie them.

In his survey of approaches to religion and media, Eisenlohr (2012) advocates those frameworks that regard religion as always already mediated. There is a case for saying that Ethiopian Orthodox Christians have always known this. A corollary of this insight, as I hope to have shown, is the conviction that prayer is at heart a shared, public endeavor that translates effectively between local and long-distance materialities. Tales of the efficacy of prayer almost always possess the public dimension: a priest in Addis Ababa telling me how the prayers of the church brought victory to Ethiopia at the Battle of Adwa in 1896, for example, or local ideas in Zege that the prayers of priests enact an ongoing covenant with God to protect the local environment and make sure that the rains fall.

The polemicization of Ethiopian religious discourse that some observers have described is real enough (Abbink 2011, Samson 2015), and certainly exacerbated by the speed and visceral quality of digital media. But it is important to note how frequently the flashpoints that result in prayerful declarations of Orthodox, Islamic, or Ethiopian identity involve migrants. The victims of ISIS were reported to be on their way to Europe, and the migrants in South Africa were killed for traveling to seek work. Those sharing images and money are also frequently those who have gone abroad and are reaffirming old connections and new identities of memory. The more global consciousness of people in Zege is a result not just of media technology coming to them, but of people from Zege going out into the world.

9

The Knowledge of the World

An Amharic novel called *Dertogada* became a runaway hit while I was in the field. It was popular enough that some of my friends in Zege were able to recount the plot without having read it: The hero, Dr. Miraje, raised in the monastery of Kibran Gebrel, just off the Zege shore, must travel to America to find the great Ethiopian rocket scientist Engineer Shagiz, whose work has been the basis of the American space program, and bring him back to Ethiopia. It emerges that there is a secret Ethiopian spy base under Lake Tana armed with state-of-the-art spy planes and submarines, and Shagiz is needed to help run the place and make the Ethiopian secret service the equal of the CIA and Mossad, which also have large parts to play in the story. These basic elements of the plot have entered widely enough into the general consciousness that I and other friends have had people report them to us quite earnestly as fact.

The novel is a remarkable document for several reasons. It reads like a postcolonial inversion of a Dan Brown thriller, with an extra helping of picaresque farce. It confronts the aporia between Ethiopian Orthodox Christians' sense of the depth and richness of their own culture and the seeming inadequacy and underdevelopment of the Ethiopian nation-state on the international scene, and tries to build a synthesis that will pull the Tana monasteries and spy planes into the same picture. It also contains multiple instances of cross-dressing, face transplants, and mistaken identity that Elizabethan theatregoers in England would have had no trouble recognizing. Its author, Yismake Worku, is reputed to have trained in the Tana monasteries while also pursuing modern education, as so many young Christians do. The book shifts abruptly from the poetry of the twentieth-century Ethiopian laureate Tsegaye Gebremedhin and church literature to quoting "Redemption

Song," all woven into a thriller built around Kabbalistic coded messages that bear the clear influence of *The Da Vinci Code* (available in English and Amharic in Bahir Dar) and its predecessors in the American Cold War technothriller genre.

The juxtaposition of space exploration and international spy agencies with the Tana monasteries captures something integral to the dual extension of technology and religion as it is locally understood. The military and economic power of "Western" science and technology is undeniable. But this power seems to sit on a different axis from the charismatic potency of the churches and the tradition they mediate. Yismake's novel brings the two together in a way that is clearly fantasy but that captures something of the general Ethiopian Orthodox engagement with modernity: we know that our people are smart and in possession of a sophisticated cultural heritage; so why are these gifts so out of sync with the contemporary world's criteria for glory and success? How, knowing so much, can we be so humiliated? It is something that has preoccupied Ethiopian intellectuals for a century or more.

This chapter will show how, in the vein of *Dertogada*, young Zege Orthodox Christian mens' search for knowledge of the world, and hence for advancement of their prospects, continually folds back into their engagement with the churches. Perhaps this is unsurprising, since the churches have always been key points of interface between the local environment and the wider world. At the same time, I will consider the relationship between global media and the human body. It will become clear that young Zegeña experiences with global knowledge and media involve more than viewing or hearing things from afar: there is always a more active physical engagement.

SEX, LOVE, AND FOOTBALL

Once in 2009 I sat on a rock by the lakeside in Zege, chewing *khat* with Babbi and Ahebe. On their request I was trying to translate the lyrics of the Shakira song "Hips Don't Lie" ("So be wise and keep on / Reading the signs of my body / And I'm on tonight / You know my hips don't lie / And I'm starting to feel it's right / All the attraction, the tension / Don't you see baby, this is perfection"). We had decided that the title should be *"Dalé Aywashm"* and hadn't got much further, but the general gist was clear enough. Babbi remarked, "Ah, the international languages: sex, love, and football." As we will see throughout this chapter, what the international languages share is a vast, globally mediated component, along with an underlying and irreducible grounding in bodily engagement. Babbi's brother would meet a Polish woman a few years later and emigrate, with positive financial results for the whole family; the international languages have huge material importance. But the meeting would not have been possible without the young man's high level of education, skill in English, and substantial experience in tour-guiding work, as well as personal charm. All of this was in turn made possible by the education of Babbi's family, their close connections to the churches, and their involvement with local associations of tour guides and coffee growers

Another of Babbi's brothers, Menilek, has been working for several years on improving Zege's coffee output in collaboration with foreign traders. The projects have been hampered by practical and bureaucratic problems, most notably the centralizing of coffee export by the Ethiopian Coffee Exchange (ECX), which has made life more difficult for small-scale and specialty growers. Still, the work has been possible because of Menilek's English skills and close relationship with local farmers, often through church associations. In 2008–09 a major project was underway to try to harvest only the highest-quality beans, which meant expanding the picking period from the usual practice of harvesting everything in the week after Epiphany, ripe or not. Menilek's work involved assuaging some farmers' complaints about the "sayensawi" (scientific) methods, which did not account, for example, for the need not to pick on Saint George's day. To coordinate this work, involving husking machines and great drying racks stretched along the shore of Lake Tana, required the ability to go between the expectations of European traders and the local coffee growers, whose practices and understandings were built around the church calendar.

Modern education and church knowledge were once thought incompatible. Attempts in the 1940s to build a government school in Zege met entrenched opposition on the grounds that it was antithetical to Zege's tradition and the institutional autonomy of the church, and so the first school was not actually constructed until the 1960s (Binayew 2014: 44). By 2009 every young person I spoke to considered modern education the only serious route to advancement, but the Afaf school only went up to eighth grade. Any further schooling had to take place in the city, which requires either money for transport and lodging or family members willing and able to put your children up. Tefera, who read my early work and ended up helping me with a number of interviews, recalled to me his journeys to school some fifteen years before: for five years he would travel the 25 kilometers from Zege to Bahir Dar on foot, or by meruch'a (runner) canoe, setting out at midnight on Sunday if there were Monday morning classes. He and his friends would bring dry injera to eat with a little spice, and would stay the week before coming back. Tefera is the son of a churchman of noble descent, which helps to explain the value his family puts on education, and their material ability to support a son in school. He is now studying for a business diploma in Bahir Dar, though he often returns to Zege for tour guide work, and has acted as an assistant and translator for other researchers who have passed through Zege. This work and his own background have given him a keen interest in Zege's history, and he has done more than anyone to help me understand the area.

Tour guiding in Zege is run through a cooperative that shares the work and its proceeds and benefits the community greatly. This goes along with the business of selling refreshments and souvenirs to tourists, in which many local women run stalls, also organized by a collective association. This work alone cannot sustain young people with big ambitions, but it provides a significant base from which many people begin and to which most regularly return in the course of studying and working in Bahir Dar.

The point of telling these stories is to establish a sense of how the hopes and dreams of young people in Zege are formed and how they work toward the future in ways that fold back into church and coffee. Starting to think about this helps us understand in turn how Zege connects to the wider world through media, travel, and exchange, and through love and personal relationships. As people build relationships they also build their imaginings of what the world is like, and I want to highlight the role that the church, the media, and the education system play in imagining a reality wider than one's own experience, and in trying to establish one's place in it. This means sex, love, and football, but also prayer and healing, which have been drawing people to Zege for six or seven centuries, as well as trade and government bureaucracy and everything else that connects the world. The place I entered as an ethnographer was one where people already had quite developed ideas of what Europeans were like and what they might expect from me, built on concrete connections of many kinds, and it seems important to account for these understandings while developing my own analysis of what Zege is like. Ethnography goes both ways.

OF SAINTS AND SWEDES: ON KNOWING HOW TO ASK

Yibeltal was a tour guide who worked in Bahir Dar. He came with me on my first couple of visits to Zege while I was looking for somewhere to settle. He was working, and did not see helping me as much different from any other tour guiding. But helping me with research gave him a chance to talk to priests in Zege, who, he was sure, possessed good love magic. Not that he necessarily needed it, being an excellent talker with the charm and education necessary to make a living out of independent guiding. But it was an interesting opportunity and a nice side perk. (However, as he told me, all the priests in Zege had claimed ignorance of such medicines. He did not believe them.)

A few months after I had settled we were having a coffee back in Bahir Dar and he was telling me about an attractive Swedish woman he had been guiding. He told me that he had gone to Giyorgis church and made a vow to Saint George that, if he got to have sex with that Swedish girl, he would light a candle for the saint every year on his annual feast day.

Obviously it is not orthodox to ask for patently sinful things in vows, but I actually believed he had done it (and he would later lead me to believe that the vow had been granted). There is a logic to the idea that would still make for a good story even if Yibeltal were just exaggerating and had not actually gone in person to the church to ask for help getting sex. Part of it is the idea of turning saintly benefaction to unsaintly ends, but there is more. Saints and tourists share a quality of being powerful external agents who can change the course of a person's life if approached in the right way. For this you need knowledge, and knowing how to ask was Yibeltal's profession.

The context for this story is that for most tour guides in Bahir Dar, including many who are from Zege and take tourists back to visit the peninsula, foreign women offer one of the more realistic prospects of material advancement in life. Many young men talk to me about meeting an older woman and developing a relationship that would lead either to long-term financial support or, better, to taking them back to Europe. There are enough examples of this actually happening that, for many, such an escape seems a more likely prospect than finding gainful local work commensurate with their levels of education.

Yibeltal had once told me that he liked having affairs with foreign women because he learned so much: "She can tell me the things she knows." Sometimes this knowledge took the form of romantic and sexual tricks, but it also meant learning languages and generally picking up information from well-educated, middle-class visitors. Yibeltal would continuously develop his appreciation of the perspectives of others, of reality as those from other countries saw it, and of what motivated them to travel, make friends and lovers, and spend money. Each engagement would further equip him to meet more people in possession of knowledge, wealth, and opportunity. Sometimes he and other tour guides would ask visitors what guides did in other places they had visited. Most suspected that Kenyan guides, with more experience of tourism, had many more sophisticated tricks for meeting people than they did—and Yibeltal would eventually end up in Kenya after gathering one too many bad debts in Bahir Dar, or, as he would have it, once opportunities in the local area had been exhausted.

In this and every example we will see in this chapter, world imaginations and knowledge are made and transmitted as much through relatively direct human connections and transactions as through mass media; or rather, the two are mutually enabling. People decide to travel to Ethiopia after reading websites or tour brochures; people decide to talk to tourists after learning English from films and textbooks. Romantic and sexual relations can easily lead to the movement of persons and the transfer of significant wealth. There are no media without the movement of people and things, and therefore the translations and exchanges by which they come to know and understand one another.

THE WORLD'S KNOWLEDGE

Being a good tour guide, like being a priest, requires a lot of knowledge. On the one hand, they need to know a lot about the churches and about Zege's history.

On the other, they need to speak English and have a developed awareness of what visitors want. Yibeltal's story displays the degree to which extra knowledge about visitors can be beneficial. One important skill, much to the amiable puzzlement of the guides, is knowing the English name of every bird you are likely to see, because even the tourists who are not explicitly there for bird-watching tend to ask. Guides should know what each painting on the church mural depicts, and all the specialist English vocabulary to describe them. Many learn smatterings of German, Spanish, Italian, and Dutch as well.

The guides act as interfaces between two vast corpora of knowledge. On the one hand is the church tradition, which is restricted by its complexity, its use of classical language, and the ascetic requirements of training. On the other is the stuff of modern education: English grammar and vocabulary, scientific training, mathematics, and so forth. This knowledge is restricted by difficulties of access; a high school recently opened in Zege, but until it did pupils had to travel to Bahir Dar at significant expense. Even then, the schools have difficulty finding textbooks and qualified staff. And the prospects for educated young people, in Bahir Dar, across Ethiopia, and beyond, are often poor (Mains 2012).

In this context it is notable that many of the most successful guides have family histories connected to the church. I have several friends whose fathers were priests, church scholars, or dignitaries such as *mislené* and *liqered*. For example, Tefera's father was *yewist' gebez*, the official in charge of the church key, and he has played a large part in Tefera developing both an expansive modern education and deep knowledge of the peninsula and its churches. There are many others among the guides, as Tefera listed for me: Getaneh's father is a *mislené* and church singer, Masresha's father was a *liqered*, Yihenew's father was a *meggabí*, and so forth.

The relationship between Church and modern education is an important one. Ethiopia's first European-style modern school was built under Emperor Menilek in 1908, and modern education was one of Haile Selassie's major governmental priorities, as education came to be seen as a key step to gaining material and developmental parity with the West (Bahru 2002, Girma 2012). Before this, education in Orthodox areas meant church education (Chaillot 2002, Ephraim 2013: 92), which involved, as we have seen, rigorous training in the Ge'ez language, in the memorizing of holy texts, in ritual technique, and often in mastery of *qiné* devotional poetry. Orthodox Christians still hold church education in extremely high regard, and have put large amounts of time and resources into its preservation (see previous chapter). A remarkable number of students I have spoken to in Addis Ababa combine modern, secular education by day with church study by night, which requires a heroic commitment. Those I have spoken to tend to hold their church education in higher regard, being both more thorough and possessing a far stronger ethical and spiritual dimension.

In the Orthodox educational tradition knowledge and creativity are inseparable from the ascetic training of the body (Lee 2013). We have seen some indication of this in the mendicant period that students undergo. But from the moment students begin to memorize the Psalms in Ge'ez, bodily discipline, especially fasting, is an integral part of their training. For any kind of creative production of poetry or images, as we will see, the student must have both absorbed a huge amount of tradition and fasted with diligence to allow the Holy Spirit to guide them. This is an expression of the fact that both knowledge and creativity are of God, and can therefore only be accessed through prayerful discipline of the flesh.

Historically, then, education in Orthodox Ethiopia has been religious: ascetic, esoteric, and highly specialist, yet providing the literary and disciplinary skills for functionaries well beyond the church (Crummey 1972, Ephraim 2013). This tradition now meets the modernist developmental goals of education as a general good, universal primary education, and so forth—worthy goals often curtailed by practical difficulties. And yet for every young person I spoke to in Zege, modern education remains the indispensable ingredient for having any hope of progress in life. I asked one university student what one thing he would wish improved for Zege, and he replied, "Education; then we can help ourselves."

When I asked Abebe, after eighteen months of informal research assistance, what he wanted out of life that I might help with, he said, "I want to study." I did end up helping to support his studies, and Abebe's interaction with me is important and indicative. He approached a foreign visitor in the hope of accruing not just short-term profit, but opportunities for learning, cultivating relationships with outsiders, and perhaps gaining future support or being introduced to others who might support him. In part, this calls on a model of patronage that would not be alien to historical Ethiopia, in which advancement came through cultivating relations with the powerful (Levine 1965, Messay 1999, Malara & Boylston 2016). In part, it is simply a matter of curtailed opportunity elsewhere. For many talented, curious young people like Abebe, such random interventions from outside often look like the only realistic way to change one's life trajectory. This is not to say that my intervention was entirely praiseworthy—it was somewhat arbitrary, was likely to lead to questions of dependence that would be difficult to manage in the future, and frankly came as much from a sense of obligation as from openhearted generosity of spirit. But it is precisely the ability to manipulate and manage such senses of obligation—the moral responsiveness of others—that is such a crucial social skill, especially in conditions of massive inequality, but classically in the gifting practices of any kind of hierarchically tending society (Haynes 2013).

There is an important sense in which anthropologists and tourists are like saints. Not because of our moral qualities, which are dubious, but because we are powerful, unpredictable, and external agents whose stochastic actions can potentially be harnessed for the good. It is not accidental that Yibeltal prayed to St. George for sex with the Swedish visitor; in many ways, the prayer and its hoped-for result belong in the same category of action: aimed at unpredictable foreign patrons, with the hope of gaining knowledge. When young people like Abebe want to request something from a patron—to send money by Western Union, for example—they go to church and ask Mary or Saint George to protect and bless the person in question, *and* to guide them toward providing generous assistance. Then they send an email directly asking for help. But at a distance the action of the saint and the action of the communication technology have a relation to each other that is crucial in conditions of radical power imbalance.

Abebe once told me that local boys in Afaf were scared of me because I walked like the Belgian martial arts movie star Jean-Claude Van Damme. Action movies were popular in the bars and teahouses, in part because you could mostly work out what was going on without the help of language. I found the comparison odd, because I know nothing about fighting, but the young men in Zege would never accept that I did not know kung fu. Most were convinced that I was refusing to teach them because I wanted to keep the knowledge to myself, in a culture in which keeping knowledge to oneself is a key concern and a basis of the functioning of hierarchy (Levine 1965).

For these young men, who experienced a lot of wealthy tourists passing through Zege and saw Van Damme beating up villains on a regular basis, it seemed obvious that white people possessed a repository of secret knowledge that allowed them to exert dominion over the world. It is hard to disagree with the general diagnosis, which seems to have its counterparts elsewhere (Rollason 2010). I had apparently limitless amounts of money; it went without saying that I would also be a secret master of violence. Local *debtera* practiced mastery over demons by means of closely guarded knowledge, and the mastery of white people was even more obviously effective; despite Ethiopia's victory over its would-be colonizers, we still found ourselves in this situation.

In a parallel set of assumptions, young men from Bahir Dar often thought that Zegeña were in possession of especially powerful love magic. Yibeltal certainly thought so. Babbi's brother, who would end up going to Poland, told me his frustration that whenever someone from Zege had any success in love, their Bahir Dar friends would assume that it was due to magic and pester them to share their secrets. That magic might be thought to be in the possession of sorcerers, but equally, it would often be assumed to be priests and monks who possessed the secrets. The church was, after all, the repository of all the great secrets of the traditional repertoire. It was known, with perhaps more justification, that certain church scholars had knowledge of "brain medicine" that was given to the students to keep them awake and increase their powers of concentration and recall. It was also known that too much of this stuff would drive you crazy, and everyone in Ethiopia knows stories of church students and *debtera* who have gone over the edge.

The cultivating of potential patrons and the search for knowledge are conditioned partly by circumstance and the limits of the possible and partly by the distinctive Amhara theory-practice of knowledge described by Levine (1965). One of the key skills of life is knowing how to learn more things, and how to turn this knowledge into productive relationships. This is the setting in which we should understand the way that engagements with modern, secular education fold back into relationships with the churches, as in the novel *Dertogada*. In working between radically different bodies of knowledge and applying them to one another, young people are mobilizing the best resources they have available to them for developing understanding, relationships, prospects, and hope. It is in the apparent incongruities between the bodies of knowledge that some of the most interesting and productive opportunities for development emerge.

PAINTING TIME AND SPACE

It is perhaps indicative of Amhara knowledge practice that my friend Mebratu never mentioned to me that he was a church painter. When I asked him about this, having found out from someone else, he just said that he assumed I knew. Perhaps it was just his natural humility, perhaps a widely shared habit of not spontaneously sharing information unless directly asked.

Mebratu is an exemplar of the young people I have been discussing: a skilled church painter who learned the trade from his father, an occasional tour guide, and a passionate Manchester United fan. He wears long dreadlocks that most traditionalists would firmly disapprove of, and many of his friends would spend their days chewing *khat* by the lakeside, which became a key medium for my own fieldwork.

Mebratu paints icons and church murals, but spends much more of his time producing works for sale to tourists. Most are in the iconic style of the church, including images of saints and Mary. Some are from older, pre-Gondarine traditions: apotropaic carvings to scare demons and protect the home. Mebratu explained each style he had learned from his father in terms of its provenance from a period, with the earliest being the charms, which he traced to the eighth and ninth centuries (see Mercier 1997 for a broader history).

For Mebratu the different painting and carving styles were ways of instantiating and continuing knowledge of the past, whether the painting would ultimately be used in a church or displayed in some tourist's home. The methods involved were different: for church paintings you had to pray and fast, and not talk to anyone "so that the Holy Spirit passes through." This is a common theme in Orthodox epistemology: true creativity can only come from God, and people become able to channel it through fasting and discipline of the flesh, as well as through mastery of an authorized tradition (Johnson 2011, Menonville 2017). Much the same goes for the composing of *qiné* poetry by church scholars. For the souvenir paintings, on the other hand, there was no such need to fast, since "God doesn't say anything" about them.

What set Zege's painting tradition apart from others, according to Mebratu, was the paint, all of which is produced from local plants. A number of plants are used, and the dyes are mixed with egg and sometimes buried for up to six months to get the right colors. Many of the painters in Zege display palates of the relevant flowers alongside their stalls where they paint and sell their works to index their provenance. The paints and the works produced from them are thus drawn from the bequest and covenant of Saint Betre Maryam that produced the coffee forest as a whole, while for tourists they speak of a local authenticity that elevates the works above mass reproduction.

Some local artists have begun producing "Picassos." These are iconic paintings on carved wood, much in the local style, but turned Cubist in imitation of Picasso's works; we see both sides of the Virgin's face at once, or a woman with her child both internal and external to her. I am told that it was originally a tourist who requested a Picasso-style icon, and local painters, finding something that appealed to visitors, were happy to produce more—not copies, but experiments with a new style. Two artists I spoke to described the Cubist style of combining multiple perspectives in a single image, and kept producing new pieces with subtle variations on the ones gone before (see the art on the cover of this book).[1]

The pieces are sold as souvenirs, but they capture something of the lives of Zege's painters: of a cosmopolitan awareness and a searching focus on the outside world, with a deep relationship with church tradition, which is performatively demonstrated for history-seeking tourists but also profoundly felt. The ability to learn from visitors is crucial—not just to know what other visitors will want to buy, but to broaden one's own perspectives.

Church paintings already perform interesting tricks with time and space. One mural in Azwa Maryam depicts Pharaoh's soldiers being drowned in the Red Sea as Moses and his followers look back on them; the soldiers' rifles can be seen floating away on the waves. Is this anachronism due to unawareness on the part of the eighteenth-century painters? Or does it equate the armies of the Pharaoh with contemporary foreign groups in Ethiopia (Koselleck 1985)? The paintings carry bits of other places and epochs into the here and now, but they do so in a dialogic, interactive fashion. Many of the murals of saints are not passive; churchgoers bow to them and address prayers to them, and priests perform venerations before them as they perform the liturgy. The paintings are active; their relationship to their object is one of complex indexicality (Mercier 1997, Gell 1998, Bosc-Tiessé 2008, Belting 2014).

In Orthodox terminology, the veneration bestowed on the icon is received by the prototype (Roudometof 2014). Some people describe icon paintings as "windows" rather than representations; they show us another world. In the words of

Abune Paulos (1988: 155), "an icon is not simply a religious painting designed to arouse appropriate emotions in the holder; it is one of the ways whereby God is revealed to humanity . . . Behind the painting of the saint is the person of the saint, and behind the saint God Himself." Iconic paintings, that is, are mediation points of human-divine contact.

On the doors and window blinds of churches there are many charcoal outlines of half-drawn saint and angels, the product of deacons and church students practicing their iconography (Griaule 2001). These practice etchings give us an indication of iconic religious practice in the course of being formed; they are part of a living tradition. However, I have the general impression that the veneration of icons is less prominent in Zege than, for example, in the Orthodoxies of Russia or Eastern Europe (e.g., Hanganu 2010, Luehrmann 2010). Priests give veneration to the icons on church walls during the performance of the liturgy, and carry large iconic paintings along with the *tabot* on saints' days and Epiphany. But at these times it is the *tabot,* not the icons, that is the main focus of lay and priestly attention. Lay people, meanwhile, often carry images of saints on small pieces of card or stored in their mobile phones, but these are not sanctified and are more like reminders than icons; I have never seen anyone pray to an image on their phone. I have been told that portable, painted, sanctified icons were used by traveling missionaries, but have never known anybody to carry one.

Likewise, the souvenir paintings destined for sale may look like icons, but they do not require any special treatment. But still they condense elements from great swathes of space and time in their construction. This is achieved through traditions of skill and the recognizable styles that tie them to twelfth-century Gonder or twentieth-century Spain, all produced with dyes from Zege plants. Enskilled knowledge allows the painters to fashion materials in ways that tie them to scales far beyond immediate experience. They turn the materials into indexes—tangible evidence—of the spatiotemporal transmission of knowledge, as well as of the relationship between Zege, its saints, and its history. The finished items are then taken away to other countries, where they will become evidence of the new owners' travels and encounters.

CONCLUSION: THE LIFE OF KNOWLEDGE

One thing that I have attempted to do in this chapter is to undermine the notion that the monasteries of Zege are necessarily conservative or backward-looking. While they are certainly regarded as guardians of history, the status of the monasteries as centers of skill and knowledge means that they tend to find themselves quite close to the unfolding of new events. At the same time, there is a clear progression of class privilege in the transmission of education and skills related to the church. As tourism has grown in economic importance, it is the sons of churchmen who have been in positions to make the most of new opportunities. It is important to state that most of these people are not wealthy by any standards, and many have undergone extreme privations in pursuit of education. But they have nonetheless become the people who introduce outsiders to the monasteries of Zege, from which other connections may ensue.

During my last visit in 2014 electricity cables were beginning to be brought into parts of the Zege peninsula as far as Ura. Until then, the main source of electricity had been the solar panel in the churchyard of Ura Kidane Mihret. The monastery had been able to purchase the panel with income from tourism, and as a result people from the surrounding area would go there when they needed to charge their mobile phones. There is nothing incongruous about this, much as it may seem to run against the grain of monastic seclusion and withdrawal. In fact the monasteries have often been points of engagement with the present, as testified to by the crowns, shields, water jugs, and other gifts from emperors that are now displayed in the new museum that has been built on the grounds of Ura Kidane Mihret.

What is perhaps more novel is the meeting of ascetic traditions of education and painting with contemporary forms of secular education at schools and universities. While students must travel to Bahir Dar for later high school and university, the people who are able to do so often come from church traditions and maintain relationships with the church-monasteries as tour guides, as we have seen. Traditional knowledge streams do not run counter to modern education, but people who are successful or privileged in one tradition are likely to find relative success in the other.

Again, this point is less surprising once we recognize how detailed and rigorous monastic traditions of education are. This is one of the central points of the novel *Dertogada*; the scholastic heritage of the monasteries should be comparable to those of NASA and modern spy agencies. The question is then what the contemporary world would look like if reimagined from a position where Ethiopian Orthodox scholarly traditions gained their rightful place alongside contemporary science.

NOTES

1. According to Johnson (2011: 44), the famous Ethiopian painter Afework Tekle also cites Picasso as an influence (and Picasso, in turn, was heavily influenced by African art). It is quite possible that the painters in Zege are aware of this work.

Conclusion

On this mountain the Lord almighty will prepare
a feast of rich food for all peoples,
a banquet of aged wine—
the best of meats and the finest of wines.

On this mountain he will destroy
the shroud that enfolds all peoples,
the sheet that covers all nations;
he will swallow up death forever

—ISAIAH 25:6–8

What is perhaps most remarkable about Orthodox practice in Zege is the degree to which fasting, prohibitions, and commensality produce an integrated ritual ecology. Orthodox practice offers structured, synchronized techniques for working on the material world and the body, and develops them into the appropriate states for the conduct of life. If the human condition is that we all live in the world of the flesh, then it behooves us to work on that world, and to mark out times and spaces where we are not completely immersed in its desires. We must dispense with the idea that the inward condition of practitioners does not matter in ritualistic systems, because it matters very much what fasting feels like: the tiredness and the happiness that practitioners describe, and the resultant effect on one's thoughts and one's soul. You work on the soul by working on the body.

The synchronized nature of fasting and feasting means that the foundations of religious practice happen on the scale of the collective, not the individual. For better or for worse, this amounts to a powerful normative force. But within this overarching synchronicity there remains a core of autonomy that stems from the nature of fasting. As Bynum (1987) notes, few religious practices give individuals so much say over what happens to their bodies. While there is little scope for violating the fasts without attracting social opprobrium, people are quite able to increase the intensity or frequency of their fasting, or indeed to formulate their own understandings of what a particular act of fasting will achieve. As we have seen, these practices prove quite variable over the trajectory of an individual life. While it is clear that deep rifts remain in Zege from the history of slavery, diligent fasting remains a way, ultimately irrefutable, in which slave descendants can demonstrate their moral constitution and their equal status as Orthodox Christians.

In feasting, too, there are different registers of inclusion and exclusion, from the purity of the Eucharist, to the avoidance of Muslim meat but the sharing of other kinds of hospitality, to the *zikir* feasts that build relations with saints without stringent purity regulations that apply to more official rituals.

Successive Ethiopian governments and other modernizers since 1974 have opposed certain practices that they consider unproductive or harmful; the most obvious examples being large-scale funerary feasting and, with less success, the refusal to work on saints' days. But it is quite difficult to stop people from fasting, if they don't want to be stopped.

Not all prohibitions concern food, and it is important to understand fasting and food restrictions within the broader regime of Orthodox observance. But in one way or another, feeding and fasting have been the dominant idioms by which people in Zege have described how life has changed and how the really important things get sorted out. Dietary restrictions distinguish Orthodox Christians from others, while eating together and eating in memory of people and saints establish and affirm the basic obligations that are vital to existence. Refusing to eat together, on the other hand, is the ultimate form of stigma, exclusion, and fear.

We have seen that knowledge in Ethiopian Orthodox tradition is closely dependent on the physical and spiritual condition of the knower. Religious poets and artists must fast in order to become channels for creation. Scholars must observe ascetic practices so that angels will guide their learning. This connection between knowledge and the condition of the body provides a clue to understanding the wider paradigm of Orthodox materiality in Zege. Prohibitions are part of the moral formation and conditioning of matter so as to make it amenable to the mediation of divine knowledge. Belief, then, is not opposed to practice but is dependent upon it.

There is one final point to make about Ethiopian traditions of knowledge: they are never complete. Ethiopian Biblical commentary does not attempt to reconcile contradictory interpretations, but adds them one upon the other, and expects further commentaries to be added in the future (Cowley 1989). I hope that this work will be accepted in the same spirit, as a contribution to an open discussion on a topic that can never be fully known. The people of Zege have shared their food and knowledge with me, and they will always have my gratitude. I look forward to our future meals and conversations.

REFERENCE LIST

Ethiopian authors are listed by first name.

Abbink, Jon. 2011. "Religion in Public Spaces: Emerging Muslim-Christian Polemics in Ethiopia." *African Affairs* 110 (439): 253–74.

———. 2014. "Religious Freedom and the Political Order: The Ethiopian 'Secular State' and the Containment of Muslim Identity Politics." *Journal of Eastern African Studies* 8 (3): 346–65.

Abdussamad H. Ahmad. 1997. "Priest Planters and Slavers of Zägé (Ethiopia), 1900–1935." *International Journal of African Historical Studies* 29 (3): 543–56.

———. 1999. "Trading in Slaves in Bela-Shangul and Gumuz, Ethiopia: Border Enclaves in History, 1897–1938." *Journal of African History* 40 (3): 433–46.

Afework Hailu Beyene. 2014. *The Shaping of Judaic Identity of the Ethiopian Orthodox Tawahado Church: Historical and Literary Evidence.* London: School of Oriental and African Studies.

Alemayehu Moges. 1973. "Language, Teaching, and Curriculum in Traditional Education of the EOC." *Ethiopian Journal of Education* 6 (1): 87–114.

Ancel, Stéphane. 2005. "Mahbär et Sänbäte: Associations Religieuses en Éthiopie." *Aethiopica* 8:95–111.

Ancel, Stéphane, and Éloi Ficquet. 2015. "The Ethiopian Orthodox Tewahedo Church (EOTC) and the Challenges of Modernity." In *Understanding Contemporary Ethiopia: Monarchy, Revolution, and the Legacy of Meles Zenawi,* edited by Gérard Prunier and Éloi Ficquet. London: Hurst.

Andreas Eshete. 2012. "Modernity: Its Title to Uniqueness and Its Advent in Ethiopia." In *What Is Zemenawinet? Perspectives on Ethiopian Modernity.* Addis Ababa: Friedrich-Ebert-Stiftung.

Antohin, Alexandra E. S. 2014. *Expressions of Sacred Promise: Ritual and Devotion in Ethiopian Orthodox Praxis.* London: University College London.

Ardener, Edwin. 1987. "Remote Areas: Some Theoretical Considerations." In *Anthropology at Home,* edited by Anthony Jackson. London: Tavistock.

Argenti, Nicolas. 2007. *The Intestines of the State: Youth, Violence, and Belated Histories in the Cameroon Grassfields.* Chicago: University of Chicago Press.

Arras, V. 1974. *De Transitu Mariae Apocrypha Aethiopice, II.* Corpus Scriptorum Christianorum Orientalum. Leeuven: Peeters.

Aspen, Harald. 2001. *Amhara Traditions of Knowledge: Spirit Mediums and Their Clients.* Wiesbaden: Harrassowitz.

Austen, Ralph A. 1993. "The Moral Economy of Witchcraft: An Essay in Comparative History." In *Modernity and Its Malcontents: Ritual and Power in Postcolonial Africa,* edited by Jean Comaroff and John Comaroff. Chicago: University of Chicago Press.

Ayala Takla-Haymanot. 1981. *The Ethiopian Church and Its Christological Doctrine.* Addis Ababa: Graphic Printers.

Aymro Wondmagegnu and Joachim Motovu. 1970. *The Ethiopian Orthodox Church.* Addis Ababa: Ethiopian Orthodox Mission.

Bahru Zewde. 2002. *Pioneers of Change In Ethiopia: Reformist Intellectuals of the Early Twentieth Century.* Athens: Ohio University Press.

Bairu Tafla. 1986. "Titles, Ranks, and Offices in the Ethiopian Orthodox Tawahdo Church: A Preliminary Survey." *Internationale Kirchliche Zeitschrift* 76:293–304.

Bandak, Andreas. 2015. "Exemplary Series and Christian Typology: Modelling on Sainthood in Damascus." *Journal of the Royal Anthropological Institute* 21 (S1): S47–63.

Bandak, Andreas, and Tom Boylston. 2014. "The 'Orthodoxy' of Orthodoxy: On Moral Imperfection, Correctness, and Deferral in Religious Worlds." *Religion and Society: Advances in Research* 5:25–46.

Bataille, Georges. 1991. *The Accursed Share: An Essay on General Economy.* Vol. 1, *Consumption.* Translated by Robert Hurley. Cambridge, MA: Zone.

Bayart, Jean-François. 2009. *The State in Africa: The Politics of the Belly.* 2nd ed. Cambridge: Polity.

Baynes-Rock, Marcus. 2015. "Ethiopian Buda as Hyenas: Where the Social Is More Than Human." *Folklore* 126 (3): 266–82.

Bialecki, Jon. 2014. "Does God Exist in Methodological Atheism? On Tanya Luhrmann's When God Talks Back and Bruno Latour." *Anthropology of Consciousness* 25 (1): 32–52.

———. 2017. *A Diagram for Fire: Miracles and Variation in an American Charismatic Movement.* Berkeley: University of California Press.

Bielo, James S. 2009. *Words upon The Word: An Ethnography of Evangelical Bible Group Study.* New York: New York University Press.

———. 2011. *Emerging Evangelicals: Faith, Modernity, and the Desire for Authenticity.* New York: New York University Press.

Binayew Tamrat Getahun. 2014. *A History of Zegie Peninsula, 1902–1991.* Lambert Academic.

Binns, John. 2002. *An Introduction to The Christian Orthodox Churches.* Cambridge: Cambridge University Press.

———. n.d. *In High Mountains, Set Apart.* Unpublished Manuscript.

Bloch, Maurice. 1971. *Placing the Dead: Tombs, Ancestral Villages and Kinship Organization in Madagascar.* London: London Seminar.

———. 2005. "Ritual and Deference." In *Essays on Cultural Transmission*, 123–38. LSE Monographs on Social Anthropology. Oxford: Berg.

———. 2008. "Why Religion Is Nothing Special but Is Central." *Philosophical Transactions of the Royal Society B: Biological Sciences* 363 (1499): 2055–61.

———. 2012. *Anthropology and the Cognitive Challenge*. Cambridge: Cambridge University Press.

Bloch, Maurice, and Jonathan Parry. 1982. "Introduction: Death and the Regeneration of Life." In *Death and the Regeneration of Life*. Cambridge: Cambridge University Press.

Boddy, Janice. 1989. *Wombs and Alien Spirits: Women, Men, and the Zar Cult in Northern Sudan*. Madison: University of Wisconsin Press.

Bonacci, Giulia. 2000. *The Ethiopian Orthodox Church and the State, 1974–1991: Analysis of an Ambiguous Religious Policy*. London: Centre of Ethiopian Studies.

Bosc-Tiessé, Claire. 2008. *Les îles de La Mémoire: Fabrique des Images et Écriture de l'histoire des Églises du Lac Tana, Ethiopie, XVIIe–XVIIIe Siècle*. Paris: Publications de la Sorbonne.

Bourdieu, Pierre. 1977. *Outline of a Theory of Practice*. Cambridge: Cambridge University Press.

boyd, danah. 2007. "Social Network Sites: Public, Private, or What?" *Knowledge Tree* 13.

Boyer, Dominic. 2012. "From Media Anthropology to the Anthropology of Mediation." In *The SAGE Handbook of Social Anthropology*, edited by Richard Fardon et al. Thousand Oaks, CA: SAGE.

Boylston, Tom. 2014. "What Kind of Territory? On Public Religion and Space in Ethiopia." *ImmanentFrame*. http://blogs.ssrc.org/tif/2014/08/26/what-kind-of-territory-on-public-religion-and-space-in-ethiopia/.

———. 2017. "Things Not for Themselves: Idolatry and Consecration in Orthodox Ethiopia." In *Christianity and the Limits of Materiality*, edited by Minna Opas and Anna Haapelainen. London: Bloomsbury.

Brown, Peter. 1988. *The Body and Society: Men, Women and Sexual Renunciation in Early Christianity*. London: Columbia University Press.

Budge, Sir E. A. Wallis, trans. 2000. *The Queen of Sheba and Her Only Son Menyelek (Kebra Nagast)*. Ethiopian Series. Cambridge, Ontario: In Parenthesis.

Bynum, Caroline Walker. 1987. *Holy Feast and Holy Fast: The Religious Significance of Food to Medieval Women*. Berkeley and London: University of California Press.

———. 1995. *The Resurrection of the Body in Western Christianity, 200–1336*. New York and Chichester: Columbia University Press.

Candea, Matei. 2012. "Derrida En Corse? Hospitality as Scale-Free Abstraction." *Journal of the Royal Anthropological Institute* 18 (S1): S34–48.

Candea, Matei, and Giovanni Da Col. 2012. "The Return to Hospitality." *Journal of the Royal Anthropological Institute* 18 (S1): S1–19.

Cannell, Fenella. 2006. "Introduction: The Anthropology of Christianity." In *The Anthropology of Christianity*, edited by Fenella Cannell, 1–50. Durham: Duke University Press.

Carsten, Janet. 2013. "Introduction: Blood Will Out." *Journal of the Royal Anthropological Institute* 19 (S1): S1–23.

Cerulli, Enrico. 1946. "Gli Atti Di Batra Maryam (Fine)." *Rassegna Di Studi Etiopici* 5:42–66.

Chaillot, Christine. 2002. *The Ethiopian Orthodox Tewahedo Church Tradition: A Brief Introduction to Its Life and Spirituality*. Paris: Inter-Orthodox Dialogue.

Cheesman, Robert E. 1936. *Lake Tana and the Blue Nile: An Abyssinian Quest.* London: Macmillan.

Chua, Liana. 2011. *The Christianity of Culture: Conversion, Ethnic Citizenship, and the Matter of Religion in Malaysian Borneo.* Basingstoke, UK: Palgrave Macmillan.

Clapham, Christopher. 1969. *Haile Selassie's Government.* New York: Praeger.

———. 1988. *Transformation and Continuity in Revolutionary Ethiopia.* Cambridge: Cambridge University Press.

———. 2017. "The Ethiopian Developmental State." *Third World Quarterly* published online June 2, 2017:1–15. doi: https://doi.org/10.1080/01436597.2017.1328982.

Cohen, Leonardo. 2009. *The Missionary Strategies of the Jesuits in Ethiopia.* Wiesbaden: Harrassowitz.

Cole, Jennifer. 2001. *Forget Colonialism? Sacrifice and the Art of Memory in Madagascar.* Berkeley: University of California Press.

Comaroff, Jean, and John L. Comaroff. 1999. "Occult Economies and the Violence of Abstraction: Notes from the South African Postcolony." *American Ethnologist* 26 (2): 297–303.

Cowley, Roger W. 1972. "Attitudes to the Dead in the Ethiopian Orthodox Church." *Sobornost* 6 (4): 241–56.

———. 1983. *The Traditional Interpretation of the Apocalypse of St John in the Ethiopian Orthodox Church.* Cambridge: Cambridge University Press.

———. 1989. *Ethiopian Biblical Interpretation: A Study in Exegetical Tradition and Hermeneutics.* Cambridge: Cambridge University Press.

Crummey, Donald. 1972. *Priests and Politicians: Protestant and Catholic Missions in Orthodox Ethiopia, 1830–1868.* Oxford: Clarendon.

———. 1988. "Imperial Legitimacy and the Creation of Neo-Solomonic Ideology in 19-Century Ethiopia." *Cahier Des Études Africaines* 28 (109): 13–43.

———. 2000. *Land and Society in the Christian Kingdom of Ethiopia: From the Thirteenth to the Twentieth Century.* Oxford: James Currey; Athens: Ohio University Press; Addis Ababa: Addis Ababa University Press.

Debray, Régis. 1991. *Cours de Médiologie Générale.* Paris: Gallimard.

———. 1996. *Media Manifestos: On the Technological Transmission of Cultural Forms.* London: Verso.

Derat, Marie-Laure. 2003. "Batra Maryam." In *Encyclopaedia Aethiopica,* vol. 1, *A–C.* Wiesbaden: Harrassowitz.

Descola, Philippe. 2013. *Beyond Nature and Culture.* Chicago: University of Chicago Press.

Donham, Donald L. 1999. *Marxist Modern: An Ethnographic History of the Ethiopian Revolution.* Berkeley: University of California Press; Oxford: James Currey.

———. 2002. "Introduction." In *Remapping Ethiopia: Socialism & After,* edited by Wendy James, Donald L. Donham, Eisei Kurimoto, and Alessandro Triulzi, 1–8. Oxford: James Currey; Athens: Ohio University Press; Addis Ababa: Addis Ababa University Press.

Douglas, Mary. 1966. *Purity and Danger: An Analysis of Concepts of Pollution and Taboo.* London: Routledge & Kegan Paul.

———. 1999. *Leviticus as Literature.* Oxford: Oxford University Press.

———. 2003. *Natural Symbols: Explorations in Cosmology.* London: Routledge.

Duffy, Eamon. 1992. *The Stripping of the Altars: Traditional Religion in England, 1400–1580*. New Haven: Yale University Press.

Dulin, John. 2016. "Intelligible Tolerance, Ambiguous Tensions, Antagonistic Revelations: Patterns of Muslim-Christian Coexistence in Orthodox Christian Majority Ethiopia." University of California, San Diego.

———. 2017. "Transvaluing ISIS in Orthodox Christian Majority Ethiopia: On the Inhibition of Violence." *Current Anthropology* 58 (6): 785–804.

Eickelman, Dale F., and Jon W. Anderson. 2003. *New Media in the Muslim World: The Emerging Public Sphere*. 2nd ed. Bloomington: Indiana University Press.

Eisenlohr, Patrick. 2012. "Media and Religious Diversity." *Annual Review of Anthropology* 41:37–55.

Engelhardt, Jeffers. Forthcoming. "Listening and the Sacramental Life: Degrees of Mediation in Greek Orthodox Christianity." In *Praying with the Senses: Contemporary Orthodox Christian Spirituality in Practice*, edited by Sonja Luehrmann. Bloomington: Indiana University Press.

Engelke, Matthew. 2007. *A Problem of Presence: Beyond Scripture in an African Church*. Berkeley and London: University of California Press.

Ephraim Isaac. 2013. *The Ethiopian Orthodox Täwahïdo Church*. Trenton, NJ: Red Sea.

Evans-Pritchard, Edward E. 1937. *Witchcraft, Oracles and Magic among the Azande*. Oxford: Clarendon.

Feeley-Harnik, Gillian. 1981. *The Lord's Table: Eucharist and Passover in Early Christianity*. Philadelphia: University of Pennsylvania Press.

———. 1995. "Religion and Food: An Anthropological Perspective." *Journal of the American Academy of Religion* 63 (3): 565–82.

Fernyhough, Timothy. 2010. *Serfs, Slaves and Shifta: Modes of Production and Resistance in Pre-Revolutionary Ethiopia*. Addis Ababa: Shama.

Feuchtwang, Stephan. 2010. *The Anthropology of Religion, Charisma, and Ghosts: Chinese Lessons for Adequate Theory*. Berlin and New York: W. de Gruyter.

Ficquet, Éloi. 2006. "Flesh Soaked in Faith: Meat as a Marker of the Boundary between Christians and Muslims in Ethiopia." In *Islam in Africa*, 39–56. Leiden: Brill.

Finneran, Niall. 2003. "Ethiopian Evil Eye Belief and the Magical Symbolism of Iron Working." *Folklore* 114 (3): 427–32.

———. 2007. *The Archaeology of Ethiopia*. Oxford: Routledge.

Fisseha Tadesse. 2002. "The Representation of Jesus: Reflecting Attitudes of Masculinity in the Ethiopian Theological Tradition." *Journal of Ethiopian Studies* 35 (1): 67–87.

Fontein, Joost. 2011. "Graves, Ruins & Belonging: Towards an Anthropology of Proximity." *Journal of the Royal Anthropological Institute* 17 (4): 706–27.

Fortes, Meyer. 1966. "Totem and Taboo." *Proceedings of the Royal Anthropological Institute of Great Britain and Ireland* 1966:5–22. doi: https://doi.org/10.2307/3031711.

Freeman, Dena. 2003. "Conclusion I: Understanding Marginalisation in Ethiopia." In *Peripheral People: The Excluded Minorities of Ethiopia*, edited by Dena Freeman and Alula Pankhurst, 301–33. Lawrenceville, NJ: Red Sea.

Freeman, Dena, and Alula Pankhurst. 2003. *Peripheral People: The Excluded Minorities of Ethiopia*. Trenton, NJ: Red Sea.

Fritsch, Emmanuel. 2001. *The Liturgical Year of the Ethiopian Church*: Master Printing Press.

——. 2011. "Qedase." In *Encyclopaedia Aethiopica*, vol. 4, *O–X*, edited by Siegbert Uhlig. Wiesbaden: Harrassowitz.

Galt, Anthony H. 1982. "The Evil Eye as a Synthetic Image and Its Meanings on the Island of Pantelleria, Italy." *American Ethnologist* 9 (4): 664–81.

Gamst, Frederick. 1979. "Wayto Ways: Change from Hunting to Peasant Life." In *Proceedings of the 5th International Conference on Ethiopian Studies*, edited by Robert Hess. Chicago: University of Illinois Press.

Gell, Alfred. 1992. *The Anthropology of Time: Cultural Constructions of Temporal Maps and Images*. Oxford and Providence: Berg.

——. 1996. "Reflections on a Cut Finger: Taboo in the Umeda Conception of the Self." In *Things as They Are: New Directions in Phenomenological Anthropology*, edited by Michael Jackson. Bloomington: Indiana University Press.

——. 1998. *Art and Agency: An Anthropological Theory*. Oxford: Clarendon.

Gennep, Arnold van. 1960. *The Rites of Passage*. London: Routledge & Kegan Paul.

Geschiere, Peter. 1997. *The Modernity of Witchcraft: Politics and the Occult in Postcolonial Africa*. Translated by Janet Roitman and Peter Geschiere. Charlottesville: University of Virginia Press.

Getatchew Haile. 1988. "A History of the Tabot of Atronesä Maryam in Amhara (Ethiopia)." *Paideuma* 34:13–22.

——. 1990. *The Faith of the Unctionists in the Ethiopian Church*. Leeuven: Peeters Press.

——. n.d. "Vision of Mary (Raiye Maryam) under Attack." Unpublished Manuscript. www.ethiopia.org/files/Vision_of_Mary_GH.pdf. Accessed June 23.

Girma Mohammed. 2012a. "Cultural Politics and Education in Ethiopia: A Search for a Viable Indigenous Legend." *Journal of Politics and Law* 5 (1).

——. 2012b. *Understanding Religion and Social Change in Ethiopia: Toward a Hermeneutic of Covenant*. London: Palgrave Macmillan.

Graeber, David. 2011. *Debt: The First 5000 Years*. Brooklyn: Melville House.

——. 2012. "On Social Currencies and Human Economies: Some Notes on the Violence of Equivalence." *Social Anthropology* 20 (4): 411–28.

Griaule, Marcel. 2001. *Silhouettes et Graffiti Abyssins*. Paris: Maisonneuve & Larose.

Gudeman, Stephen. 2008. *Economy's Tension: The Dialectics of Community and Market*. Oxford: Berghahn.

Hacking, Ian. 1999. *The Social Construction of What?* Cambridge, MA: Harvard University Press.

Hammerschmidt, Ernst. 1965. "Jewish Elements in the Cult of the Ethiopian Church." *Journal of Ethiopian Studies* 2:1–12.

Hanganu, Gabriel. 2010. "Eastern Christians and Religious Objects: Personal and Material Biographies Entangled." In *Eastern Christians in Anthropological Perspective*, edited by Chris Hann and Hermann Goltz, 33–55. Berkeley and London: University of California Press.

Hann, Chris. 2007. "The Anthropology of Christianity Per Se." *European Journal of Sociology* 48 (3): 383–410.

Hann, Chris, and Hermann Goltz. 2010. "Introduction: The Other Christianity?" In *Eastern Christians in Anthropological Perspective*, edited by Chris Hann and Hermann Goltz, 1–32. Berkeley and London: University of California Press.

Hannig, Anita. 2013. "The Pure and the Pious: Corporeality, Flow, and Transgression in Ethiopian Orthodox Christianity." *Journal of Religion in Africa* 43 (3): 297–328.

———. 2014. "Spiritual Border Crossings: Childbirth, Postpartum Seclusion, and Religious Alterity in Amhara, Ethiopia." *Africa* 84 (2): 294–313.

———. 2017. *Beyond Surgery: Injury, Healing, and Religion at an Ethiopian Hospital.* Chicago: University of Chicago Press.

Haustein, Jörg. 2009. "Navigating Political Revolutions: Ethiopia's Churches during and after the Mengistu Regime." In *Falling Walls: The Year 1989/90 as a Turning Point in the History of World Christianity,* 117–36. Wiesbaden: Harrassowitz.

———. 2011. *Writing Religious History: The Historiography of Ethiopian Pentecostalism.* Wiesbaden: Harrassowitz.

Hayden, Brian. 2009. "Funerals as Feasts: Why Are They So Important?" *Cambridge Archaeological Journal* 19 (1): 29–52.

Haynes, Naomi. 2013. "On the Potential and Problems of Pentecostal Exchange." *American Anthropologist* 115 (1): 85–95.

Heo, Angie. 2015. "Relic Technics and the Extensible Memory of Coptic Orthodoxy." *Material Religion: The Journal of Objects, Art, and Belief* 11 (1): 50–74.

Hermann, Yodit-Judith. 2010. "Le Rituel de l'eau Bénite: Une Réponse Sociale et Symbolique à La Pandémie Du Sida." *Annales d'Éthiopie* 25:229–45.

———. 2012. L'Implication du Christianisme Éthiopien dans la Lutte contre le Sida: Une Socio-anthropologie de la "Guérison." Thesis. Université de Provence: Provence.

Hirsch, Eric, and Charles Stewart. 2005. "Introduction: Ethnographies of Historicity." *History and Anthropology* 16 (3): 261–74.

Hirschkind, Charles. 2006. *The Ethical Soundscape: Cassette Sermons and Islamic Counterpublics.* New York: Columbia University Press.

Hoben, Allan. 1970. "Social Stratification in Traditional Amhara Society." In *Social Stratification in Africa,* edited by Arthur Tuden and Leonard Plotnicov, 187–224. New York: Free.

———. 1973. *Land Tenure among the Amhara of Ethiopia: The Dynamics of Cognatic Descent.* Chicago and London: University of Chicago Press.

Hocart, A. M. 2004. *The Life-Giving Myth, and Other Essays.* London: Routledge.

Hodder, Ian. 2012. *Entangled: An Archaeology of the Relationships between Humans and Things.* Oxford: Wiley-Blackwell.

Hodges, Matt. 2008. "Rethinking Time's Arrow: Bergson, Deleuze and the Anthropology of Time." *Anthropological Theory* 8 (4): 399–429.

Ingold, Tim. 2000. "The Temporality of the Landscape." In *The Perception of the Environment: Essays on Livelihood, Dwelling and Skill,* 189–208. London: Routledge.

James, Wendy. 1986. "Lifelines: Exchange Marriage among the Gumuz." In *The Southern Marches of Imperial Ethiopia: Essays in History and Social Anthropology,* edited by Donald L. Donham and Wendy James, 119–47. Oxford: James Currey.

Johnson, Edwin Hamilton. 2011. *Patronage and the Theological Integrity of Ethiopian Orthodox Sacred Paintings in Present Day Addis Ababa, Ethiopia.* London: School of Oriental and African Studies.

Kane, Thomas Leiper. 1990. *Amharic-English Dictionary.* Vols. 1 and 2. Wiesbaden: Harrassowitz.

Kaplan, Steven. 1984. *The Monastic Holy Man and the Christianization of Early Solomonic Ethiopia*. Wiesbaden: Steiner.

———. 1986. "The Ethiopian Cult of the Saints: A Preliminary Investigation." *Paideuma* 32:1–13.

———. 1995. *The Beta Israel (Falasha) in Ethiopia: From Earliest Times to the Twentieth Century*. New York: New York University Press.

———. 2003a. "Burial." In *Encyclopaedia Aethiopica*, vol. 1, A–C, 645–48. Wiesbaden: Harrassowitz.

———. 2003b. "The Social and Religious Functions of the Eucharist in Medieval Ethiopia." *Annales d'Éthiopie* 19:7–18.

———. 2008. "Finding the True Cross: The Social-Political Dimensions of the Ethiopian Mäsqäl Festival." *Journal of Religion in Africa* 38 (4): 447–65.

———. 2014. "The Christianization of Time in Fifteenth Century Ethiopia." In *Religious Conversion: Experience and Meaning*, edited by Miri Rubin and Ira Katznelson, 81–98. Farnham, UK: Ashgate.

Keane, Webb. 2007. *Christian Moderns: Freedom and Fetish in the Mission Encounter*. Berkeley and London: University of California Press.

———. 2014. "Rotting Bodies: The Clash of Stances toward Materiality and Its Ethical Affordances." *Current Anthropology* 55 (S10).

Khan, Naveeda. 2011. "The Acoustics of Muslim Striving: Loudspeaker Use in Ritual Practice in Pakistan." *Comparative Studies in Society and History* 53 (3): 571–94.

Klepeis, Peter, Izabela A. Orlowska, Eliza F. Kent, Catherine L. Cardelús, Peter Scull, Alemayehu Wassie Eshete, and Carrie Woods. 2016. "Ethiopian Church Forests: A Hybrid Model of Protection." *Human Ecology* 44 (6): 715–30.

Koselleck, Reinhart. 1985. *Futures Past: On the Semantics of Historical Time*. Cambridge, MA, and London: MIT Press.

Kuroda, Akinobu. 2007. "The Maria Theresa Dollar in the Early Twentieth-Century Red Sea Region: A Complementary Interface between Multiple Markets." *Financial History Review* 14 (1): 89–110.

Lambek, Michael J. 1992. "Taboo as Cultural Practice among Malagasy Speakers." *Man*, New Series, 27 (2): 245–66.

———. 1993. *Knowledge and Practice in Mayotte : Local Discourses of Islam, Sorcery and Spirit Possession*. Toronto and London: University of Toronto Press.

———. 2002. *The Weight of the Past: Living with History in Mahajanga, Madagascar*. Basingstoke, UK: Palgrave Macmillan.

Larebo, Haile M. 1986. "The Orthodox Church and the State in the Ethiopian Revolution 1974–1984." *Religion in Communist Lands* 14 (2): 148–59.

———. 1988. "The Ethiopian Orthodox Church." In *Eastern Christianity and Politics in the Twentieth Century*, edited by Pedro Ramet, 375–99. Durham and London: Duke University Press.

Larkin, Brian. 2013. "The Politics and Poetics of Infrastructure." *Annual Review of Anthropology* 42:327–43.

Lee, Ralph. 2011. "Symbolic Interpretations in Ethiopic and Ephremic Literature." PhD diss., London, School of Oriental and African Studies.

———. 2013. "Ethiopian Orthodox Hermeneutics." Seminar paper delivered to Ethiopian Graduate School of Theology, March 19, 2013. Addis Ababa.

Levine, Donald N. 1965. *Wax & Gold: Tradition and Innovation in Ethiopian Culture.* Chicago: University of Chicago Press.

———. 1974. *Greater Ethiopia.* Chicago: University of Chicago Press.

Lévi-Strauss, Claude. 1964. *Totemism.* Translated by Rodney Needham. London: Merlin.

———. 1966. *The Savage Mind.* Chicago: University of Chicago Press.

Lloyd, G. E. R. 1996. *Adversaries and Authorities: Investigations into Ancient Greek and Chinese Science.* Cambridge: Cambridge University Press.

———. 2011. "Humanity between Gods and Beasts? Ontologies in Question." *Journal of the Royal Anthropological Institute* 17 (4): 829–45.

Lomnitz, Claudio. 2005. *Death and the Idea of Mexico.* Cambridge, MA: Zone.

Luehrmann, Sonja. 2010. "A Dual Quarrel of Images on the Middle Volga: Icon Veneration in the Face of Protestant and Pagan Critique." In *Eastern Christians in Anthropological Perspective,* edited by Chris Hann and Hermann Goltz, 56–78. Berkeley and London: University of California Press.

Lyons, Diane. 2014. "Perceptions of Consumption: Constituting Potters, Farmers, and Blacksmiths in the Culinary Continuum in Eastern Tigray, Northern Highland Ethiopia." *African Archaeological Review* 31:169–201.

Lyons, Diane, and Andrea Freeman. 2009. "'I'm Not Evil': Materialising Identities of Marginalised Potters in Tigray Region, Ethiopia." *Azania: Archaeological Research in Africa* 44 (1): 75–93.

Mains, Daniel. 2012. *Hope Is Cut: Youth, Unemployment, and the Future in Urban Ethiopia.* Philadelphia: Temple University Press.

Malara, Diego Maria. 2017. "A Geometry of Blessing: Embodiment, Relatedness, and Exorcism amongst Ethiopian Orthodox Christians in Addis Ababa, Ethiopia." PhD diss., University of Edinburgh.

Malara, Diego Maria, and Tom Boylston. 2016. "Vertical Love: Forms of Submission and Top-Down Power in Orthodox Ethiopia." *Social Analysis: Journal of Cultural and Social Practice.*

Marcus, Cressida. 2001. "The Production of Patriotic Spirituality: Ethiopian Orthodox Women's Experience of War and Social Crisis." *Northeast African Studies* 8 (3): 179–208.

———. 2002. "Imperial Nostalgia: Christian Restoration & Civic Decay in Gondar." In *Remapping Ethiopia: Socialism & After,* edited by Wendy James, Donald L. Donham, Eisei Kurimoto, and Alessandro Triulzi, 239–56. Oxford: James Currey; Athens: Ohio University Press; Addis Ababa: Addis Ababa University Press.

———. 2008. "Sacred Time, Civic Calendar: Religious Plurality and the Centrality of Religion in Ethiopian Society." *International Journal of Ethiopian Studies* 3 (2): 143–75.

Marcus, Harold G. 1994. *A History of Ethiopia.* Berkeley, Los Angeles, and London: University of California Press.

Marsland, Rebecca. 2015. "Keeping Magical Harm Invisible: Public Health, Witchcraft and the Law in Kyela, Tanzania." In *The Clinic and the Court: Law, Medicine and Anthropology,* edited by Tobias Kelly, Ian Harper, and Akshay Khanna. Cambridge: Cambridge University Press.

Masquelier, Adeline. 1993. "Narratives of Power, Images of Wealth: The Ritual Economy of Bori in the Market." In *Modernity and Its Malcontents: Ritual and Power in Postcolonial Africa*, edited by Jean Comaroff and John Comaroff, 3–33. Chicago: University of Chicago Press.

Mazzarella, William. 2004. "Culture, Globalization, Mediation." *Annual Review of Anthropology* 33:345–67.

———. 2009. "Affect: What Is It Good For?" In *Enchantments of Modernity: Empire, Nation, Globalization*, edited by Saurabh Dube, 291–309. New Delhi and London: Routledge.

Mbembe, Achille. 1992. "Provisional Notes on the Postcolony." *Africa* 62 (1): 3–37.

McCann, James C. 1995. *People of the Plow: An Agricultural History of Ethiopia, 1800–1900*. Madison: University of Wisconsin Press.

McLuhan, Marshall. 1964. *Understanding Media: The Extensions of Man*. London: Routledge & Kegan Paul.

Ménonville, Siena-Antonia de. 2017. "Image in Decency: An Anthropology of Christian Orthodox Image Production in Ethiopia Today." PhD diss., Paris, Université Paris Descartes.

Merawi Tebeje. 2005. "Fethat." In *Encyclopaedia Aethiopica*, vol. 2, *D–Ha*, edited by Siegbert Uhlig et al., 535–36. Wiesbaden: Harrassowitz.

Mercier, Jacques. 1997. *Art That Heals: Image as Medicine in Ethiopia*. New York and London: Prestel.

Merid Wolde Aregay. 1988. "The Early History of Ethiopia's Coffee Trade and the Rise of Shawa." *Journal of African History* 29 (1): 19–25.

Mersha Alehegne. 2010. "Täzkar." In *Encyclopaedia Aethiopica*, vol. 4, *O–X*, edited by Siegbert Uhlig et al., 882. Wiesbaden: Harrassowitz.

Messay Kebede. 1999. *Survival and Modernization: Ethiopia's Enigmatic Present: A Philosophical Discourse*. Lawrenceville, NJ: Red Sea.

Messing, Simon D. 1957. "The Highland-Plateau Amhara of Ethiopia." PhD diss., University of Pennsylvania.

Meyer, Birgit. 2011. "Mediation and Immediacy: Sensational Forms, Semiotic Ideologies and the Question of the Medium." *Social Anthropology* 19 (1): 23–39.

———. 2014. "Mediation and the Genesis of Presence." *Religion and Society: Advances in Research* 5:205–54.

Moore, Henrietta, and Todd Sanders. 2001. "Magical Interpretations and Material Realities: An Introduction." In *Magical Interpretations, Material Realities*, 1–27. London: Routledge.

Munn, Nancy D. 1992. "The Cultural Anthropology of Time: A Critical Essay." *Annual Review of Anthropology* 21:93–123.

Oosterbaan, Martijn. 2008. "Spiritual Attunement: Pentecostal Radio and the Soundscape of a Favela in Rio de Janeiro." *Social Text* 26 (3 96): 123–45.

Orlowska, Izabela. 2006. "Re-Imagining Empire: Ethiopian Political Culture under Yohannis IV (1872–89)." Phd diss., London, School of Oriental and African Studies.

———. 2013. "Forging a Nation: The Ethiopian Millennium Celebration and the Multiethnic State." *Nations and Nationalism* 19 (2): 296–316.

———. 2015. "Ethiopian Church Forests: Hubs of Social and Religious Life and Pockets of Remaining Biodiversity." Presented at the 19th International Conference of Ethiopian Studies, Warsaw.

Ortner, Sherry B. 1973. "On Key Symbols." *American Anthropologist* 75 (5): 1338–46.

Pankhurst, Alula. 1992. *Resettlement and Famine in Ethiopia: The Villagers' Experience.* Manchester: Manchester University Press.

———. 2003. "Introduction: Dimensions and Conceptions of Marginalisation." In *Peripheral People: The Excluded Minorities of Ethiopia,* edited by Dena Freeman and Alula Pankhurst, 1–26. Lawrenceville, NJ: Red Sea.

Pankhurst, Alula, and Harald Aspen. 2005. "Grave Culture in Christian Regions." In *Encyclopaedia Aethiopica, D-Ha,* edited by Siegbert Uhlig et al., 2:873–75. Wiesbaden: Harrassowitz.

Pankhurst, Alula, and Damen Haile Mariam. 2000. "The Iddir in Ethiopia: Historical Development, Social Function, and Potential Role in HIV/AIDS Prevention and Control." *Northeast African Studies* 7 (2): 35–57.

Pankhurst, Helen. 1992. *Gender, Development, and Identity: An Ethiopian Study.* London: ZED.

Pankhurst, Richard. 1968. *Economic History of Ethiopia, 1800–1935.* Addis Ababa: Haile Selassie I University Press.

———. 1987. "Some Brief Notes on the Ethiopian Tabot and Mänbärä Tabot." *Quaderni Di Studi Etiopici,* no. 8–9:28–32.

———. 1990. *A Social History of Ethiopia.* Addis Ababa: Institute of Ethiopian Studies.

———. 2011. "Slavery and Emancipation in Traditional Ethiopia: The Role of the Fetha Nagast, or Laws of the Kings." *African and Asian Studies* 10 (1): 32–40. doi: https://doi.org/10.1163/156921011X558600.

Pankhurst, Rita. 1997. "The Coffee Ceremony and the History of Coffee Consumption in Ethiopia." In *Ethiopia in Broader Perspective: Papers of the 13th International Conference of Ethiopian Studies, Kyoto, 12–17 December 1997,* edited by Katsuyoshi Fukui, Eisei Kurimoto, and Masayoshi Shigeta, 516–39. Kyoto: Shokado.

Abba Paulos Tzadua. 2009. *The Fetha Nagast: The Law of the Kings.* Edited by Peter L. Strauss Durham: Carolina Academic.

Paulos Yohannes. 1988. *Filsata: The Feast of the Assumption of the Virgin Mary and the Mariological Tradition of the Ethiopian Orthodox Tewahedo Church.* Princeton: Princeton Theological Seminary.

Persoon, Joachim. 2004. "Between Ancient Axum and Revolutionary Moscow: The Ethiopian Church in the 20th Century." In *Eastern Christianity: Studies in Modern History, Religion, and Politics,* edited by Anthony O'Mahoney, 160–214. London: Melisende.

———. 2006. "The Monastery as a Nexus of Ethiopian Culture: A Discourse of Reconstruction." In *Proceedings of the XVth International Conference of Ethiopian Studies, Hamburg 2003,* edited by Siegbert Uhlig, 679–86, Aethiopistische Forschungen 65. Wiesbaden: Otto Harrassowitz.

Peters, John Durham. 2013. "Calendar, Clock, Tower." In *Deus in Machina: Religion, Technology, and the Things in Between,* edited by Jeremy Stolow. New York: Fordham University Press.

Pina-Cabral, João de. 1986. *Sons of Adam, Daughters of Eve: The Peasant Worldview of the Alto Minho.* Oxford: Clarendon.

Pitt-Rivers, Julian. 1977. "The Law of Hospitality." In *The Fate of Shechem or the Politics of Sex: Essays in the Anthropology of the Mediterranean*. Cambridge: Cambridge University Press.

Pop, Simion. 2011. "Eastern Orthodox Christinity as Anthropological Object: Conceptual and Methodological Considerations." *Studia Ubb Sociologia* 56 (2): 93–108.

Quirin, James. 1992. *The Evolution of the Ethiopian Jews: A History of the Beta Israel (Falasha) to 1920*. Philadelphia: University of Pennsylvania Press.

Rahel Mesfin. 1999. "Zege and Its Coffee: Local Livelihoods and Natural Resource Utilization in Northwest Ethiopia." MA thesis, Addis Ababa University.

———. 2002. "Land-Related Disputes: The Case of Zege Peninsula, Northern Ethiopia." In *Resource Alienation, Militarization and Development: Case Studies from East African Drylands*, edited by Mustafa Babiker, 137–50. Addis Ababa: Organization for Social Science Research in Eastern and Southern Africa (OSSREA).

Rappaport, Roy A. 1999. *Ritual and Religion in the Making of Humanity*. Cambridge: Cambridge University Press.

Reminick, Ronald A. 1974. "The Evil Eye Belief among the Amhara of Ethiopia." *Ethnology* 13 (3): 279–91.

Rodinson, Maxime. 1964. "Sur La Question Des 'Influences Juives' En Éthiopie." *Journal of Semitic Studies* 9:11–19.

———. 1967. *Magie, Médecine et Possession à Gondar*. Paris: École Pratique des Hautes Études—Sorbonne.

Rollason, William. 2010. "Working out Abjection in the Panapompom Bêche-de-Mer Fishery: Race, Economic Change and the Future in Papua New Guinea." *Australian Journal of Anthropology* 21 (2): 149–70.

Roudometof, Victor. 2014. *Globalization and Orthodox Christianity: The Transformations of a Religious Tradition*. London and New York: Routledge.

Sahlins, Marshall. 2004. *Apologies to Thucydides: Understanding History as Culture and Vice Versa*. Chicago: University of Chicago Press.

Salamon, Hagar. 1999. *The Hyena People: Ethiopian Jews in Christian Ethiopia*. Berkeley: University of California Press.

Samson Bezabeh. 2015. "Living across Digital Landscapes: Muslims, Orthodox Christians, and an Indian Guru in Ethiopia." In *New Media and Religious Transformations in Africa*, edited by Rosalind I. J. Hackett and Benjamin F. Soares. Bloomington: Indiana University Press.

Schielke, Samuli, and Liza Debevec. 2012. "Introduction." In *Ordinary Lives and Grand Schemes: An Anthropology of Everyday Religion*. London and New York: Berghahn.

Schulz, Dorothea E. 2008. "Soundscape." In *Key Words in Religion, Media and Culture*, edited by David Morgan. New York: Routledge.

Seeman, Don. 2009. *One People, One Blood: Ethiopian-Israelis and the Return to Jerusalem*. New York: Rutgers University Press.

Setargew Kenaw. 2011. *Knowledge Production and Spiritual Entrepreneurship in Zar: A Study of Spirit Mediumship in Northeastern Ethiopia*. Saarbrücken: VDM.

Shelemay, Kay Kaufman. 2012. "Rethinking the Urban Community: (Re) Mapping Musical Processes and Places." *Urban People* 14 (2).

Shenoda, Anthony. 2013. "Public Christianity in a Revolutionary Egypt." *Cultural Anthropology Online*, Fieldsights—Hot Spots. www.culanth.org/fieldsights/234-public-christianity-in-a-revolutionary-egypt.

Simmel, Georg. 1997. "The Sociology of the Meal." In *Simmel on Culture: Selected Writings*. London: SAGE.

Solomon Dejene. 2010. "Exploring Iddir: Toward Developing a Contextual Theology of Ethiopia." In *Research in Ethiopian Studies: Selected Papers of the 16th International Conference of Ethiopian Studies, Trondheim July 2007*, edited by Harald Aspen et al. Wiesbaden: Harrassowitz Verlag.

Stewart, Charles. 1991. *Demons and the Devil: Moral Imagination in Modern Greek Culture*. Princeton and Oxford: Princeton University Press.

Stolow, Jeremy. 2012. "Introduction: Religion, Technology, and the Things in Between." In *Deus in Machina: Religion, Technology, and the Things in Between*, edited by Jeremy Stolow. New York: Fordham University Press.

Stone, Michael. 2013. *Adam and Eve in the Armenian Tradition: Fifth through Seventeenth Centuries*. Atlanta: Society of Biblical Literature.

Strathern, Marilyn. 2012. "Eating (and Feeding)." *Cambridge Journal of Anthropology* 30 (2): 1–14.

Taddesse Tamrat. 1972a. "A Short Note on the Traditions of Pagan Resistance to the Ethiopian Church (14th and 15th Centuries)." *Journal of Ethiopian Studies* 10 (1): 137–50.

———. 1972b. *Church and State in Ethiopia, 1270–1527*. Oxford: Clarendon.

———. 1994. "Ethiopia in Miniature: The Peopling of Gojam." In *New Trends in Ethiopian Studies: Papers of the 12th International Conference of Ethiopian Studies*, edited by Harold Marcus, 1:951–62.

Täklä Iyäsus WaqGera (Aläqa). 2014. *The Goggam Chronicle*. Edited and translated by Girma Getahun. Oxford: Oxford University Press for the British Academy.

Taylor, Charles. 2007. *A Secular Age*. Cambridge, MA, and London: Belknap Press of Harvard University Press.

Teshale Tibebu. 1995. *The Making of Modern Ethiopia: 1896–1974*. Trenton, NJ: Red Sea.

Tihut Yirgu Asfaw. 2009. *Gender, Justice and Livelihoods in the Creation and Demise of Forests in North Western Ethiopia's Zeghie Peninsula*. Vancouver: University of British Columbia.

Triulzi, Alessandro. 1981. *Salt, Gold and Legitimacy: Prelude to the History of No-Man's Land, Belū Shangul, Ii Al-Laggā, Ethiopia (ca.1800–1898)*. Naples: Istituto Universitario Orientale.

Tsehai Berhane-Selassie. 2008. "Socio-Politics of Ethiopian Sacred Groves." In *African Sacred Groves: Ecological Dynamics and Social Change*, edited by Michael J. Sheridan and Celia Nyamweru. Oxford: James Currey.

Tubiana, Joseph. 1991. "Zar and Buda in Northern Ethiopia." In *Women's Medicine: The Zar-Bori Cult in Africa and Beyond*, edited by I. M. Lewis, Ahmed El Safi, and Sayed Hamid A. Hurreiz, 19–36. Edinburgh: Edinburgh University Press for the International African Institute.

Turner, Edith. 1987. *The Spirit and the Drum: A Memoir of Africa*. Tucson: University of Arizona Press.

Turner, Victor. 1969. *The Ritual Process: Structure and Anti-Structure*. London: Routledge & Kegan Paul.

Ullendorff, Edward. 1968. *Ethiopia and the Bible*. Oxford: Published for the British Academy by the Oxford University Press.

Valeri, Valerio. 2000. *The Forest of Taboos: Morality, Hunting, and Identity among the Huaulu of the Moluccas*. Madison: University of Wisconsin Press.

Verdery, Katherine. 2000. *The Political Lives of Dead Bodies: Reburial and Postsocialist Change*. New York: Columbia University Press.

Vries, Hent de. 2001. "In Media Res: Global Religion, Public Spheres, and the Task of Contemporary Comparative Religious Studies." In *Religion and Media*, edited by Hent de Vries and Samuel Weber, 3–43. Stanford: Stanford University Press.

West, Harry. 2005. *Kupilikula: Governance and the Invisible Realm in Mozambique*. Chicago: University of Chicago Press.

Wright, Marta C. 2002. "At the Limits of Sexuality: The Femininity of Ethiopian Nuns." *Journal of Ethiopian Studies* 35 (1): 27–42.

Young, Allan. 1975. "Magic as a 'Quasi-Profession': The Organization of Magical Healing among Amhara." *Ethnology* 14 (3): 245–65.

———. 1977. "Order, Analogy, and Efficacy in Ethiopian Medical Divination." *Culture, Medicine and Psychiatry* 1 (2): 183–99.

Abdussamad Ahmad, 26, 29, 78, 79
abstinence: church attendance and, 8;
    communicants and, 5, 125; Orthodox
    calendar and, 37, 42, 55; suppression and,
    11–12; temporality of, 6
Acts of Betre Maryam, Saint, 34–35, 65–66, 67,
    73, 85n1, 113
Adam, 1, 7, 16, 20n6, 75
Addis Ababa: amplification technology in, 140;
    buda (evil spirit) in, 92; burial practices in,
    112; communion practices in, 125; Mesqel
    in, 51; modern education in, 149; Orthodox
    activists in, 142; as trade hub, 29, 78. See also
    Betre Maryam monastery
Afaf: dingay masmereq (graduating stone) in,
    33; festivals in, 49–54; government school
    in, 118, 146; mass media technologies in,
    139; mosque construction, 66, 132, 134–35,
    139, 142, 143; Muslim community in, 8, 88,
    132–34, 139; slave trade in, 29, 33; taverns
    in, 121–22. See also buda (evil spirit) issue;
    concrete grave issue; Fure Maryam, church
    of; market, Afaf
agabi (marriage-making), 31–32
Agew language, 24
Aläqa Täkle Iyäsus, 78–79
alemawi (worldly). See worldly (alemawi) space
Amde Sion, Emperor, 23, 73
Amharic language: Abyssinian reference, 24;
    Dertogada (Yismake Worku), 144–45; hymns,

140, 143; mamalled (mediation), 14; newir
    (prohibition), 8; prayer, 138; pronunciation,
    vii; qurban, 123; sile (because), 43; use of, 51;
    zikir, 127
amplification technology, 131, 132, 134,
    139–40, 142
analogical reasoning, 6–7, 20nn7–8, 40,
    107, 113, 119
andimta (laity), 14
angels: actions of, 5, 54; comparisons to, 61,
    64; fallen angels, 58; guidance of, 70, 157;
    images of, 58, 76, 129, 154; nature of, 57, 61,
    70; in Protestantism, 59–60; role of, 57–58.
    See also Gabriel the Archangel; Michael the
    Archangel; Raphael the Archangel
animals: animal husbandry prohibitions, 1;
    animal products fasts, 7, 38, 43; buda (evil
    spirit) and, 88, 89, 96–97, 100; cattle ban,
    74–75; consumption of, 10, 35; human/animal
    binary distinction, 10; mediators with,
    61; ploughing prohibitions and, 73, 74–75;
    protection from, 65, 73; purity and, 36n9;
    sacrifice of (meswat), 34–35, 36n8, 66, 74, 84,
    107, 117, 118
anointing, 5, 24, 25, 82
aqni abbatocch (original fathers), 27, 36n6
aqwaqwam (chants). See chants (aqwaqwam)
Ark of the Covenant (Tabote S'ion), 25
asceticism, 20, 63–65, 107, 149, 150, 155, 157
Aspen, Harald, 16, 112

Assumption (*Filseta*), 13, 55n1
authority structures: angels, 54; clerical
    authority, 61–62; feasting and, 96, 105–6;
    land reforms and, 30–33, 70; media use and,
    142–43; monastic authority, 22, 26–30, 64,
    76; of Orthodox church, 4, 5, 7, 15, 22, 49, 66;
    political power, 3, 22, 23, 65–67; power of the
    land (*yager* power), 27–28; ritual and, 124;
    Solomonic authority, 25; transformations of,
    19, 60; universal, 7. *See also* hierarchy
avoidance acts, 2, 7, 11, 12, 43, 90, 157
Awde Negest (*Circle of Kings*), 69
Azwa Maryam, church of, vi map 1, 12, 17, 153

Bahir Dar: burial practices in, 112; education,
    79, 146, 149, 155; love magic and, 151; map,
    vi map 1; media use in, 140; St. George,
    church of, 135; tour guides in, 146–48; trade
    and, 99; Weyto in, 94. *See also* St. George,
    church of
balabbat (patriarch), 22
balabbatocch (landlords), 27, 28, 34
baptism: blessings with holy water and, 127;
    Christ's divinity and, 47; clergy and, 62, 64;
    forty-eighty rule, 6–7, 20n4; grace and, 5;
    Pentecostal revivals and, 59; of slaves, 95
beer (*tella*): *buda* (evil spirit) and, 96; Easter
    hospitality and, 119–20; at *fit'hat* (mortuary
    rites), 110; hospitality relations and, 77; *tezkar*
    feasts and, 105
bellringer (*deway*), 28
Beta Israel (*Falasha*), 24, 79, 86, 88, 89, 94, 95, 98
Betre Maryam, Saint: Acts of, 34–35, 65–66, 67,
    73, 85n1, 113; coffee and, 75, 83; covenant
    (*kidan*) and, 1, 73, 153; feasts for, 52;
    historical information on, 23; images of,
    76; as intercessor, 61; pact with God, 65; as
    patron, 14
Betre Maryam monastery, vi map 1, 17, 112, 116
Binayew Tamrat, 26, 28, 29, 30, 77, 85n3
blackness concepts, 80
bleeding restrictions, 4, 5, 6, 125
blessings, 2, 63, 126, 127
Bloch, Maurice, 106
blood sacrifice, 35, 66, 74, 84–85, 107, 117, 137
Bosc-Tiessé, Claire, 22, 76, 85n3
boundaries: blood and, 84–85; management of,
    2, 4, 12, 64, 70–71; media communication
    and, 141; mediation and, 2–3, 61, 66, 85;
    P'agumén and, 54; prohibitions and, 8, 70;
    tabot and, 4; violations of, 68, 89–90

buckthorn (*ades*), 73, 75, 77, 85n1
buda (evil spirit) issue: attacks by, 18; *buda* (evil
    spirit) accusees, 88–89, 94–95, 97–98; *buda*
    (evil spirit) aspects, 88–91; cannibalism
    and, 9; defining *buda* (evil spirit), 87–88;
    hospitality relations and, 95–97, 122; as
    interpersonal phenomenon, 91–94, 101–2;
    marginalization and, 9, 96; overview, 86–87;
    as term of shame, 99; *tezkar* feasts and, 105;
    value production modes and, 99–101
Bynum, Caroline Walker, 157

cannibalism, 9, 96
Carsten, Janet, 84
celibacy, 61, 62, 64
Cerulli, Enrico, 75
Chalcedon, Council of, 24
chants (*aqwaqwam*), 5, 49, 62, 67, 70, 140–41, 143.
    See also hymns; *mergéta*
ch'ewa (proper), 8–9, 11, 28, 78–79, 92, 98
chiqa shum (tax collector), 28, 30
Christmas: fasting and, 40, 48, 49, 55n1; feasting
    and, 40, 130; *fel* practices, 34; Orthodox
    calendar and, 40, 47–48, 49; *tezkar* and, 117;
    vigils of, 40
church-monasteries: concrete graves in, 111–14;
    defined, 20n2; foundational covenant (*kidan*)
    and, 73; imagery in, 58; landholders and,
    22–23; as material history, 84; prohibition
    and, 1–3; tourism and, 2, 155. *See also*
    coffee forest; monasteries (*gedam*); *specific*
    church-monasteries
clean (*nes'uh*), 8, 9, 78, 91, 92
clergy: deacons, 6, 61, 62, 69; Engelhardt on, 5;
    fasting and, 8, 61; fees and stipends of, 62–63,
    110; laity's reaffirmation of, 60; monks, 12, 27,
    28, 60, 61, 62, 64; role of, 12; sacraments and,
    5, 61; work of priests, 61–65. *See also* priests
coffee: drinking of, 48, 121; hospitality relations
    and, 72, 77, 82–83, 96, 117; Muslims and, 77,
    82, 117
coffee forest: church protection of, 76–77;
    covenant (*kidan*) and, 1, 72, 73, 153;
    deforestation, 75; ecological uniqueness of,
    1; forest cleaners (*ment'ari*), 27; history of,
    26–27, 29, 85nn1–2; as material history, 73,
    80–81; ploughing prohibitions and, 1–2, 73,
    75; preservation of, 75; sacredness of, 1
coffee trade: *buda* (evil spirit) issue, 93, 97;
    centralization/expansion of, 77–78, 93;
    clergy and, 14; covenant (*kidan*) and, 75,

85nn1–2; environmental mediation and, 65–67; foreign traders and, 21, 93, 97, 146; harvest season, 40–41; history of, 29, 73–74, 75, 77; interdependence and, 1; *liqered* and, 23, 27–28, 29; monasteries and, 75; output declines, 31; rich trader narrative, 73–74, 78; silver coins (*t'egera*) and, 81–83; slavery and, 78–79, 80–81, 85, 93; social divisions and, 80

commemorations: fasting and, 13, 43; feasting and, 13; funeral practices, 114, 116, 118; Orthodox calendar and, 54–55; *Qwisqwam* (exile from Egypt), 13, 39, 55n1; saints' days as, 52, 130n3; *sigdet* (prostration) and, 45; *zikir* feasts as, 39, 127–29. *See also* Marian feasts

commensality: *buda* (evil spirit) and, 95; covenant (*kidan*) and, 129–30, 156; Eucharist and, 119, 123; feeding and, 129–30; hospitality and, 122; integrated ritual ecology and, 156; slaves and, 95; *zikir* feasts and, 127, 130

commodity economics, 72, 74, 77, 80, 82–83, 99

Communion: abstinence and, 125; activities after, 5; Communion marriages, 32; communion practices, 124–25; grace and, 5; prohibitions and, 56; receiving rules, 20n3. *See also* Eucharist

concrete grave issue, 108, 109, 111–14

covenant (*kidan*): as foundation of social thought, 129–30; ploughing prohibitions and, 73

Cowley, Roger, 15, 61

Crucifixion, 40, 43, 45, 52, 85, 125, 126

Debray, Régis, 132

Debre Silasé, church of, vi map 1

debtera, 62, 67–69, 80, 151

Dejene, Solomon, 114

demons, 15, 37, 57, 67–68, 70, 82, 84, 126, 152. *See also buda* (evil spirit) issue

Derg government: concrete grave issue, 108, 113; fall of, 108, 113; land reforms of, 2, 29, 30, 33, 64, 99; modernization, 104–5; Orthodox Christianity and, 33–34, 60; political power and, 17, 22, 33; religious appropriation by, 33–34, 47, 60; rise of, 2, 30; *tezkar* (funeral feasts) and, 104

Dertogada (Yismake Worku), 144–45, 155

Descola, Philippe, 7, 10, 20n8

dingay masmereq (graduating stone), 33

dinkwan merèt (tent land), 27

dirty (*koshasha*), 12

disgust reactions, 11, 12

Divine Liturgy, 62

division of labor, 12, 14, 19, 56, 127, 139

Douglas, Mary, 7, 10, 20n7

Dulin, John, 138

Easter season: Eucharist and, 125–26; excess and, 41, 120, 124, 126; fasting and, 40, 43, 44, 55n1; feasting and, 40, 46, 124, 125, 130; *fel* practices, 34; hospitality and, 119–20; market days and, 41, 44; Orthodox calendar and, 40; *tezkar* and, 117; vigils (*gehad*), 40, 43

education: access to, 149, 154–55; *agabí shimaglé* and, 32; in Bahir Dar, 79, 146, 149, 155; church education, 28, 63–65, 68, 135, 149–50; fundraising for church education, 64–65, 135; global knowledge and, 20, 145–47; "grain students/grain schools," 63–64; importance of, 145–46, 150; laity's religious education, 14; modern education, 17, 20, 144, 145–47, 149, 150, 155; secular government education, 30, 33, 65, 118, 146, 149, 152; of slave owners, 78

Egypt, 6, 13, 24, 39, 48, 55n1, 138

Eisenlohr, Patrick, 143

elder panel (*shimgelna*), 31–32

Engelhardt, Jeffers, 4–5

Engelke, Matthew, 4

environment: boundary management and, 61, 102; *buda* (evil spirit) issue and, 86–87, 90, 102; fasting and, 46; forest preservation, 75; funeral practices and, 113, 118; global knowledge and, 145; as material history, 72–73, 81, 84; material history in, 73, 83–84; media communication and, 131–32, 142; mediation and, 35, 61, 65–67, 67; Orthodox calendar and, 37, 40–41; Orthodoxy and, 15, 19; prohibitions and, 3, 6, 9, 10, 37; protection of, 65, 67, 77, 143; sanctity and, 54, 72. *See also* coffee forest

Ephraim Isaac, 25, 36n8, 62

Epiphany (*T'imqet*), 25, 41, 49, 52–53, 55n1, 127

EPRDF (Ethiopian People's Revolutionary Democratic Front) government: *buda* (evil spirit) accusations, 97–98; divisive symbols and, 39; Ethiopian Millennium, 47; land reforms and, 30–31; modernization and, 47, 104; religious appropriation by, 2, 47; religious equality policies and, 134; *tezkar* feasts and, 104

Ethiopian Orthodox Tewahido Church, 24, 47

Ethiopian People's Revolutionary Democratic Front (EPRDF) government. *See* EPRDF (Ethiopian People's Revolutionary Democratic Front) government

Eucharist: commensality and, 129–30; Easter hospitality and, 125–26; echoing of, 19, 119, 125–28; Engelhardt on, 5; excess and, 124; holy of holies (*meqdes/qiddiste qiddusan*), 6; holy water and, 126; hospitality and, 127; prohibitions around, 6, 56, 125; purity and, 12, 56, 157; rate of receiving, 5; as sacrifice, 123–27; *zikir* feasts, 127–29

evil spirit (*buda*). *See buda* (evil spirit) issue

Exaltation of the Cross (*Mesqel*), 40, 44, 49–52

excess, 41, 120, 124, 126

exclusion: *buda* (evil spirit) issue, 88, 92, 94, 95, 100; creation of, 9; feasting and, 157; refusal to eat and, 157. *See also* marginal groups

excommunication (*wigzet*), 64, 69

Ezana of Axum, King, 23

Facebook, 132, 136–39, 142–43

Falasha (Beta Israel group), 24, 79, 86, 88, 89, 94, 95, 98

fasting: as channel for creativity, 157; Christmas and, 40, 48, 49, 55n1; of clergy, 61; coexistence of, 9; communion prohibitions and, 125; as a discipline, 37, 42, 44, 55, 125, 150; Easter season, 43, 44; Eucharist and, 6; fasting/nonfasting binary, 10; government regulation and, 157; importance of, 2; integrated ritual ecology and, 156; Orthodox calendar and, 3, 37–44, 49; participation levels, 39; Pentecost and, 55n1; or religious poets and artists, 157; understanding of as act that suppresses, 11

fasts: *Abiy S'om* (great fast), 55n1; Advent season, 129; of the Apostles, 55n1; Assumption (*Filseta*), 13, 55n1; church attendance and, 7–8; clergy and, 39, 61; Communion fast, 43, 61; Easter season and, 43, 44; eating, work and sexuality subjected to, 2; *Filseta* (Assumption), 13, 55n1; of Heraclius, 55n3; laity and, 39; Lenten fasts, 7, 39, 41, 44, 55nn2–3, 125; of Nineveh, 39, 55n1; Pasch fast, 55n3; of the prophets, 55n1; *Qwisqwam* (exile from Egypt), 13, 39, 55n1; of salvation, 55n1; seven major fasts, 7, 55n1; Wednesday/Friday fasts, 7, 39, 40, 43, 55n1

feasting: communion prohibitions and, 56; as dominant idioms, 157; Easter season, 41,

46; inclusions/exclusions, 157; Orthodox calendar and, 3, 37–41, 44–46; temporality of, 6. *See also* Marian feasts

feasts, 130

fel practices, 34–35, 66, 135

festivals: amplification technology and, 142; Epiphany (*T'imqet*) and, 41, 53; Ethiopian Millennium and, 47; Exaltation of the Cross (*Mesqel*), 40, 49–52; Marian feasts and, 12; market days and, 41; saints' days and, 127

Fetha Negest (Law of Kings), 11, 20n4, 29, 95

Feuchtwang, Stephan, 106, 124

Filseta (Assumption), 13, 55n1

fit'hat (mortuary rites), 109, 110, 115

Fortes, Meyer, 10, 11–12

forty-eighty rule, 6–7, 20n4

Freeman, Dena, 89

Fritsch, Emmanuel, 40, 62

fruit, 2, 26, 75, 77, 85n1

fukera (bragging, praise songs), 108

fundraising, for church education, 64–65

funerals: clerical payments, 110; funeral tents, 110; grave digging, 109–10; graveyard politics, 111–14; *iddir* groups and, 109; *igzîo*, 109–10; memorials, 115–17; mortuary rites (*fit'hat*), 109, 110; remembrance, 117–18; as social participation, 108–9. *See also* funerary feasting (*tezkar*)

funerary feasting (*tezkar*): animal sacrifice (*meswat*), 107; *buda* crisis and, 105; church authority and, 107; decline of, 19, 23, 34–35, 104–5, 107; *fukera* (bragging, praise songs) and, 108; government opposition to, 157; hospitality and, 105; lavishness of, 106; logic of, 105; overview, 103–4; power and, 106–7; proper relationships and, 96. *See also* funerals

Fure, 63, 132, 133, 136

Fure Maryam, church of, vi map 1, 8, 12, 16, 52, 63, 111, 136

Gabriel the Archangel, 39, 57–58, 73, 128–29, 141

gedam (monastery), 20n2. *See also* church-monasteries

Ge'ez language: amulet inscriptions in, 90–91; church education and, 131, 149, 150; classical hymns in, 140; *debtera* and, 67–69; foundation stories in, 75; modern education and, 17; scripture in, 20n4, 24, 58

Gell, Alfred, 10

George, Saint, 39, 73, 135, 147, 150–51

Getatchew Haile, 69

Ginbot Lideta (birthday of Mary), 12, 121, 129, 130
Girma Mohammed, 63
Giyorgis monastery, 17
Glory of Kings (Kibre Negest), 25
Gojjam region, 24, 29, 35n3, 77–78, 86, 94–95
grace (*sega*), 5, 12, 25, 56, 61
graduating stone (*dingay masmereq*), 33
Graeber, David, 82, 117
grassroots participation, 34, 47–48, 60
Gregorian calendar, 38, 40, 47
gult rights, 36n6

hagiographies, 26, 75, 108, 115
Haile Selassie, Emperor, 22, 30, 105, 112, 113
Hannig, Anita, 44
Haustein, Jörg, 59
Hegel, Georg Wilhelm Friedrich, 4
Heraclius, fast of, 55n3
hierarchy: as authority, 5; church-agrarian hierarchy, 82; decline of, 34; distance maintenance and, 15; in economics, 82; local government bureaus (*qebellé*), 31, 75, 104, 105; of mediation, 5, 60; *tezkar* (funeral feasts) and, 108
Hoben, Alan, 36n6, 78
holy orders, 5, 12, 56, 61, 63, 64
Holy Spirit, 24, 47, 59, 150, 152
Holy Trinity (*qiddist selassé*), 57, 128, 130n3
holy water, 4, 5, 54, 97, 125, 126
Holy Week, 44, 45, 46
hops, 73, 75, 77, 82, 85n1
hospitality: beer (*tella*) and, 77, 119–20; *buda* (evil spirit) and, 95–97; coffee and, 72, 77, 82–83; commercial industry of, 121; decline of, 19, 21, 23, 34–35, 96, 103, 105, 118; Eucharistic feast and, 119–21; excess and, 41, 120, 124, 126; *Ginbot Lideta* (birthday of Mary), 121; guest/stranger status, 121–23; inclusion and, 157; moral values and, 34, 82–83; prohibitions and, 8; sacrifice and, 123–27; social decline and, 119. *See also* funeral feasting (*tezkar*)
humans: human/animal binary, 10; human body/world interface, 2; human/divine relations, 2, 9, 15, 61; human economics, 82–83, 117; human/God binary, 10
hybrid mediators, 57
hymns: in Amharic language, 140, 143; classical Ge'ez hymns, 140; for *Filseta* (Assumption), 13; recorded hymns, 140–41, 142; votive hymns, 6. *See also* chants (*aqwaqwam*)

ice guardian (*yebered tebaqí*), 65–66
iddir groups, 68, 106, 109, 114
images: in the home, 141; icons, 4, 153–54; of interreligious cooperation, 138; of martyrs, 137; of murdered Christians, 136–38; practice images, 154; of saints, 152; of South African killings, 137, 138; souvenir paintings, 152–54, 155n1
impurity, 4, 15, 64, 74, 78, 87, 90, 92, 98, 125
Incarnation, 13, 24, 51
incest: as *newir* (prohibition), 8; seventh generation rule, 79, 91
inclusion: blackness concepts, 80; creation of, 9; feasting and, 121, 129–30; levels of, 92, 157; overlapping of, 88; scripture and, 20n8
intercession, 4–5, 12–15, 59, 61
Islam: challenges from, 60, 65, 135–36; hospitality and, 133; marginal groups and, 11; meat restrictions and, 133; Orthodox Church and, 2, 66, 133. *See also* Muslims
Italian occupation, 30, 34, 47, 81–82, 134
Iyasu I, Emperor, 28, 77

Jesus Christ: baptism of, 47; Crucifixion, 40, 45, 52, 85, 125, 126; crucifixion of, 85; divinity/humanity of, 24, 47; Engelhardt on, 5; fast of Christ, 55n3; Incarnation, 13, 24, 51; as mediator, 59, 61; Resurrection, 40, 45, 46, 124, 125; suffering of, 43; titles of, 59
Jewish-Hebraic influences, 25, 36n8, 85, 128

Kane, Thomas Leiper, 14
Kaplan, Steven, 38, 61, 64, 65, 89, 115
Keane, Webb, 5
keeper of the outside (*yewist' gebez*), 28
khat use, 32, 50, 133, 152
Kibre Negest (Glory of Kings), 25
Kidane Mihret (Covenant of Mercy), 13, 128
Kidane Mihret monastery, 128
knowledge: divine knowledge, 157; human exchange and, 147–48; image creation and, 152–54, 155n1; and knower's condition, 157; knowledge buffet, 16; knowledge traditions, 157; media communication and, 148; mediation and, 70–71; modern education and, 145–47, 149; overview, 144–45; patron cultivation and, 150–52; progressiveness of, 154–55; tourism and, 148–49, 150–51, 155; world's knowledge, 148–52

koshasha (dirty), 12

labor relations, 2, 10, 31, 39, 72, 157
laity: activism of, 60; in chain of authority, 28; fasts and, 39; lay religious societies, 60; on Protestants, 12; religious education of, 14; religious texts and, 60; saints' images and, 154. *See also mahber* (monastic associations)
Lambek, Michael, 10, 11–12, 21n11, 93, 95
landlords (*balabbatocch*), 28, 80, 99
land reforms: appropriations/taxations, 29–30; *buda* (evil spirit) crisis and, 99; church holdings and, 2; counterbalances to, 77; of Derg government, 2, 29, 30, 33, 64, 99; hospitality decline and, 118; local class relations and, 2
Law of Kings (Fetha Negest), 11, 20n4, 29, 95
Lenten fasts, 9, 39, 41, 44, 55nn1–2, 125
Levine, Donald N., 63, 152
Lévi-Strauss, Claude, 10, 21n11
Leviticus, 6–7, 20nn4–7
líqered position, 23, 27–28, 29, 117
liturgical ritual, 14, 60, 105, 124
Lloyd, G. E. R., 20n8

magic: *Awde Negest* (*Circle of Kings*), 69; *debtera* and, 67–69, 80; ice guardian (*yebered tebaqí*), 65–66; love magic, 147, 151; magico-religious scrolls, 7; Orthodox Christianity and, 15; specialists of, 18; use of, 67–70, 79; witchcraft discourse, 99. *See also buda* (evil spirit) issue
mahber (monastic associations), 22, 31–32, 98, 110, 135
Malara, Diego Maria, 44, 92, 126
mamalled (mediation), 14
marginal groups: accounts of, 11; Beta Israel group (*Falasha*), 24, 79, 86, 88, 89, 94, 95, 98; *buda* (evil spirit) accusees as, 97–98; *buda* (evil spirit) as, 9, 89; Islam and, 11; market traders as, 99; Orthodox Christianity and, 11, 79; potters, 8; weavers, 8; Weyto, 8–9, 24, 93, 94. *See also* slave descendants
Marian feasts: annual feasts of, 13, 44; *Filseta* (Assumption), 13; *Ginbot Lideta* (birthday of Mary), 12, 121, 129, 130; Orthodox calendar and, 26; *Qwisqwam* (exile from Egypt), 13; *tabots* and, 52
market, Afaf: *buda* (evil spirit) issue, 86–89, 92–93, 96, 99; *fel* practices and, 34; growth of, 33; market days, 17, 41, 44; market traders, 93, 96, 99, 100; *Mesqel* (Exaltation

of the Cross) festival, 48; Muslim minority in, 88; Orthodox calendar and, 41, 44; taxation of, 27
marriage: *agabí shimaglé* and, 31–32; Communion marriages, 32; fasts and, 45; grace and, 5; marriage arrangements, 31, 53; *sir'ate teklil* ceremony, 32
marriage prohibitions: asymmetry in, 11; *buda* (evil spirit) issue, 95; cannibalism and, 9; *Falasha* (Beta Israel group) and, 95; food prohibition comparison, 8–9; godparents and, 21n9; incest, 8; inclusion/exclusion levels, 92; slave descendants and, 9, 11, 79, 92, 98
Marsland, Rebecca, 124
Mary, Blessed Virgin, Saint. *See* Virgin Mary
masmammat (to bring others to agreement), 29, 32
Medhane Alem, church of, 134
media communication: amplification technology, 131, 132, 134, 139–40, 142; anthropological works and, 3; authority structures and, 142–43; Christian-Muslim relations and, 133, 136; *Dertogada* (Yismake Worku), 144–45; expanded accessibility, 139–42; Facebook, 132, 136–39, 142–43; internet access, 132, 133–39; knowledge and, 148; overview, 131–32; prayer books, 141; recordings, 139–40; territoriality and, 132; as unmediated connection, 60
mediation: anthropological works and, 3; definitions, 15; general theory of, 2; hierarchy and, 12–15; as maintenance of hierarchical distance, 15; as material actualization of a relationship, 15; mediation/intercession distinction, 15; political authority structure and, 3; prohibition and, 2, 9; protections, 2, 65; regulatory function of, 5; restrictive function of, 5; theory of, 4
mediators: hybrid mediators, 57; importance of, 2; need for, 71; nonpriestly mediators, 65–66; patron saints, 14; prayer and, 15, 63; proliferation of, 61; specialists as, 14
Mehal Zege, 17, 27, 62, 111
Mehal Zege Giyorgis, church of, vi map 1, 17, 49, 52, 73, 111, 116
mendicants, 63–64, 150
Menilek I, Emperor, 22, 25, 73, 77, 112, 149
ment'ari (forest cleaners), 27
meqdes/qiddiste qiddusan (holy of holies), 6
Mercier, Jacques, 7

mergéta, 16, 21n19, 48, 66. *See also* chants (*aqwaqwam*)

Mes'hafe Ginzet (Book of Remembrance), 110, 112

Mesqel (Exaltation of the Cross) festival, 40, 44, 49–52, 123

mesqel adebabay (Square of the Cross), 35, 66

Messing, Simon D., 105

meswat (animal sacrifice), 34–35, 36n8, 66, 74, 84, 117, 118

Michael the Archangel, 39, 53, 54, 57–58, 128

mislené position, 27–28, 117

mist'irat (sacraments). *See* sacraments

modernization: concrete grave issue and, 111–14; Derg government and, 104–5; EPRDF government and, 47, 104; funerary feasts and, 104–5; modern education, 17, 20, 144, 145–47, 149, 150, 155; modernizers, 157; opposition to, 2

monasteries (*gedam*): asceticism in, 63–64; coffee forest and, 75–76, 77; decline of landholding, 33; *Dertogada* (Yismake Worku) and, 144–45; feasting and, 52; founding of, 23–26, 77; land politics and, 26–30; material history of, 76; monastic associations (*mahber*), 22; monastic authority, 19, 22–23, 33, 37, 64, 76–77; monastic prayer, 14; monks, 12, 27, 28, 60, 61, 62, 64; patriarchiate and, 23, 25, 26, 36n5; progressiveness of, 154–55; Protestantism and, 59; saints' relics in, 115–16; spatial correlations and, 135; support for, 65; taxation and, 77, 85n3; tourism and, 84, 118, 154–55. *See also* Betre Maryam, Saint; church-monasteries; coffee forest; *specific monasteries*

moral values: control and, 11; decline of, 34; difference distinctions and, 9; fast observance and, 38; formation of, 157; slave sacrifice and, 74, 85; slave trade and, 83–85

morning prayers (*mahlet*), 62, 141

mosque construction, 66, 132, 134–35, 139, 142, 143

Munn, Nancy, 38, 46, 49

Muslims: in Afaf, 88, 132, 133; amplification technology and, 139; Christian-Muslim relations, 117, 133–39; coffee trade, 77, 82; *dhikr* comparison, 127; equality status, 134; fasting of, 35; festivals of, 47; in Fure, 132; *khat* use, 133–34; land claims of, 35; mosque construction, 134–35, 139; Muslim meat avoidance, 8, 9, 11, 157; Muslim traders, 29,

74, 78, 95; prohibitions and, 8; public media and, 136–39; religious equality claims, 60, 66; as traders, 74; Weyto as, 93, 94

Neo-Solomonids, 26

newir (prohibition), 8, 9

Nineveh fasts, 39, 55n1

"of the bone" (*be at'int*) status, 27

ordination, 5, 12, 56, 61–62, 63, 64

Oriental Orthodox churches, 24

original fathers (*aqní abbatocch*), 27

Orthodox calendar: Advent season, 40; Christmas, 40, 47–48, 49, 55n1; countercalendars, 46–49; Easter season, 40; Ethiopian Millennium, 47; fasting and, 7–8, 42–45; feasting and, 37–41, 44–46; harvest season and, 40–41; Lenten season, 40; market days and, 41; overview, 3, 37–38, 54–55; sacred rituals and, 49–54; saints' days, 39–40; vigils, 40. *See also* Epiphany (T'imqet); Exaltation of the Cross (*Mesqel*); saints' days

Orthodox Church: anthropological works and, 3–4; boundary mediation of, 2; church-agrarian hierarchy, 82; church poverty, 64; church training decline, 17; constitutional equality of, 2; EPRDF and, 2; land reforms and, 2, 33; local political hierarchies and, 105; marginal groups and, 11; materiality and, 4, 157; participation surge in, 33; Pentecostalism and, 58–59; poverty of, 64; Protestantism and, 3–4, 12; resource decline, 65; spatial correlations, 6

P'agumén, 38–39, 54

Pankhurst, Alula, vii, 89, 112, 114

Pankhurst, Richard, 85n2, 109

Patriarchiate: monastics and, 25; of Paulos, 36n5; subjugation of, 33

Paulos Yohannes, Patriarch, 13–14, 26, 36n5, 56, 154

Pentecostalism, 3–4, 58–59

ploughing prohibitions, 1, 73, 74–75

prayer: angels and, 57; authority structures and, 35; Divine Liturgy, 62; efficacy of, 143; *fel* practices as, 34; mediators and, 15, 63; in Pentecostalism, 59; prayer books, 141; priests and, 5, 14, 54, 64; *Widassé Maryam* (Praises of Mary), 62, 141. *See also* chants (*aqwaqwam*)

pride, prohibitions as control mechanism over, 9

priests: anthropological works and, 3; blessings by, 63; Divine Liturgy, 62; Eucharist and, 124; noncelibate priests, 62; poverty of, 64; spatial correlations, 6; training, 63; work of, 61–65
prohibitions: affective dimensions, 11; analogical reasoning and, 6–7; anthropological works and, 3; bodies/environment and, 9; chewa distinctions, 8–9; on Christians eating Muslim meat, 8; classification/order, 10; as control mechanisms over pride and desire, 9; as enabling relationship with God, 2; gendering of, 6, 9; holy of holies (meqdes/qiddiste qiddusan) and, 6; human/divine relations and, 9; inappropriate times and, 4; moral formation and, 157; negative nature of, 10; negators and, 11–12; observance of, 2; political authority structure and, 3; and understanding of religious life, 2. See also fasting; marriage prohibitions
proper (chewa), 8–9, 11, 28, 78–79, 92, 98
Protestantism: anthropological works and, 3–4; competition from, 65; as existential threat, 12; expansion of, 58; Mary and, 12; on mediators, 58–59, 61, 71; on monasticism, 59; opposition to, 2; Orthodox Church and, 2, 3, 12, 66; Orthodox fasts and, 35; on Raphael the Archangel, 54; on sacraments, 61; secularism and, 59; semiotic transparency and, 60; transubstantiation and, 12; as worldly (alemawi), 12
purity: animal sacrifice and, 36n9; communicants and, 5; Eucharist and, 6, 56; holy water and, 126; repurification of mothers, 20n4; temporal conditions and, 5–12; of Virgin Mary, 13; zikir feasts, 157

qebellé offices, 31, 104
qése gebbez (tabot guardian), 28
qiddist selassé (Holy Trinity), 57, 128, 130n3
Quirin, James, 89
Qwisqwam (exile from Egypt), 13, 39, 55n1

Rahel Mesfin, 18, 26, 66
Raphael the Archangel, 5, 54, 57–58
Ras Haylu, King of Gojjam, 29, 77–78
Regnier, Denis, 92
remembrance, 111–14, 116, 117–18, 127
Reminick, Ronald A., 93
research methodology, 15–19
Resurrection, 40, 45, 46, 124, 125
rich trader narrative, 73–74, 81, 81–83, 83, 84, 99

rist land rights, 27, 36n6
ritual regime, 3
Rufael, church of, 134

Sabbath, Ethiopian, 25
Sabbath bread, 126
sacraments (mist'irat): clerical authority and, 61; effects of, 56. See also specific sacraments
sacrifice(s): decline of, 35; Eucharistic sacrifice, 123–27; hospitality and, 123–27; imagery of, 85; Lévi-Strauss's theory of, 21n11; slave trade and, 83–85. See also animals, sacrifice of
saints: anthropological works and, 3; boundary management and, 12; Engelhardt on, 5; importance of, 2; as mediators and patrons, 14, 57, 65; relics of, 115–16; tesaminnet (being listened to by others), 15; zikir feasts, 157. See also saints' days; specific saints
saints' days: annual feasts, 44; echoing and, 127; holy water and, 126; Raphael the Archangel, 54; refusal to work on, 157; Saint George's Day, 146; tabots and, 39, 127, 129, 154; zikir feasts, 127–29
Samson Bezabeh, 136
sanctity: liminal times and, 54; of matter, 4–5; regulation of, 5, 49; slavery parallels, 19, 72, 74
seclusion, 1, 2, 4, 116, 155
secularism: church power and, 27; government encroachments of, 22, 29; opposition to, 2; Protestantism and, 59; secular government education, 65
sega (grace), 5, 12, 25, 56, 61
seventh generation rule, 79, 91
shimgelna (panel of elders), 31–32
silet (vows), 39, 43
silver coins (t'egera), 81–83, 82, 84
sir'ate teklil ceremony, 32
slave descendants: accounts of, 11, 79, 80; fasting and, 157; marriage and, 9, 11, 79, 92, 98; as material history, 80; point of division, 8–9; presence of, 18; status differences, 74, 157; stigma and, 78, 79
slaves: in Afaf, 29; baptism of, 11, 95; chewa and mislené roles and, 28, 78; sacrifice of, 74, 84; stigma and, 74
slave trade: in Afaf, 33; buda (evil spirit) and, 91, 93; coffee trade and, 78, 93; history of, 18, 72; parallel history of, 72; rifts caused by, 19, 88, 92, 157; sacrifice and, 83–85; silver coins (t'egera) and, 81–83; Zege as importer of, 1

Solomon, King, 23, 25

St. George, church of, 135

stigmatization: of *buda* (evil spirit) accusees, 97–98; *Falasha*, 86, 89, 94, 95, 98; isolation and, 11; refusal to eat and, 157; of slave descendants, 78, 79

Sunday school movement, 14, 39, 60

taboos: on eating, 10; on killing, 10; on looking at, 10; on sexual intercourse, 10; on touching, 11

tabots: access to, 56; boundaries and, 4; holy of holies (*meqdes/qiddiste qiddusan*), 6; importance of, 25; power of, 4, 31; *qése gebbez* and, 28; saints' days and, 39, 127, 129, 154; Tabote S'ion (Ark of the Covenant), 25; transit of, 39, 52–54

taxation: Afaf market and, 99; relief from, 22, 77, 85nn3–4; tax collector (*chiqa shum*), 28, 30

Taylor, Charles, 59

t'egera (silver coins), 81–83, 84

Tekle Haymanot, King of Gojjam, 29, 77–78

t'ella (homebrewed beer): *buda* (evil spirit) and, 96; Easter hospitality and, 119–20; at *fit'hat* (mortuary rites), 110; hospitality relations and, 77; *tezkar* feasts and, 105

tent land (*dinkwan merét*), 27

tesamínnet (being listened to by others), 15, 29, 32

Tewodros II, Emperor, 26

thalers (silver coins), 81–83

Tihut Yirgu Asfaw, 18, 26, 31, 66

T'imqet (Ephiphany). *See* Epiphany (*T'imqet*)

tourism: church-monasteries and, 76; global knowledge and, 146–48; income from, 79, 112; knowledge and, 148–49, 150–51, 155; monasteries (*gedam*) and, 84, 118, 154–55; pilgrimage sites, 2; thalers and, 81, 84

trade: *buda* (evil spirit) crisis and, 99; Muslim traders, 29, 74, 78, 95; rich trader narrative, 73–74, 81–83, 83, 84, 99; silver coins (*t'egera*) and, 81–83; trade routes, 1, 81

transubstantiation, 5, 12, 123

Turner, Victor, 50

Unctionism, 24, 47–48

unction of the sick (anointing), 5

Ura, 17, 20n2, 27

Ura Kidane Mihret, church of, vi map 1, 13, 17, 49, 111, 155

Valeri, Valerio, 10, 11, 21n12

value production modes, 99–101

vigils (*gehad*), 40, 43, 62

Virgin Mary: boundary management and, 12; clergy's relationship with, 63–64, 76; empathy of, 13; feasts of, 52; *Ginbot Lideta* (birthday of Mary), 12, 121, 129, 130; images of, 152–53; as incorrupt, 13; intercession of, 12, 14; Kidane Mihret (Covenant of Mercy), 128; as mediator, 12, 57, 59, 61, 64; petitions for protection, 138; prayers for patrons, 151; Protestantism and, 12; special characteristics of, 13; status of, 21n17; suffering of, 14; *Widassé Maryam* (Praises of Mary), 62, 141

Wanjeta Mikael, church of, 128–29

Weyto (marginalized ethnic group), 8–9, 24, 93, 94

Widassé Maryam (Praises of Mary), 62, 141

wigzet (excommunication), 64, 69

worldly (*alemawi*) space, 12, 49, 53, 55, 59, 63, 134, 141

yager líqered, 27–28

yager power, 27–28

yebered tebaqí (ice guardian), 65–66, 135

yemahber líqered, 28

yemahber power, 27–28

yeqollo temarí ("grain students"), 63–64

yeqollo timhirt bét ("grain school"), 63

yesét mahber (women's association), 27

yewist' gebez (keeper of the outside), 28

Yiganda, 20n2

Yiganda Tekle Haymanot monastery, vi map 1, 17

Yismake Worku, 144–45, 155

Yohannes IV, Emperor, 133

Young, Allan, 7

Zara Yaqob, Emperor, 26, 38, 44

Zege Peninsula, vi map 1

zer (seed, race), 78, 87–88, 91, 98

zikir feasts, 12, 39, 104, 127–29, 157